Lecture Notes in Economics and Mathematical Systems

Managing Editors: M. Beckmann and W. Krelle

246




Pieter W. Otter

# Dynamic Feature Space Modelling, Filtering and Self-Tuning Control of Stochastic Systems

## A Systems Approach with Economic and Social Applications


Springer-Verlag
Berlin Heidelberg New York Tokyo

**Author**

Dr. Pieter W. Otter
Institute of Econometrics, University of Groningen
P.O. Box 800, 9700 AV Groningen, The Netherlands

ISBN 3-540-15654-2 Springer-Verlag Berlin Heidelberg New York Tokyo
ISBN 0-387-15654-2 Springer-Verlag New York Heidelberg Berlin Tokyo



Printing and binding: Beltz Offsetdruck, Hemsbach/Bergstr.
2142/3140-543210

*The progress of science consists in observing these interconnections and in showing with a patient ingenuity that the events of this evershifting world are but examples of a few general connections or relations called laws. To see what is general in what is particular and what is permanent in what is transitory is the aim of scientific thought.*

*(A.N. Whitehead, 'An Introduction to Mathematics'.)*

*To Katharina, Jan and Wilmy*

*In memory of Harmine*

# Preface

The literature on systems seems to have been growing almost exponentially during the last decade and one may question whether there is need for another book. In the author's view, most of the literature on 'systems' is either technical in mathematical sense or technical in engineering sense (with technical words such as noise, filtering etc.) and not easily accessible to researchers is other fields, in particular not to economists, econometricians and quantitative researchers in social sciences. This is unfortunate, because achievements in the rather 'young' science of system theory and system engineering are of importance for modelling, estimation and regulation (control) problems in other branches of science. State space modelling; the concept of observability and controllability; the mathematical formulations of stability; the so-called canonical forms; prediction error estimation; optimal control and Kalman filtering are some examples of results of system theory and system engineering which proved to be successful in practice. A brief summary of system theoretical concepts is given in Chapter II where an attempt has been made to translate the concepts into the more 'familiar' language used in econometrics and social sciences by means of examples.

By interrelating concepts and results from system theory with those from econometrics and social sciences, the author has attempted to narrow the gap between the more technical sciences such as engineering and social sciences and econometrics, and to contribute to either side. In Chapter III, for instance, a general linear model, called the structural model with feature space, is formulated. This model gives the opportunity to describe relations parsimoniously by formulating processes (systems) mathematically and statistically in the so-called feature space. The idea of introducing an auxiliary space to describe relations parsimoniously, is not new and can be found in social sciences in which it is known as factor space; in system theory in which it is called state space and in pattern recognition in which it is called feature space, see e.g. Andrews (1972). It is called intrinsic modelling by Kalman (1981) and is - in the author's view - closely related to Popper's idea of simplicity. It is shown that models assumed implicitly in 'data-oriented' techniques such as factor analysis and canonical correlation are special feature space models but theoretically postulated (economic) models such as regression models, rational expectation models, permanent income models appear to be special feature space models too. It is shown that the reduced form version of the model is equivalent in structure to a linear stochastic state space model with stochastic inputs, which may be of interest to engineers (control problems). By using techniques from system theory and social sciences, such as Kalman filtering, prediction error estimation, canonical correlation, factor analysis, tests on eigenvalues and canonical correlation coefficients, the model can be identified.

Another example of an integrated approach is found in Chapter VII, when self-tuning control is discussed. For instance, the in system engineering terms formulated 'persistent excitation' of signals in order to identify parameters, is reformulated in terms of the parameter identifiability concept used in econometrics.

The reader, unfamilair with engineering 'language' (a short dictionary is given in Chapter I), but familair with (statistical) language used in econometrics and social sciences, may read the examples of the various Chapters first and also Chapter III, section 4.2 of Chapter IV, Chapter VI and section 7.7. An attempt has been made to make the book 'self-contained' for practical use.

Herewith I would like to express my gratitude to several persons. I would like to thank Professor Jan Willems for his guidance and our sometimes philosophical discussions. I am obliged to Prof.Dr. K.J. Åström for his hospitality and his enthusiastic support during my visit to the Lund University of Technology. Furthermore I want to thank the 'younger' generation for their enthusiasm and (computer) assistance, in particular Lourens Aalders, Jacob Engwerda, Zwier Medendorp, Jan Schuur and Dirk Tempelaar.

I also would like to mention Dr. Theo Dijkstra, Drs. Geert Joosten, Drs. Marten Kuiper and Drs. Ton Steerneman, all from the Institute of Econometrics and the doctoral students following courses in 'system theory and econometrics' for the stimulating discussions. Last but certainly not least I am grateful to Rina Koning for her accurate typing and her patience with my sometimes 'Etruscan' language and Wilmy van Balen for her constant (moral) support.

# Table of Contents

## Notation and Symbols

| | |
|---|---|
| $\triangleq$ | by definition equal to |
| $A > 0$, $A \geqq 0$ | The real symmetric or Hermitian matrix A is positive definite or nonnegative-definite respectively. |
| $A = \mathrm{diag}(a_1,\ldots,a_n)$ | Diagonal matrix with diagonal entries $a_1,\ldots,a_n$. |
| $A'$ or $A^T$ | Tranpose of the matrix A. |
| $\det(A)$ or $\lvert A\rvert$ | Determinant of the matrix A. |
| $\mathrm{tr}(A)$ | Trace of A. |
| $r(A)$ | Rank of A. |
| $\lVert A\rVert$ | Norm of the matrix A defined by $\lVert A\rVert = \max\limits_{x \neq 0} \lVert Ax\rVert / \lVert x\rVert$ <br> $\lVert A\rVert$ bounds the 'amplifying power' of $\lVert Ax\rVert \leqq \lVert A\rVert\,\lVert x\rVert$ for all vectors x, and equality holds for at least one non-zero x. |
| $\delta_{ks}$ | Kronecker delta: $\delta_{ks} = 1$ for $k = s$ and $\delta_{ks} = 0$ for $k \neq s$. |
| $\overset{N}{\Sigma} y(i)$ | $\sum_{i=1}^{N} y(i)$ |
| $\underline{x}$ | $\underline{x}$ is a stochastic (random) variable or vector. |
| $E\{\underline{x}\}$ | 'Expectation' of $\underline{x}$. |
| $p(.,\theta)$ | The probability density function (p.d.f.) of a random variable/vector with parameter vector θ. |
| $\underline{x} \sim N(\mu,\Sigma_x)$ | $\underline{x}$ has a normal (Gaussian) distribution with mean μ and covariance matrix $\Sigma_x$. |
| $\xrightarrow{L}$ | 'converges in law to' <br> Let $\{\underline{x}_n\}$ be a sequence of random variables, n = 1,2,... . Let $\underline{x}_n$ have |

distribution $F_n$ and $\underline{x}$ distribution F
Then $\underline{x}_n \overset{L}{\rightarrow} \underline{x}$ if $\lim_{n \rightarrow \infty} F_n(.) = F(.)$ for all continuity points of F.

$\operatorname{plim}_{n \rightarrow \infty}(\underline{x}_n) = c$ — 'convergence in probability'
$\lim_{n \rightarrow \infty} P(|\underline{x}_n - c| < \varepsilon) = 1$ for every $\varepsilon > 0$. 'P' is an abbreviation for 'Probability'.

$\underline{x}_n \xrightarrow{a.s.} \underline{x}$ — The sequence of random variables/vectors $\{\underline{x}_n\}$ is said to converge almost surely (or with probability one) to $\underline{x}$, if given $\varepsilon, \delta > 0$ there exists a $k_o(\varepsilon,\delta)$ such that
$P(|\underline{x}_n - \underline{x}| < \varepsilon,\ \forall k \geqq k_o) > 1 - \delta$

$\underline{x}(k) = x(k)$ — A discrete stochastic process $\{\underline{x}_k : k \in Z\}$, $\underline{x}_k \in \mathbb{R}^n$, is a family of random vectors indexed by the parameter k and defined on a common probability space $(\Omega, A, P)$ where $\Omega$ is the sample space, A some $\sigma$-algebra and P a probability measure defined on A. For each k, $\underline{x}_k(\omega)$ with $\omega \in \Omega$ is a random variable, notation: $\underline{x}(k)$. For each $\omega$, $x_k(\omega)$ is called a realization of the process, notation: $\underline{x}(k) = x(k)$.

$\otimes$ — Kronecker product:

$$A \otimes B \triangleq \begin{bmatrix} a_{11}B & \dots & a_{1m}B \\ \vdots & & \vdots \\ a_{p1}B & \dots & a_{pm}B \end{bmatrix}$$

# I. Introduction

It is worthwhile noting that - although sometimes known under different names - certain features of systems[1] and of system modelling appear to be the same in different fields of research. The stability of a system is such a feature arising in almost every field of research, e.g. in biology, physics, economics, cybernetics, etc. The description of a system in terms of variables acting upon the system, called stimuli in psychology, predetermined variables in econometrics and input variables in system engineering and variables describing the response of the system, called endogenous variables in econometrics and output variables in system engineering is an example of a system modelling feature. It is not surprising, that in a variety of cases, statistical models, although from different fields of research, have the same structure. In order to give an impression of such a structure equivalence, a 'basic' decomposition $\underline{y}(k) = \underline{s}(k) + \underline{v}(k)$ is considered. Here $\underline{y}(k)$ denotes some observable random vector which is decomposed into a systematic part $\underline{s}(k)$ and a non-systematic part $\underline{v}(k)$, for instance $\underline{v}(k)$ is a normally distributed random vector, uncorrelated with $\underline{v}(s)$ for $k \neq s$, to be referred to as white noise. The index (k) may be time, regions, persons, etc. In engineering $\underline{y}(k)$ may be a signal $s(k)$ corrupted with white noise. In econometrics, the decomposition is called a linear regression equation, when the systematic part $s(k)$ is modelled as $s(k) = x(k)\beta$, in which $x(k)$ is some given row vector of exogenous variables and $\beta$ is the parameter vector. The decomposition may be a simple 'errors-in-variables' model, with $\underline{s}(k)$ as the 'true' unobservable variable. When $\underline{s}(k) = P\underline{f}(k)$, in which P is a deterministic matrix and $\underline{f}(k)$ is standard white noise with dimension less or equal to the dimension of $\underline{y}(k)$ consisting of what is called in psychology factors, we have a factor-analytic model.

It is shown in Chapters III and VI that many postulated (economic)

---

[1] A system is according to the Oxford illustrated dictionary (1975) to be understood as 'the complex whole, set of connected things or parts, or organized body of material or immaterial things'.

models, e.g. a rational expectation model, a time-series model, a regression model, etc., we have basically the same structure and appear to be special cases of two general models defined in Chapter III and to be discussed in the sequel.

It is also worthwhile noting the remarkable equivalence in structure of two 'data oriented' models, namely Jöreskog's linear structural model, which is closely related to factor-analytic modelling and widely used in psychology and more recently in econometrics and the so-called state space model from system theory introduced by Kalman, see. e.g. Kalman (1981). Both models consist of two equations namely the so-called process equation, which describes the (dynamic) relations between unobservables and a measurement or output equation which relates the unobservables to observable quantities. In principle the number of unobservables is smaller than the number of observables. This equivalence in structure suggests some common underlying idea how to model processes (systems). In the author's view this common idea is called 'simplicity' by Popper (1977), a concept which according to Hesse (1974, page 231) is inversely related to the number of freely adjustable parameters but also to 'the notion of invariance between different coordinate systems as an economy of parameters', Hesse (1974, page 233).
It is interesting in this respect to relate the concept of 'simplicity' to modelling techniques such as factor analysis and state space modelling, in particular to the so-called canonical forms and Kronecker invariants to be discussed in Chapter II. According to Van der Geer (1967), the basic idea of factor analysis is a reduction of the dimensionality of vector space (by coordinate transformation) with a resulting gain in the parsimony of the description of the relations. State space modelling refers - roughly speaking - to a parsimonious modelling of past inputs and current and future outputs. The essential information from the, in principle, large number of past inputs is contained in a memory function, called the state vector. Here too is a dimensionality reduction by means of the introduction of a memory function. It may be concluded that the simplicity of both models is because of a dimensionality reduction and a modelling of 'information preserving' functions in a lower dimensional space called factor space in psychology and state space in system theory.

The same approach has also been followed in pattern recognition, where according to Andrews (1972, page 9) 'the objective in defining feature space is to reduce the dimensionality of pattern space yet maintaining discriminatory power for classification purposes', in which feature space is defined to be an intermediate domain between the data gathering space and the classification process. The pattern space is essentially that domain which is defined by the discretization of sensor data, observing the real world and is usually of high dimensionality.

In Chapter III it is shown that both the discussed models are special cases of two general models, called the linear structural feature[2)] space (LSF) model and the reduced form feature space (LRF) model. The general name, feature space, is used which, for a specific application, may have a specific name, e.g. factor space, parameter space, canonical space, etc. In Chapter IV the question under what conditions and how the unobservable feature vector can be 'reconstructed' from observables, is investigated. This reconstruction problem is known as Kalman filtering, which is discussed in detail for a special feature space model, namely the classical regression model. In Chapter V the parameter identifiability problem and the prediction error estimation technique is discussed and is applied to the feature space models. It turns out that the Kalman filter and the prediction error estimation are each other's 'complements', in the sense that the filter generates prediction errors, which are used and minimized in the prediction error estimation algorithm, whereas the prediction error algorithm serves as a feed-back mechanism for the filter in this way preventing the divergence of the filter. The (LSF) model, or the (LRF) model, the Kalman filter and the prediction error estimation technique are the general 'tools' to model, identify and filter specific feature space models, of which examples are given in Chapter VI. However, in the analysis we need definitions, theorems and concepts from system theory which are summarized in Ch. II.

In the control part of the booklet a rather new area in control theory is introduced, which is known as adaptive or self-organizing control. Self-organizing control deals with a recursive simultaneous process of regulation and identification of systems. The so-called self-

---

[2)] Feature is according to the Oxford illustrated dictionary (1975) to be understood as 'the distinctive or characteristic part of a 'thing'', in our case the characteristic part of a model.

tuning control approach of Åström is generalized to multi-input, multi-output systems and is studied for two controllers; one with a one-period ahead cost functional and a variant of the steady-state optimal linear quadratic Gaussian (LQG) control. By means of a simulation study, the self-tuning control is applied to a macro-economic model of the US-economy. The concept of linear closed loop modelling is formulated in order to identify parameters because linear closed loop controllers may give rise to identifiability and estimation problems.

We begin by giving a short dictionary to facilitate a better communication between the different fields of research.

| System Theory/Engineering | Social Sciences/Econometrics |
|---|---|
| input variable | predetermined variable, exogenous variable, stimulus, instrumental variable |
| output variable | endogenous variable, response variable, target variable |
| system identification | (parameter) identifiability and estimation of a model |
| filtering | estimation, smoothing |
| impulse response functions | impact, total multipliers |
| white noise (standard) | normally distributed random variable(s), uncorrelated with time (with unit covariance) |
| coloured noise | autocorrelated normally distributed random variable(s) |
| process noise | disturbances, unique factor(s), transitory variable |
| measurement noise | disturbances, 'errors-in-variables' |
| noisy observations | observables corrupted with measurement noise |
| state space variable | - |

New is the term feature variable, which for specific applications stands for state space variable, regression parameter, factor, expectation variable, latent variable, canonical variable, policy variable, etc.

# II. Elements of System Theory

## 2.1. Definitions of Dynamic Input-Output Models and State Space Models.

According to the Oxford illustrated dictionary (1975), a system is defined as 'a complex whole, set of connected things or parts, organized body of material or immaterial things'. The system can be represented by a model (or a collection of models). A relation exists between the system and its environment, represented in the model by the so-called input and output variables. In system theory system and model are used synonymously. Models are classified into the following categories: (i) deterministic-stochastic (ii) discrete-continuous (iii) linear-non-linear (iv) stationary-non-stationary. Models can be described either in the time domain or in the frequency domain.

In system theory two important classes of models are considered; the dynamic input-output models denoted by $\Sigma I/O$ and dynamic systems with state space, denoted by $\Sigma m$. As we shall see the second one is an 'efficient' description of the $\Sigma I/O$. Realization theory deals with the connection between the two models, which will be discussed later on. Following Willems (1974) we have that $\Sigma I/O$ is defined as:

<u>Definition (2.1)</u> : $\Sigma I/O \triangleq \{T, U, \mathcal{U}, Y, \mathcal{Y}, F\}$ with

1) $T \subset \mathbb{R}$: the time axis
2) $U$ : the convex set of input values
3) $\mathcal{U}$ : the set of functions with $u \in \mathcal{U}$, $u: T \rightarrow U$. It is supposed that $\mathcal{U}$ is closed under 'concatenation', that is if $u_1, u_2 \in \mathcal{U}$ and $t' \in T$ then $u \in \mathcal{U}$ where

$$u(t) \triangleq \begin{cases} u_1(t), & t < t' \\ u_2(t), & t \geq t' \end{cases}$$

4) $Y$ : the set of output values
5) $\mathcal{Y}$ : the set of output functions $y \in \mathcal{Y}$ with $y: T \rightarrow Y$
6) $F$ : is called the system function with $F: \mathcal{U} \rightarrow \mathcal{Y}$. It is assumed that $F$ is non-anticipating, i.e. if

$u_1, u_2 \in \mathcal{U}$ and $u_1(t) = u_2(t)$ for $t \leqq t'$ then $(Fu_1)(t') = (Fu_2)(t')$.

Definition (2.2) : A ΣI/O is called *linear* if: (i) $U, \mathcal{U}, Y, \mathcal{Y}$ are vector spaces in $\mathbb{R}$ or $\mathbb{C}$ and (ii) F is linear.

Definition (2.3) : If $T = \mathbb{R}$ or $[t_o, \infty]$ we speak of (time) continuous models. If $T = Z$ or $\{k \in Z \mid k > k_o\}$ we speak of a (time) discrete model.

Definition (2.4) : A ΣI/O is called time-invariant if $t_1, t_2 \in T \Rightarrow$ $\Rightarrow t_1 + t_2 \in T$; $u \in \mathcal{U} \Rightarrow S_t u \in \mathcal{U}$ where $S_t$ denotes $(S_t u)(t') = u(t+t')$ thus $S_t \mathcal{U} \subset \mathcal{U}$; $S_t \mathcal{Y} \subset \mathcal{Y}$ and $S_t F = F S_t$.

Linear Discrete Systems.

Suppose $T = Z$, $U \in \mathbb{R}^m$, $Y \in \mathbb{R}^p$ and $\mathcal{U} = \{u(k)\}_{-\infty}^{\infty}$ is the set of all input vectors with zero value if $k = -\infty$ and $\mathcal{Y} = \{y(k)\}_{-\infty}^{\infty}$ is the set of all output vectors with zero values for $k = -\infty$ and $F: \mathcal{U} \rightarrow \mathcal{Y}$ is linear and non-anticipating.

It can be proved, see e.g. Willems (1974), that all linear discrete systems can be written as the following sum:

$$y(k) = \sum_{j=-\infty}^{k} W_{k,j}\, u(j), \qquad k,j \in Z.$$

F is determined by a set of matrices $W_{k,j}$ (defined to be zero if $j > k$). All stationary discrete systems can be written as the so-called convolution sum:

$$y(k) = \sum_{j=-\infty}^{k} G_{k-j}\, u(j), \qquad j \in Z$$

with $G_k = W_{k,o}$. The matrices $\{G_k\}_o^{\infty}$ are called Markov parameters, impulse response functions, etc.

Linear Continuous Systems.

Suppose $T = \mathbb{R}$, $U = \mathbb{R}^m$, $Y = \mathbb{R}^p$.
$\mathcal{U}$ = all piece-wise continuous functions,
$\mathcal{Y}$ = all piece-wise continuous functions,
$F: \mathcal{U} \rightarrow \mathcal{Y}$ is defined by the convolution sum

$$y(t) = \int_{-\infty}^{t} W(t,\tau)\, u(\tau)\, d\tau, \qquad t,\tau \in \mathbb{R}$$

where $W(.,.): \mathbb{R}_+^2 \to \mathbb{R}^{p\times m}$ is locally bounded, i.e. for every bounded region in $\mathbb{R}_+^2 \triangleq \{(t_1,t_o) \in T^2 \mid t_1 > t_o\}$ there is a $k < \infty$, such that $\|W(.,.)\| \leqq k$ in this region, where $\|.\|$ denotes a matrix norm. All stationary linear continuous systems can be written as

$$y(t) = \int_{-\infty}^{t} G(t-\tau)u(\tau)d\tau .$$

<u>Example (2.1):</u>

Consider the reduced form econometric model without disturbances

$$y(k) = \Pi z(k), \qquad k = 0,1,2,...$$

where $y(k) \in \mathbb{R}^m$, $z(k) \in \mathbb{R}^p$. $y(k)$ is an output vector and $z(k)$ a vector of predetermined variables including m output variables lagged one period. The equation can be rewritten as

$$y(k) = Ay(k-1) + Bu(k).$$

If we lag this equation one period, substitute the right-hand side back into the original equation, the equation takes after s-times the form

$$y(k) = A^{s+1}y(k-s-1) + \sum_{\tau=0}^{s} C_\tau u(k-\tau),$$

with $C_\tau = A^\tau B$. If $s \to \infty$ and suppose $\lim_{\tau\to\infty} A^\tau = 0$ then the so-called final form equation will be obtained

$$y(k) = \sum_{\tau=0}^{\infty} C_\tau u(k-\tau) \text{ or } y(k) = \sum_{j=-\infty}^{k} C_{k-j} u(j).$$

This is a stationary discrete $\Sigma I/O$ with input vectors $\{u(k)\}_0^\infty$ and output vectors $\{y(k)\}_0^\infty$ and $F \approx \{C_\tau\}_0^\infty$. It is noticed that a more 'efficient' description is given by the original first-order difference equation. This will be discussed later.

<u>Example (2.2):</u>

According to the *Wold*-decomposition a stationary stochastic scalar process $\underline{z}(k)$ can be written as

$$\underline{z}(k) = \sum_{j=0}^{\infty} a_j \underline{\varepsilon}(k-j),$$

where $\{\underline{\varepsilon}(i)\}_{-\infty}^{k}$ is a white noise process. This is a stationary $\Sigma I/O$ with input $\underline{\varepsilon}(i)$, output $\underline{z}(k)$ and $F \approx \{a_j\}_0^\infty$.

Frequency Description of Systems.

We begin by defining the (one-sided) Laplace transform of a real-valued continuous function F(t) in the interval $[0,\infty]$. It is assumed that F(t) is of exponential order, i.e. $|F(t)| < Me^{\alpha t}$ for $t > T$ where M, $\alpha$ and T are positive constants. The one-sided Laplace transform is defined by

$$L\{F(t)\} = \hat{f}(s) = \int_0^\infty F(t)e^{-st}dt$$

where $s \in \mathbb{C}$, $s = \sigma + iw$ with $i^2 = -1$. It is assumed that $L\{F(t)\}$ exists for $\mathrm{Re}(s) \geqq \sigma_0$, some constant. If $\mathrm{Re}(s) = 0$ and

$$\int_{-\infty}^\infty |F(t)|dt < \infty$$

we have a *Fourier* transform.

As we have seen a continuous stationary linear $\Sigma I/O$ can be represented as: the convolution integral

$$y(t) = \int_{-\infty}^t G(t-\tau)u(\tau)d\tau$$

where it is assumed that u(t) is absolutely continuous on $[-\infty,t]$.

Assuming that the Laplace transform of y(t) and u(t) exists we have

$$\int_0^\infty y(t)e^{-st}dt = \int_{t=0}^\infty \int_{\tau=0}^\infty G(\tau)u(t-\tau)e^{-st}d\tau dt$$

$$= \int_\tau \int_t G(\tau)e^{-s\tau}u(t-\tau)e^{-s(t-\tau)}dtd\tau$$

thus

$$\hat{y}(s) = \hat{G}(s)\hat{u}(s)$$

Hence the Laplace transform of the output is the product of the Laplace transforms of the impulsresponse function $G(\tau)$ and the input u(t).

The *z-transform* can be related to the Laplace transform as follows, see Standard Mathematical Tables (1973). Let F(t) be a continuous function of time, sampled at regular intervals $\Delta$. In picture:

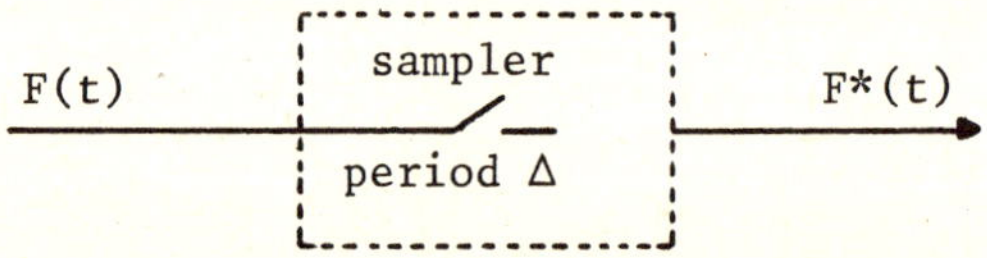

From the picture it can be seen that this is an input-output system with input F(t) and output F*(t). The sampling frequency is $w = 1/\Delta$. Define the set of impuls functions $\delta_\Delta(t)$ by

$$\delta_\Delta(t) \triangleq \sum_{n=0}^{\infty} \delta(t-n\Delta)$$

where $\delta(s) = 0$ for $s \neq 0$ and $\int_a^b \delta(s)ds = 1$, for $a < 0 < b$.
The ΣI/O is

$$F^*(t) = F(t)\delta_\Delta(t) = \sum_{n=0}^{\infty} F(n\Delta)\delta(t-n\Delta).$$

The Laplace transform is

$$L\{F^*(t)\} = \hat{f}^*(s) = \int_0^\infty \sum_{n=0}^{\infty} F(n\Delta)\delta(t-n\Delta)e^{-st}dt$$

$$= \sum_{n=0}^{\infty} F(n\Delta)e^{-n\Delta s}$$

The variable z is introduced by means of the transformation $z = e^{\Delta s}$. Since any function of s can now be replaced by a corresponding function of z we have

$$f(z) \triangleq \sum_{n=0}^{\infty} F(n\Delta)z^{-n}$$

which defines the z-transform for a sequence of discrete signals $\{F(n\Delta)\}$. The inverse of z can be seen as the back-ward shift operator, i.e. $z^{-1}F(n\Delta) = F((n-1)\Delta)$ because $z^{-k} = \delta(t-k\Delta)$. For example $z^{-k}F^*(t) = \delta(t-k\Delta)\sum_{n=0}^{\infty} F(n\Delta)\delta(t-n\Delta) = F(t-k\Delta)$.

Notice that z depends on the length of the sampling interval Δ. It is assumed, however, that the series converges for $|z| \geq z_o$.

Dynamic Systems with State Space (Σm).

Deterministic Σm.

A dynamic system with state space is defined by:

Definition (2.5) : $\Sigma m \triangleq \{T,U,\mathcal{U},Y,\mathcal{Y},\chi,\varphi,r\}$ where

1) $T,U,\mathcal{U},Y,\mathcal{Y}$ are the same as in definition (2.1)
2) $\chi$ is the set of all possible states
3) $\varphi$ is the state space evolution function

with $\varphi$: $T_+^2 \times \chi \times \mathcal{U} \to \chi$ where

$T_+^2 = \{(t_1,t_o) \in T^2 \mid t_1 > t_o\}$

and with the following properties:

(i) $\varphi(t_o,t_o,x_o,u) = x_o \qquad x_o \in \chi$

(ii) $\varphi(t_2,t_1,\varphi(t_1,t_o,x_o,u),u) = \varphi(t_2,t_o,x_o,u)$

(iii) if for $u_1,u_2 \in \mathcal{U}$, $u_1(t) = u_2(t)$ and for $t_o \leqq t < t_1$ then $\varphi(t_1,t_o,x_o,u_1) = \varphi(t_1,t_o,x_o,u_2)$

(iv) r is the reading function:

$r: \chi \times U \times T \to Y.$

$\varphi(t_1,t_o,x_o,u) = x_1$ is the state obtained at time $t_1$ by starting from $x_o$ and applying input u where $x_1 \in \chi$. $r(\varphi(t_1,t_o,x_o,u),u(t),t) = y(t)$ is the output we 'read' if the system is in 'state' $x_o$ applying input u(t).

Definition (2.6) : $\Sigma m$ is called a *linear* state space model if $U,\mathcal{U},Y,\mathcal{Y}$ are vector spaces in $\mathbb{R}$ and if $\varphi(t_1,t_o,\ldots): \chi \times \mathcal{U} \to \chi$ is linear and $r(.,.,t): \chi \times U \to Y$ is linear for all t.

Definition (2.7) : $\Sigma m$ is called *stationary* if $\varphi(t_1+t,t_o+t,x_o,u) = \varphi(t_1,t_o,x_o,S_t u)$ and $r(x,u,t)$ independent of t.

If T = Z or $\{k \in Z \mid k \geqq k_o\}$ and $\mathcal{U} = \{u(k)\}_{-\infty}^{\infty}$ and $\mathcal{Y} = \{y(k)\}_{-\infty}^{\infty}$ we have starting from $x_{k_o}$ with input $u_{k_o}$ the following one-step evolution function

$$\varphi(k_o+1,k_o,x_o,u_{k_o}) = f_{k_o}(x_{k_o},u_{k_o})$$

The following recurrent relations determine the model completely

$$x(k+1) = f_k(x(k),u(k)), \text{ initial condition } x(k_o) = x_{k_o}$$
$$y(k) = p_k(x(k),u(k)).$$

Here $f_k: \chi \times \mathcal{U} \to \chi$ and $p_k: \chi \times U \to Y$.

If $f_k$ and $p_k$ are linear they can be represented by matrices.

The linear discrete state space model can be written as:

process equation: $x(k+1) = A(k)x(k) + B(k)u(k)$

output equation : $y(k) = C(k)x(k) + D(k)u(k)$

where $k \in Z$, $x \in \mathbb{R}^n$, $u \in \mathbb{R}^p$, $y \in \mathbb{R}^m$, initial condition $x(0) = x_o$. The stationary, linear, discrete state space models can be written as proces

process equation: $x(k+1) = Ax(k) + Bu(k)$, initial condition $x(0) = x_o$.

output equation : $y(k) = Cx(k) + Du(k)$.

Remark: In system theory the process eq. is also called the state eq.

Example (2.3):

From example (2.1) we have the reduced form model

$$y(k) = \Pi z(k), \qquad k = 1,2,\dots$$

with $y(k) \in \mathbb{R}^m$ and $z(k) \in \mathbb{R}^p$. If $z(k)$ includes a lagged endogenous vector $y(k-1)$ we have

$$y(k) = Ay(k-1) + Bu(k).$$

$\Pi$, A and B are parameter matrices. Rearrange the rows of

$$\Pi = \begin{bmatrix} \pi_{11} & \cdots & \pi_{1p} \\ \vdots & & \vdots \\ \pi_{m1} & \cdots & \pi_{mp} \end{bmatrix}$$

into the vector: $\tilde{\pi} \triangleq (\pi_{11},\dots,\pi_{1p},\pi_{21},\dots,\pi_{2p},\pi_{m1},\dots,\pi_{mp})$. The parameter vector $\tilde{\pi}$ satisfies the trivial difference equation:

$\tilde{\pi}(k) = \tilde{\pi}(k-1) = \tilde{\pi}(k-2) = \dots = \tilde{\pi}(0) = \tilde{\pi}$

The above reduced form model can be rewritten as the following non-stationary m with $A(k) = I$, $B(k) = 0$, $D(k) = 0$ and

$$C(k) = Z(k) \triangleq \begin{bmatrix} z'(k) & 0 & 0 \\ 0 & z'(k) & 0 \\ \vdots & & \vdots \\ 0 & \dots & z'(k) \end{bmatrix}$$

and $\tilde{\pi}(k)$ as the state vector

$$\tilde{\pi}(k) = \tilde{\pi}(k-1), \quad \text{initial condition } \tilde{\pi}(0) = \tilde{\pi}.$$
$$y(k) = Z(k)\tilde{\pi}(k)$$

Another trivial state space description of the reduced form model

$$y(k) = Ay(k-1) + Bu(k), \qquad k = 1,2,\dots$$

is by considering the output vector $y(k)$ to be the state vector giving the following stationary $\Sigma m$

$$x(k+1) = Ax(k) + Bu(k), \qquad \text{initial condition } x(0) = y_o$$
$$y(k) = x(k)$$

This trivial rewriting of the reduced form model as a state space model is often done in order to perform control experiments.

Stochastic Systems with State-Space.

A stochastic system with state space is defined by:

Definition (2.8) : $\Sigma s \triangleq \{T,U,\mathcal{U},Y,\mathcal{Y},\chi,\phi,s,r\}$.

$T,U,\mathcal{U},Y,\mathcal{Y},\chi$ are defined in definitions (2.1) and (2.5).

1) $\Phi$: is a set of distribution functions on the state space $\chi$ and output space Y; every element $\varphi \in \Phi$ is a potential initial distribution function.

2) s: is a stochastic state evolution function, which defines for every $x_o \in \chi$ and every $t',t \in T$ with $t' \geqq t$ and every $u \in \mathcal{U}$ a distribution function.

$s: T_+^2 \times \chi \times \mathcal{U} \to \Phi$

s must fulfill two conditions for a finite dimensional state space. Let $F(x',t' \mid x_o,t_o,u)$ be the conditional distribution function of the state at time $t'$, $x_o$ the state of time $t_o$ and u the input. Let $u,\tilde{u} \in \mathcal{U}$ with $u(t) = \tilde{u}(t)$ for every $t \in [t_o,t'] \cap T$ then for every $x',x_o \in \chi$ the following conditions must hold:

(i) $F(x',t' \mid x_o,t_o,u) = F(x',t' \mid x_o,t_o,\tilde{u})$

(ii) For every $t_o,t_1 \in T$ with $t_o \leqq t_1 < t_2$ and for every $x_o,x' \in \chi$ and for every $u \in \mathcal{U}$;

$$F(x',t_2 \mid x_o,t_o,u) = \int_{\chi} F(x',t_2 \mid \xi,t_1,u) \times F(\xi,t_1 \mid x_o,t_o,u)d\xi$$

This equation is called the equation of *Chapman-Kolmogorov* and can be seen as an extension of the semi-group property of the state evolution function in deterministic systems with state space.

Roughly speaking it states that the conditional distribution function at time $t_2$ starting at time $t_o$ equals the one obtained through the intermediate state $\xi$.

3) r: is a output function and defines for every $x \in \chi$ and for every $u(t) \in U$ a distribution function on Y.

$r: \chi \times U \times T \rightarrow \Phi$

The deterministic discrete state space models were determined by the recurrent equations

$$x(k+1) = f_k(x(k),u(k)), \qquad \text{initial condition } x(0) = x_o$$
$$y(k) = p_k(x(k),u(k))$$

A similar construction applies for discrete stochastic state space models. A *class* of stochastic state space models can be represented by

$$\underline{x}(k+1) = f_k(\underline{x}(k),u(k),\underline{w}(k))$$
$$\underline{y}(k) = p_k(\underline{x}(k),u(k),\underline{v}(k))$$

Here $\underline{w}(k)$ and $\underline{v}(k)$ represent stochastic processes with outcome space $\Omega$. It is usually assumed that $\underline{w}(k)$ and $\underline{v}(k)$ are gaussian. For every outcome $\underline{w} = w \in \Omega$ and $\underline{v} = v \in \Omega$ we have a deterministic system.
A general *non-linear* stochastic state space model can be represented by the following equations, see Sage and Melsa (1971):

$$\underline{x}(k+1) = \Phi(\underline{x}(k),k) + \Gamma(\underline{x}(k),k)\underline{w}(k) + \Theta(u(k),k)$$

$$\underline{y}(k) = \psi(\underline{x}(k),k) + \Xi(\underline{x}(k),k)\underline{v}(k) + \pi(u(k),k)$$

with initial condition $\underline{x}(0) \sim N(\mu_x(0),\Sigma_x(0))$.
If $\Phi(\underline{x}(k),k) = A(k)\underline{x}(k)$, $\Gamma(\underline{x}(k),k) = B(k)\underline{x}(k)$, $\psi(\underline{x}(k),k) = C(k)\underline{x}(k)$, $\Xi(\underline{x}(k),k) = 0$ or $I$ we have the so-called *bilinear* model, see Priestley (1978). If $\Phi(\underline{x}(k),k) = A(k)\underline{x}(k)$, $\Gamma(\underline{x}(k),k) = I$, $\psi(\underline{x}(k),k) = C(k)\underline{x}(k)$, $\Xi(\underline{x}(k),k) = I$, $\Theta(u(k),k) = B(k)u(k)$ and $\pi(u(k),k) = D(k)u(k)$ we obtain the important class of discrete linear stochastic state space models fully specified as:

$$\underline{x}(k+1) = A(k)\underline{x}(k) + B(k)u(k) + \underline{w}(k)$$

$$\underline{y}(k) = C(k)\underline{x}(k) + D(k)u(k) + \underline{v}(k), \qquad k = 1,2,\ldots$$

where $\underline{x}(k) \in \mathbb{R}^n$, $u(k) \in \mathbb{R}^p$, $\underline{y}(k) \in \mathbb{R}^m$. The initial distribution of $\underline{x}(0)$ is gaussian with mean $\mu_x(0)$ and covariance $\Sigma_x(0)$. The stochastic noise vector $(\underline{w}(k)'\underline{v}(k)')'$ is gaussian with zero mean and covariance

$$\operatorname{cov}\begin{bmatrix}\begin{bmatrix}\underline{w}(k)\\ \underline{v}(k)\end{bmatrix} & (\underline{w}'(s)\underline{v}'(s))\end{bmatrix} = \begin{bmatrix}\Sigma_w(k) & \Sigma_{wv}(k)\\ \Sigma_{vw}(k) & \Sigma_v(k)\end{bmatrix}\delta_{ks}.$$

The noise vector $\underline{w}(k)$ is called the *process noise* and $\underline{v}(k)$ represents the *measurement noise*. The state vector $\underline{x}(k)$ is usually not observable.

Example (2.4):

Consider the following regression equation

$$\underline{y}(k) = x'(k)\underline{\beta}(k) + \underline{\varepsilon}(k),$$

where $x(k) \in \mathbb{R}^p$ is a vector of exogenous variables and $\underline{\varepsilon}(k)$ is a white noise process. Assume the parameter vector $\underline{\beta}(k)$ to be first order Markov process, $\underline{\beta}(k) = \underline{\beta}(k-1) + \underline{w}(k-1)$, with initial distribution $\underline{\beta}(0) \sim N(\beta_o,\Sigma\beta_o)$ and $\underline{w}(k-1)$ a white noise vector. By considering the parameter vector $\underline{\beta}(k)$ to be the state vector, we have the linear state space model

$$\underline{\beta}(k) = \underline{\beta}(k-1) + \underline{w}(k-1)$$

$$\underline{y}(k) = x'(k)\underline{\beta}(k) + \underline{\varepsilon}(k), \qquad k = 1,2,\ldots$$

with initial distribution $\underline{\beta}(0) \sim N(\beta_o,\Sigma\beta_o)$.

Discrete Time Systems Obtained by Sampling Continuous Systems.

Equivalent to a discrete time $\Sigma m$, a time-continuous $\Sigma m$ can be written as

$$\dot{x}(t) = Ax(t) + Bu(t), \qquad \text{initial condition } x(0) = x_o$$

$$y(t) = Cx(t) + Du(t), \qquad t \geqq t_o$$

where $\dot{x}(t) \triangleq dx(t)/dt$ and $x(t)$, $u(t)$ and $y(t)$ are continuous functions of time. The so-called transition matrix for this system is, see Kwakernaak (1972)

$$\Phi(t,t_o) \triangleq e^{A(t-t_o)}$$

where the exponential of a square matrix is defined as

$$e^M = I + \frac{1}{2!} M^2 + \frac{1}{3!} M^3 + \ldots$$

When this continuous system is sampled at equidistant intervals $\Delta$, the discrete time $\Sigma m$ is given by

$$\tilde{x}(k+1) = A_d\tilde{x}(k) + B_d\tilde{u}(k)$$
$$\tilde{y}(k) = C_d\tilde{x}(k) + D_d\tilde{u}(k), \qquad k \geqq t_o$$

where

$$A_d = e^{A\Delta} \quad , B_d = (\int_0^{\Delta} e^{A\tau} d\tau)B$$
$$C_d = Ce^{A\Delta} \quad \text{and } D_d = C(\int_0^{\Delta} e^{A\tau} d\tau)B + D$$

Note that the matrices $A_d$, $B_d$, $C_d$ en $D_d$ depend on the sampling interval.

Example (2.5):

Consider the system $\dot{x}(t) = Ax(t)$, $t \geqq t_o$, with $A = \text{diag}(-1/2\theta - 1/\theta)$. Suppose the system is sampled at intervals $\Delta$, then at period $t_o+\Delta$ the transition matrix is given by

$$\Phi(t,t_o) = \Phi(\Delta) = A_d = \text{diag}(e^{\frac{-\Delta}{2\theta}} e^{\frac{-\Delta}{\theta}})$$

and hence $A_d$ depends on the sampling interval $\Delta$.

Transfer Functions.

Before defining tranfer functions, the z-transform introduced before is briefly restated. The z-transform, $\hat{X}(z)$ of a sequence of vectors $x(k)$, $k = 0,1,\ldots$ is

$$\hat{X}(z) = \sum_{k=0}^{\infty} z^{-k} x(k)$$

where $z \in \mathbb{C}$. This transform is defined for those values of z for which the sum converges, see Kwakernaak (1972). Applying the z-transform to the convolution sum $y(k) = \sum_{\tau=0}^{\infty} G_\tau u(k-\tau)$ yields $\hat{Y}(z) = \hat{G}(z)\hat{U}(z)$. $\hat{G}(z)$ is called the *transfer function* and consists of elements which are proper rational functions of z.

Example (2.6):

Suppose the following stationary discrete $\Sigma m$

$$x(k+1) = Ax(k) + Bu(k), \qquad k = 0,1,\ldots$$

where $x(k) \in \mathbb{R}^n$ and $u(k) \in \mathbb{R}^m$. Multiplication of both sides by $z^{-k}$ and summation over $k = 0,1,\ldots$ yields

$$z\sum_{k=0}^{\infty} x(k)z^{-k} - zx(0) = A\hat{X}(z) + B\hat{U}(z)$$

or $(zI-A)\hat{X}(z) = B\hat{U}(z)$ for $x(0) = 0$. Suppose the output is given by $y(k) = Cx(k) + Du(k)$ then $\hat{Y}(z) = \hat{H}(z)\hat{U}(z)$, where $\hat{H}(z) = C(zI-A)^{-1}B + D$. Let $\tilde{A}(z) = (zI-A)$ then $\tilde{A}^{-1}(z) = \tilde{A}^*(z)/\det(\tilde{A}(z))$ where $\tilde{A}^*(z)$ is the adjoint and $\det(\tilde{A}(z))$ is a finite polynomial in z. The tranfer function is generally of the form $\hat{H}(z) = P(z)/\det(\tilde{A}(z))$, where $P(z)$ is a polynomial matrix in z. The roots of $\det(\tilde{A}(z))$ are called the *poles* of $\hat{H}(z)$. The elements of $\hat{H}(z)$ are rational functions of z. The denominator of the transfer function $\hat{H}(z)$ is $\det(\tilde{A}(z))$, unless cancellation occurs of factors of the form $(z-\lambda_i)$, where $\lambda_i$ is a characteristic value of A, in all elements of $\hat{H}(z)$. It can be shown, see Kwakernaak (1972) that if $\hat{H}(z)$ is a square matrix we have $\det(\hat{H}(z)) = \psi(z)/\Phi(z)$ where $\Phi(z) = \det(\tilde{A}(z))$ and $\psi(z)$ is a polynomial in z. The roots of $\psi(z)$ are called the *zeroes* of the system.

## 2.2. Observability, Reconstructability and Controllability.

These concepts are defined for state space models and are important for control and filtering theory. The concepts are briefly discussed for the deterministic case, following Willems (1974) and Kwakernaak (1972) and for the stochastic case, following Jazwinski (1970).

Let $\Sigma m$ be a deterministic system defined in section (2.1).

Definition (2.9) : A $\Sigma m$ is called (completely) *reachable* at time $t_o \in T$ from state $x^* \in \chi$ if for every $x_o \in \chi$ there is a

$t_{-1} \leqq t_o$ and $u \in U$ such that $x_o = \varphi(t_o, t_{-1}, x^*, u)$.

Definition (2.10): $\Sigma m$ is called *controllable* at time $t_o \in T$ towards state $x^* \in \chi$ if for every $x_o \in \chi$ there is a $t_1 \geqq t_o$ and $u \in U$ such that $x^* = \varphi(t_1, t_o, x_o, u)$.

Definition (2.11): Suppose $u \in U$, $y \in Y$ such that for some $x(.)$: $(-\infty, t_o] \cap T \to \chi$, $x(t_1) = \varphi(t_1, t_{-1}, x(t_{-1}), u)$ for $t_{-1} \leqq t_1 \leqq t_o$ and $y(t) = r(x(t), u(t), t)$ for $t \leqq t_o$. Then the state space $\chi$ is called *reconstructable* at time $t_o \in T$ if $x(t_o)$ is uniquely determined from *every* such a u and y.

Definition (2.12): Suppose $u \in U$ and $y \in Y$ are such that there is a $x(.)$: $[t_o, \infty) \cap T \to \chi$ such that $x(t_1) = \varphi(t_1, t_o, x(t_o), u)$ for $t_1 \geqq t_o$ and $y(t) = r(x(t), u(t), t)$ for $t \geqq t_o$. $\chi$ is called *observable* at time $t_o$ if $x(t_o)$ is uniquely determined from every such a u and y.

From the above definitions it can be seen that in case of reconstructability one deals with the question of a unique reconstruction of the present state from the *past* inputs and outputs, whereas the observability deals with the unique determination of the present state from *future* inputs and outputs.

Theorem (2.1) : Suppose the following $\Sigma m$

$$x(k+1) = Ax(k) + Bu(k), \qquad x \in \mathbb{R}^n$$

$$y(k) = Cx(k) + Du(k)$$ then

(i) (reachability from zero) $\Leftrightarrow \text{rank}(B:AB:..A^{n-1}B) = n$

(ii) (controllability) $\Leftrightarrow R(B:AB:...:A^{n-1}B) \subset R(A^n)$ where $R$ denotes the range, i.e. if $L: v_1 \to v_2$ is linear then $R(L) \triangleq \{v_2 \in V_2 \mid \text{there is a } v_1 \in V_1 \text{ with } v_2 = Lv_1\}$

(iii) (observability) $\Leftrightarrow \text{rank}(C'(CA)'...(CA^{n-1})')' = n$

(iv) (reconstructability) $\Leftrightarrow \Pi(C'(CA)'...(CA^{n-1})')' \subset$ $\subset \Pi(A^n)$ where $\Pi$ denotes the null space, i.e., $\Pi(L) \triangleq \{v_1 \in V_1 \mid Lv_1 = 0\}$.

For a non-stationary $\Sigma m$

$$x(k+1) = A(k)x(k) + B(k)u(k)$$
$$y(k) = C(k)x(k)$$

we have, according to Kwakernaak (1972) the following. Define a real $(n\times n)$ transition matrix

$$\varphi(k,k_o) \triangleq \begin{cases} A(k-1)A(k-2)\dots A(k_o) & k \geq k_o+1 \\ I & k = k_o \end{cases}$$

<u>Theorem (2.2)</u> : $\Sigma m$ is completely controllable if and only if for every $k_o$ there is a $k_1 \geq k_o+1$ such that the symmetric non-negative definite matrix

$$W(k_o,k_1) \triangleq \sum_{k=k_o}^{k_1-k} \varphi(k_1,k+1)B(k)B'(k)\varphi'(k_1,k+1) \text{ is non-singular.}$$

<u>Theorem (2.3)</u> : $\Sigma m$ is completely reconstructable if and only if for every $k_1$ there is a $k_o \leq k_1-1$ such that the symmetric non-negative definite matrix

$$M(k_o,k_1) \triangleq \sum_{k=k_o+1}^{k_1} \varphi'(k,k_o+1)C'(k)C(k)\varphi(k,k_o+1) \text{ is non-singular.}$$

<u>Example (2.7):</u>

Consider the following reduced form model without disturbances $y(k) = Ay(k-1) + Bu(k-1)$, $y(k),u(k) \in \mathbb{R}^2$, where $y(k)$ is a vector to be controlled towards zero. From the controllability condition we have that $y(k)$ is controllable if $\mathcal{R}(B{:}AB) \subset \mathcal{R}(A^2)$ which is fulfilled iff rank $\text{rank}(B{:}AB) = 2$. The if part can seen as follows. Suppose we want to reach state $y^* = 0$ in a finite number of steps by manipulating $u(.)$. After two periods we have $y(2) = Ay(1) + Bu(1) = A^2y(0) + ABu(0) + Bu(1)$. Now $(B{:}AB)\begin{bmatrix} u(1) \\ u(2) \end{bmatrix} = -A^2y(0)$, which has a solution if $(B{:}AB)^{-1}$ exists and hence if $\text{rank}(B{:}AB) = 2$.

<u>Example (2.8):</u>

Casti (1977) considers a simplified Leontief system in which the production period is measured in discrete time units. Let the model be $x(k+1) = Ax(k) + Ml(k)$, $x \in \mathbb{R}^n$, $l \in \mathbb{R}^p$ where the production matrix A is of the form

$$A = \begin{bmatrix} 0 & \cdots\cdots & 0 & a_1 \\ a_2 & 0 & \cdots & 0 \\ 0 & & & \vdots \\ \vdots & & & \vdots \\ 0 & \cdots\cdots & a_n & 0 \end{bmatrix} \qquad a_i \geqq 0$$

The vector x(k) represents the various products $x_i(k)$, i = 1,...,(n-1) with $x_n(k)$ being the finished product and $x_i(k)$ being intermediate products. The matrix M = diag($m_1,\ldots,m_n$), $m_i \geqq 0$. The vector l(k) is the labour input. Assume that, based on the knowledge of the finished product $x_n(k)$, we want to determine the level of production of the intermediate products. The measured output is given by $y(k) = x_n(k) = Cx(k)$ where $C = (0 \ldots 0\ 1)$. So $x_i(k)$, i = 1,...,(n-1) have to be reconstructed from the output $x_n(k)$. According to theorem (2.1) we have that $x_i(k)$ is reconstructable if

$$\mathrm{rank}(C':A'C'\ldots(A')^{n-1}C') = \mathrm{rank}\begin{bmatrix} 0 & \cdots\cdots\cdots & \prod_{i=2}^{n} a_i \\ \vdots & a_n a_{n-1} & 0 \\ \vdots & a_n & \vdots \\ \vdots & & \vdots \\ 1 & \cdots\cdots\cdots & 0 \end{bmatrix} = n$$

that is only if $a_i \neq 0$ for i = 2,...,n.

Example (2.9):

Consider the following 'regression' equation is state space form without disturbances

$$\beta(k+1) = \beta(k)$$
$$y(k) = x'(k)\beta(k), \qquad k = 1,2,\ldots$$

where $\beta(k) \in \mathbb{R}^p$ is the parameter vector; x(k) is a p-dimensional vector of exogenous variables and $y(k) \in \mathbb{R}$ is the output variable. From theorem (2.3) we know that β(k) is reconstructable from the past observations if for $k_0 = 0$ the (p×p) matrix $M(0,k_1) = \sum_{k=1}^{k_1} x(k)x'(k)$ is non-singular. This condition coincides with the condition for least squares estimation. The least squares 'estimator' $b(k_1)$ is given by

$b(k_1) = (\sum_{k=1}^{k_1} x(k)x'(k))^{-1} \sum_{k=1}^{k_1} x(k)y(k)$ for $k_1 \geqq 1$ and hence $\sum_{k=1}^{k_1} x(k)x'(k)$ must be non-singular.

Stochastic Controllability and Reconstructability.

In Jazwinski (1970) some conditions are given for the following stochastic model to be controllable and reconstructable.

$$\underline{x}(k+1) = A(k)\underline{x}(k) + \underline{w}(k)$$

$$\underline{y}(k) = C(k)\underline{x}(k) + \underline{v}(k)$$

It is assumed that the white noise processes $\underline{w}(.)$ and $\underline{v}(.)$ are uncorrelated with covariances respectively $\Sigma_w(k)$ and $\Sigma_v(k)$.

Theorem (2.4) : The model (the pair $A(k),\sqrt{\Sigma_w}(k)$) is completely stochastically controllable if

$$\widetilde{W}(k_o,k_1) \triangleq \sum_{k=k_o}^{k_1-k} \varphi(k_1,k+1)\Sigma_w(k)\varphi'(k_1,k+1)$$

is positive definite for $k_o \geqq 0$. The model is said to be uniformly completely controllable if there is a positive integer N and positive constants $\alpha$ and $\beta$ such that $0 < \alpha I \leqq \widetilde{W}(k-N,k) \leqq \beta I$ for *all* $k \geqq N$.

Theorem (2.5) : The model (the pair $A(k),C(k)$) is completely stochastically reconstructable if

$$\widetilde{M}(k_o,k_1) \triangleq \sum_{k=k_o+1}^{k_1} \varphi'(k,k_o+1)C'(k)\Sigma^{-1}v(k)C(k)\varphi(k,k_o+1)$$

is positive definite. The model is uniformly completely stochastically reconstructable if there is positive integer N and positive constants $\alpha$ and $\beta$ such that $0 < \alpha I \leqq \widetilde{M}(k-N,k) \leqq \beta I$ for all $k \geqq N$.

## 2.3. Realization Theory.

It is not the intention to study realization theory in depth, because the theory for stochastic dynamical systems is still in motion and somewhat random, but merely to give an impression of this important concept in system theory. The problem in realization theory is to obtain a state space model from input-output data, or in other words, given an input-output description, find a state space model with the same behaviour as the input-output model. The problem will be illustrated for the following deterministic ΣI/O

$$y(k) = \sum_{j=-\infty}^{k} G_{k-j} u(j), \quad k,j \in Z,\ y(k) \in \mathbb{R}^p \text{ and } u(k) \in \mathbb{R}^m.$$

The problem is to realize this system as the following state space model

$$x(k+1) = Ax(k) + Bu(k)$$

$$y(k) = Cx(k) + Du(k)$$

with initial state $x^* = 0$. (Notation: $(\Sigma m, x^*) \Leftrightarrow \Sigma I/O$).)
The realization is called *minimal* if $G_k = CA^{k-1}B$ and $G_o = D$. For this model the realization has been solved and will now be given. Define the following matrices:

1) Hankel matrix

$$H \triangleq \begin{bmatrix} G_1 & G_2 & \cdots & G_j & \cdots \\ G_2 & G_3 & & \vdots & \\ \vdots & \vdots & & \vdots & \\ G_k & G_{k+1} & \cdots & G_{k+j-1} & \cdots \\ \vdots & \vdots & & \vdots & \end{bmatrix}$$

2) the finite Hankel matrix

$$H_{N,N'} \triangleq \begin{bmatrix} G_1 & G_2 & \cdots & G_{N'} \\ \vdots & \vdots & & \vdots \\ G_N & G_{N+1} & \cdots & G_{N+N'-1} \end{bmatrix}$$

3) the shifted Hankel matrix

$$\sigma H \triangleq \begin{bmatrix} G_2 & G_3 & \cdots & G_{j+1} & \cdots \\ G_3 & \vdots & & \vdots & \\ \vdots & \vdots & & \vdots & \\ G_{k+1} & G_{k+2} & \cdots & G_{k+j+1} & \cdots \\ \vdots & \vdots & & \vdots & \end{bmatrix}$$

The rank of H is defined as $\text{rank}(H) = \sup_{N,N'} \text{rank}(H_{N,N'}) = \lim_{N,N' \to \infty} \text{rank}(H)$.

It can be proved that for *given* impulse response functions $\{G_k\}_o^\infty$ we have

<u>Theorem (2.6)</u> : (i) there is a (A,B,C,D) such that $\dim(x) < \infty$ and $(A,B,C,D) \Rightarrow \{G_k\}_o^\infty \Leftrightarrow \text{rank } H < \infty$

(ii) there is a realization with $\dim(x) = \text{rank}(H)$

(iii) Suppose $\text{rank}(H) < \infty$ then $\dim(x) = \text{rank}(H) \Leftrightarrow$ the realization is observable and controllable $\Leftrightarrow$ the realization is minimal

(iv) If $\{A_1,B_1,C_1,D_1\} \Leftrightarrow \{G_k\}_o^\infty$ and $\{A_2,B_2,C_2,D_2\} \Leftrightarrow$ $\Leftrightarrow \{G_k\}_o^\infty$ with $\dim(x_1) = \dim(x_2) = \text{rank}(H) < \infty$ then the two realizations are T-equivalent, that is, there is a non-singular matrix T such that $A_2 = TA_1T^{-1}$, $B_2 = TB_1$, $C_2 = C_1T^{-1}$ and $D_2 = D_1$.

<u>Remark.</u> When discussing canonical forms a procedure will be given to select a unique number in the class of T-equivalent realizations.

<u>Realization algorithm:</u>

<u>Step I</u> : Determine N,N' such that $n = \text{rank}(H) = \text{rank}(H_{N,N'})$

Step II : Factorize $H_{N,N'}$ as $H_{N,N'} = PQ$ with P a (Np×n) matrix and Q a (n×N'm) matrix. Let $P_1$ be the (p×n) matrix of the first p rows of P and $Q_1$ be the (n×m) matrix of the m first columns of Q

Step III: Determine a left inverse of P, $P^{\#}$ and a right inverse of Q, $Q^{\#}$, e.g. $P^{\#} = (P'P)^{-1}P'$ and $Q^{\#} = Q'(QQ')^{-1}$

Step IV : $A = P^{\#}(\sigma H)_{N,N'}Q^{\#}$, $B = Q_1$, $C = P_1$ and $D = G_o$.

<u>Remark 1</u>: The determination of the rank of H may be difficult if $\{G_k\}_o^\infty$ is estimated from noisy observations $\{y(i)\}$ and $\{u(i)\}$, see e.g. Van Kok and Van Wijk (1978). We return to this problem in chapter III.
<u>Remark 2</u>: The procedure is mechanical and no attention is paid to prior restrictions on (A,B,C,D) induced by 'physical' laws or theoretical considerations. The set of minimal realizations may not include prior admissible realizations.

For stochastic systems no unifying approach exists. In the author's view the realization concept relates to a wider concept of reduction of high dimensional data by 'information-preserving' functions to be discussed in chapter III. One such function is the state space vector which accumulates information from past inputs. Other functions may be sufficient statistics, 'factors' from factor analysis, canonical variables, predictors etc.

The following example gives an impression of the relation between realization and sufficient statistics.

Example (2.10):

Suppose we have the following regression model

$$\underline{y}(k) = x'(k)\beta + \underline{\varepsilon}(k), \qquad k = 1,2,\ldots$$

where $\underline{y}(k) \in \mathbb{R}$ and $x(k) \in \mathbb{R}^p$ and $\underline{\varepsilon}(.)$ white noise. The least squares estimator for $\beta$, based on N-observations $\underline{y}(1),\ldots,\underline{y}(N)$ and N-observations $x(1),\ldots,x(N)$, with $N \geqq 1$, is given by

$$\underline{b}(N) = (X'_{(N)}X_{(N)})^{-1}\sum_{i=1}^{N} x(i)\underline{y}(i)$$

where $X_{(N)} = (x(1)',\ldots,x(N)')$. The least squares estimator is $\Sigma I/O$ with $\{\underline{y}(i)\}$ as input and $\{\underline{b}(N)\}$ as output and can be written as the convolution sum $\underline{b}(N) = \sum_{i=-\infty}^{N} G_{N,i}\underline{y}(i)$ where $G_{N,i} \triangleq (X'_{(N)}X_{(N)})^{-1}x(i)$ assumed to be zero for $i \leqq 0$. From mathematical statistics it is known that $\underline{b}(N)$ is sufficient, that is all statistical information from the observations $\underline{y}(1),\ldots,\underline{y}(N)$ with respect to $\beta$ is accumulated in $\underline{b}(N)$, so we may 'forget' the observations $\{\underline{y}(i)\}_1^N$.

In chapter IV it will be shown that the recursive version of the least squares estimator can be written as

$$\underline{b}(N) = \underline{b}(N-1) + K(N)\underline{r}(N), \qquad N > 1$$

where $K(N)$ is a weighting matrix and $\underline{r}(N) \triangleq \underline{y}(N) - x(N)\underline{b}(N-1)$ is the prediction error. This equation is a state space model with $\underline{r}(N)$ as input and with an observable state vector $\underline{b}(N)$. The recursive least squares is a more 'efficient' description than the $\Sigma I/O$ description of the least squares estimator.

## 2.4. Canonical Forms.

In general our only information about the system is through the input-output data, i.e., the tranfer function. Consider a $\Sigma m$,

$$x(k+1) = Ax(k) + Bu(k)$$
$$y(k) = Cx(k) + Du(k)$$

with transfer function $G(z) = C(zI-A)^{-1}B + D$ and another $\Sigma m$,

$$\tilde{x}(k+1) = \tilde{A}\tilde{x}(k) + \tilde{B}u(k)$$
$$y(k) = \tilde{C}\tilde{x}(k) + Du(k)$$

where $\tilde{A} = TAT^{-1}$, $\tilde{B} = TB$, $\tilde{C} = CT^{-1}$. The tranfer function of the second $\Sigma m$ is $\tilde{G}(z) = \tilde{C}[zI-\tilde{A}]^{-1}\tilde{B} + D = CT^{-1}[zI-TAT^{-1}]^{-1}TB + D =$ $= CT^{-1}[T(zI-A)T^{-1}]^{-1}TB + D = C[zI-A]^{-1}B + D = G(z)$ and hence all $\Sigma m$'s, related by a similarity transformation $(A,B,C,D) \overset{T}{\rightarrow} (TAT^{-1},TB,CT^{-1},D)$ have the same tranfer function $G(z)$.

Which one should be chosen? A natural choice is to select a unique member, which remains invariant under (coordinate) transformation, but preserves the basic 'property', in this case the transfer function. This unique member is called a *canonical* form. More formally we have the following:

Definition (2.13): Two systems $(A_1,B_1,C_1,D_1)$ and $(A_2,B_2,C_2,D_2)$ are said to be T-equivalent if there is a non-singular matrix T such that $A_2 = TA_1T^{-1}$, $B_2 = TB_1$, $C_2 = C_1T^{-1}$ and $D_2 = D_1$.

Definition (2.14): The set of systems equivalent to a particular system is called an *orbit* in the parameter space (A,B,C). A *canonical* form is then a subset of the parameter space which intersects each orbit exactly once.

Example (2.11):

Glover (1973) considers the scalar system

$$x(k+1) = ax(k) + bu(k), \qquad b \neq 0$$
$$y(k) = cx(k)$$

with transfer function $G(z) = c(z-a)^{-1}b$ together with a system $(a_1,b_1,c_1)$ with $a_1 = a$, $b_1 = tb$ and $c_1 = ct^{-1}$ for $t \neq 0$. The orbits are given for fixed a by $b_1 = tb$ and $c_1 = ct^{-1}$.
In figure for one orbit:

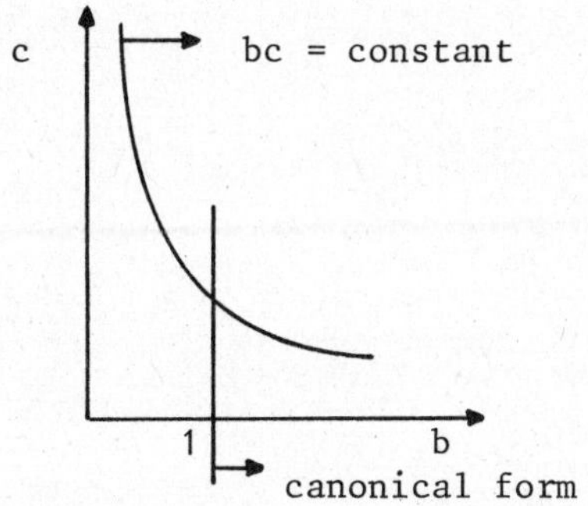


A canonical form can be obtained by a prior value selection for b, e.g. $b = 1$, $a \in \mathbb{R}$, $c \in \mathbb{R}$.

Example (2.12):

In econometrics we often deal with structural models, in simplified version without disturbances: $Ay(k) = Bu(k)$, $y \in \mathbb{R}^p$, $u \in \mathbb{R}^m$, where it is assumed that $A^{-1}$ exists. The structural model is characterized by (A,B). The reduced form is given by $y(k) = A^{-1}Bu(k) = \Pi u(k)$ and hence characterized by the transfer function $\Pi$. Now all structural systems $(A_1,B_1) \overset{T}{\rightarrow} (TA,TB)$ are T-equivalent because $TAy(k) = TBu(k)$ gives the same transfer function $\Pi_1 = (TA)^{-1}TB = A^{-1}B = \Pi$. A canonical form can be obtained by a prior selection of certain values for the parameters of (A,B), leading to the usual rank conditions for what is known in econometrics as the identifiability problem. The basic property for the structural model is the transfer function $\Pi$. See for a discussion Kalman (1981).

Following Casti (1977) we have that basic 'properties' of systems should be independent of the coordinate system used to describe them. Hence we try to isolate and describe coordinate free properties of the system. From the foregoing we have:

(i) choose system features $P$ as candidates for basic properties, e.g. $P$ = {transfer functions}

(ii) specify a transformation group G, which is to act on the system , e.g. G = {all linear coordinate transformations}

(iii) investigate whether the features $P$ remain invariant under transformation from G and if so, choose that system, which describes the system features as 'simply' as possible.

Following Glover (1973) a procedure will be given in order to obtain a canonical form. It is shown in Luenberger (1967) that if the pair (A,B) is controllable then there is an ordered set of integers $\kappa = (k_1,\ldots,k_m)$ such that $k_1 + k_2 + \ldots + k_m = n$, and $\det(P(A,B,\kappa)) \neq 0$ where n is the dimension of the state vector and

$$P(A,B,\kappa) = (b_1, Ab_1, \ldots, A^{k_1-1} b_1, \ldots, b_m, Ab_m, \ldots, A^{k_m-1} b_m).$$

Now if we assume that such a set of integers, $\kappa$, is given then we can state the following result.

Theorem (2.7) : Given the set $\kappa = (k_1,\ldots,k_m)$ and under the assumption on (A,B) that $\det(P(A,B,\kappa)) \neq 0$ the following pair $(\tilde{A},\tilde{B})$ constitutes a canonical form for (A,B) under the transformation $(A,B) \overset{T}{\rightarrow} (TAT^{-1},TB)$

$$\tilde{A} = \begin{bmatrix} A_{11} & \cdots & A_{1m} \\ A_{21} & & \vdots \\ \vdots & & \vdots \\ A_{m1} & \cdots & A_{mm} \end{bmatrix}, \quad \tilde{B} = \begin{bmatrix} B_{11} & \cdots & B_{1m} \\ B_{21} & & \vdots \\ \vdots & & \vdots \\ B_{m1} & \cdots & B_{mm} \end{bmatrix},$$

$$\underset{(k_j \times k_i)}{A_{ji}} = \begin{cases} \left[\begin{array}{c:c} 0_{1,k_i-1} & \alpha_{ii0} \\ \hdashline & \vdots \\ I_{k_i-1} & \alpha_{iik_i-1} \end{array}\right] & j = i \\[2ex] \left[\begin{array}{c:c} & \alpha_{ij0} \\ 0_{k_j,k_i-1} & \vdots \\ & \alpha_{ijk_j-1} \end{array}\right] & j \neq i \end{cases}$$

$$B_{ji}_{(k_j \times 1)} = \begin{cases} \begin{bmatrix} 1 \\ 0 \\ \vdots \\ 0_{k_i,1} \end{bmatrix} & \begin{matrix} j = i \\ j \neq i,\ k_i \neq 0 \end{matrix} \\ \begin{bmatrix} \alpha_{ij0} \\ \alpha_{ij1} \\ \vdots \\ \alpha_{ijk_j-1} \end{bmatrix} & j \neq i,\ k_i = 0 \end{cases}$$

See for a proof Glover (1973). For a detailed study we refer to Glover and Willems (1974).

Remark 1: Basic properties of a state space model are the so-called Kronecker invariants $\{k_i\}$. These invariants are, however, difficult to obtain from noisy observations, because they are sensitive to numerical errors, see e.g. Van Kok and Van Wijk (1978).

Remark 2: As stated before canonical forms may contradict prior admissible structures, induced by physical knowledge about the process.

## 2.5. Stability.

The stability concept is one of the major concepts, arising in all branches of science, because any 'organization' is concerned with its stability as that part of the organization, which maintains it. Historically, stability analysis deals with the question whether a system returns to an equilibrium position after (small) external perturbations, whereas in modern system theory one is concerned with the question of a *controlled* bringing into an equilibrium position, thus applying *actively* perturbations.

Stability is immediately related to the *feed-back* concept. This feedback may be passive, which is related to the *internal* dynamics of a system or active, which is related to *control laws*.

Note the parallel between the historical evolution of stability analysis in system theory and the evolution of economic theory, e.g. the theory

of the 'invisible' hand of Adam Smith (internal passive feed-back) and the theory of Keynes, a more active feed-back theory.
In the sequel various stability concepts and conditions for stability will be introduced. Intuitively stability is associated with a bounded response of a system, depending in general on four quantities, namely (i) time (ii) the initial state (iii) the input and (iv) the functional form of a system. We begin by considering zero-input deterministic systems.

Stability of Zero-Input Deterministic Systems.

Definition (2.15): A *flow* $\Sigma f \triangleq \{T,X,\Phi\}$ with

(i) $T \subset \mathbb{R}$ the time axis

(ii) $X$ a normed space

(iii) $\Phi$ a stated space evolution function: $T_+^2 \times X \to X$ satisfying

1) $\phi(t_1,t_1,x) = x$ (consistency)

2) $\phi(t_2,t_o,x_o) = \phi(t_2,t_1,\phi(t_1,t_o,x))$ with $t_o \leqq t_1 \leqq t_2$ (semi group property).

A typical example of a flow is a differential equation $\dot{x} = f(x,t)$ with $x \in \mathbb{R}^n$ and $f\colon \mathbb{R}^n \times \mathbb{R} \to \mathbb{R}^n$.

Definition (2.16): Suppose $\Sigma f = \{T,X,\Phi\}$ with X a normed space and $x^*(t)$ a *trajectory* of $\Sigma f$. This trajectory is called stable in the sense of *Lyapunov* if for any $t_o$ and $\varepsilon > 0$ there is a $\delta(\varepsilon,t_o) > 0$ such that $\|x(t_o)-x^*(t_o)\| \leqq \delta$ implies $\|x(t)-x^*(t)\| < \varepsilon$ for all $t \geqq t_o$. Here $\|.\|$ denotes a norm on X.

Definition (2.17): $x^*(t)$ is called asymptotically stable if

(i) it is stable in the sense of Lyapunov

(ii) for all $t_o$ there is a $\rho(t_o) > 0$ such that $\|x(t_o)-x^*(t_o)\| < \rho(t_o)$ implies $\|x(t)-x^*(t)\| \to 0$ as $t \to \infty$.

Definition (2.18): $x^*(t)$ is called asymptotically stable in the large if

(i) it is stable in the sense of Lyapunov

(ii) for any $x(t_o)$ and any $t_o$ $\|x(t)-x^*(t)\| \to 0$ as

$t \to \infty$.

Definition (2.19): The linear time-varying differential equation $\dot{x}(t) = A(t)x(t)$ is *exponentially* stable if there are positive constants $\alpha$ and $\beta$ such that

$$\|x(t)\| \leq \alpha e^{-\beta(t-t_o)} \|x(t_o)\|, \qquad t \geq t_o$$

for every initial state $x(t_o)$.

Note that the definitions, except the last one, apply for a *trajectory* $x^*(t)$. This is necessary for non-linear systems, but for linear systems we can speak of stability of systems rather then stability of trajectories. This can be seen as follows.
Let $x^*(t)$ be a solution of the linear differential system $\dot{x}(t) = A(t)x(t)$, and let $x(t)$ be another solution then $d(x(t)-x^*(t))/dt = A(t)(x(t)-x^*(t))$ is also a solution. In order to study the stability of $x^*(t)$ we can study the stability of the zero solution, i.e. $x^*(t) = 0$. If the zero solution is stable any solution is stable.
Because we often deal with linear differential or difference equations, some conditions for stability are given. Suppose $\Sigma f$ is of the form $\dot{x} = Ax(t)$, $x \in \mathbb{R}^n$. The solution is of the form $x(t) = e^{AT}x(0)$, where $e^A = I + A + \frac{1}{2!}A^2 + \ldots$ and $x(0)$ is the initial value. Assume that A has n distinct characteristic values $\lambda_1,\ldots,\lambda_n$. Let the corresponding eigenvectors be $e_1,\ldots,e_n$. Define $T \triangleq (e_1,\ldots,e_n)$ and $\Lambda \triangleq \operatorname{diag}(\lambda_1,\ldots,\lambda_n)$ then (i) $e^{AT} = Te^{\Lambda t}T^{-1}$ and (ii) $e^{\Lambda t} = \operatorname{diag}(e^{\lambda_1 t},\ldots,e^{\lambda_n t})$. The solution can be expressed as $x(t) = \sum_{i=1}^{n} e^{\lambda_i t} e_i f_i x(0) = \sum_{i=1}^{n} \mu_i e^{\lambda_i t} e_i$ where the rows $f_i$ are the rows of $T^{-1}$. The stability of the solution $x(t) = 0$ clearly depends on the eigenvalues $\lambda_1,\ldots,\lambda_n$ obtained from the characteristic polynomial $\det(\lambda I-A) = 0$, denoted by $p(\lambda)$. For the more general case in which some eigenvalues are the same we have the following:

Theorem (2.8) : The linear system $\dot{x}(t) = Ax(t)$ is stable in the sense of Lyapunov if and only if

(i) $\operatorname{Re}(\lambda_i) \leq 0, \qquad i = 1,\ldots,n$

(ii) to any characteristic value with $\operatorname{Re}(\lambda_i) = 0$ and multiplicity m there correspond exactly m independent characteristic vectors of A

(iii) the system is asymptotically stable in the large

if and only if the characteristic values of A have strictly negative real parts.

Condition (ii) is always satisfied if A has not multiple characteristic values on the imaginary axis (m=1). A procedure to test whether $Re(\lambda_i) < 0$ and based on the characteristic polynomial $p(\lambda) = p_n + \dots + p_1\lambda + p_o$ is given by the so-called *Routh-Hurwitz* criterion:

Theorem (2.9) : Let $p_n > 0$, then the roots of $p(\lambda)$ have negative real parts if and only if $\Delta_i > 0$, $i = 1,\dots,n$ where

$$\Delta_1 = \det(p_n-1),\ \Delta_2 = \det\begin{bmatrix} p_{n-1} p_n \\ p_{n-3} p_{n-2} \end{bmatrix},$$

$$\Delta_i = \begin{bmatrix} p_{n-1} & p_n & 0 & 0 & 0 \\ p_{n-3} & p_{n-2} & p_{n-1} & p_n & 0 \\ \vdots & & & & \vdots \\ p_{n+1-2i} & & \cdots & & p_{n-i} \end{bmatrix},$$

$$\Delta_n = \begin{bmatrix} p_{n-1} & p_n & 0 \\ p_{n-3} & p_{n-2} & \vdots \\ \vdots & & p_2 \\ 0 & \cdots & p_o \end{bmatrix}$$

For the discrete difference equation $x(k+1) = Ax(k)$, $x \in \mathbb{R}^n$ we have the following. The solution of the difference equation with $k = 0$ and initial state $x(0)$ is of the form $x(k+1) = A^k x(0)$ or $x(k+1) = \sum_{i=1}^{n} \lambda_i^k e_i f_i x(0)$ where $e_i$ and $f_i$ are defined for the continuous case.

Theorem (2.10) : The time-invariant linear discrete system $x(k+1) = Ax(k)$ is stable in the sense of Lyapunov if and only if

(i) $|\lambda_i| \leq 1$

(ii) to any characteristic value with $|\lambda_i| = 1$ and multiplicity m there correspond exactly m independent characteristic vector of A. The system is asymptotically stable in the large if and only if $|\lambda_i| < 1$, $i = 1,\dots,n$.

The Routh-Hurwitz criterion defined for a continuous system applies mutatis mutandis for the discrete system.

Local Stability for non-linear Systems.

Consider a flow $\Sigma f$: $\dot{x} = f(x(t))$ with equilibrium point $x^* \in \mathbb{R}^n$, an interior point of the state space X, $(f(x^*) = 0)$ and f a differentiable function in the neighbourhood of $x^*$. The linearized flow $\Sigma l$ around $x^*$ is given by $\Sigma l$: $\Delta\dot{x} = \left.\frac{\partial f}{\partial x}\right|_{x=x^*}\Delta x$, where the matrix $\partial f/\partial x$ is the Jacobian evaluated at $x = x^*$.

According to theorem (2.8) we have that if $\mathrm{Re}(\lambda_i) < 0$, $i = 1,\dots,n$ for all eigenvalues $\lambda_i$ of $\left.\frac{\partial f}{\partial x}\right|_{x=x^*}$, then $x^*$ is an asymptotically stable equilibrium point of $\Sigma f$.

For the discrete system $\Sigma^d f$: $x(k+1) = g(x(k))$ with equilibrium point $x^*$, $(g(x^*) = 0)$ we have the linearized flow $\Sigma^d l$: $\Delta x(k+1) = \left.\frac{\partial g}{\partial x}\right|_{x=x^*}\Delta x(k)$. If $|\lambda_i| < 1$ for all eigenvalues of the Jacobian $\left.\frac{\partial g}{\partial x}\right|_{x=x^*}$, the equilibrium point $x^*$ is an asymptotically stable point of $\Sigma^d f$.

Example (2.14):

A general structural model can be written, with suppressed time index, as $g(x_1,\dots,x_l) = 0$, where $x_i$, $i = 1,\dots,l$ are endogenous or predetermined variables. Many economic variables are measured as Value = price × quantity, e.g. $C = p_c c$, where C denotes the consumption, $p_c$ the consumption price and c the 'real' consumption. Assume e.g. $x_1 = C$, $x_i = p_c$ and $x_j = c$ then g is a non-linear function, which may be linearized as follows. Let the reference values (trajectory) be $C^*(k) = p_c^*(k)c^*(k)$, $k = 1,2,\dots$ . Applying a Taylor series around the reference values we have

$$C(k) = g[(p_c(k),c(k)] \approx g[p_c^*(k),c^*(k)] + \frac{\partial g[p_c^*(k),c^*(k)]}{\partial p_c(k)} \cdot$$

$$\cdot\ [p_c(k)-p_c^*(k)] + \frac{\partial g[p_c^*(k),c^*(k)]}{\partial c(k)} \cdot [c(k)-c^*(k)] + \dots$$

$$\approx g[p_c^*(k),c^*(k)] + c^*(k)[p_c(k)-p_c^*(k)] +$$

$$+\ p_c^*(k)[c(k)-c^*(k)] + \dots$$

Suppose the reference values $p_c^*(k) = p_c(k-1)$, $C^*(k) = C(k-1)$ and $c^*(k) = c(k-1)$, where $p_c(k-1)$, $C(k-1)$ and $c(k-1)$ are the observed values at period $(k-1)$, then dividing the left-hand and right-hand side by $C(k-1)$ yields

$$\frac{C(k)-C(k-1)}{C(k-1)} \approx \frac{c(k-1)[p_c(k)-p_c(k-1)]}{p_c(k-1)c(k-1)} + \frac{p(k-1)[c(k)-c(k-1)]}{p_c(k-1)c(k-1)}$$

$$\tilde{C}(k) \approx \tilde{p}_c(k) + \tilde{c}(k)$$

where $\tilde{C}(k)$, $\tilde{p}_c(k)$ and $\tilde{c}(k)$ denote the relative first differences. Stability analysis for the linearized model tells something about the stability around the equilibrium points, being the observed time-series of the nominal variables, but nothing about the trajectory itself. Care should be taken when applying stability conditions in the linearized model. This can be seen from the following simple analysis. Suppose the consumption $C(k)$ grows exponentially with time, i.e. $C(k) = \alpha C(k-1)$ with $\alpha > 1$ (clearly unstable). The relative first difference equation is $\tilde{C}(k) = \tilde{C}(k-1) = \alpha - 1$ because $\tilde{C}(k) = (C(k)-C(k-1))/C(k-1) = \alpha - 1$. It can be immediately noticed that this equation is *always* Lyapunov stable for every trajectory $\{C(i)\}$. Note that $\{C(i)\}$ is not a equilibrium *point*.

External Stability; BIBO Stability.

A type of stability, which may be important for economic systems, is the so-called external stability or BIBO stability (Bounded Input Bounded Output). Only linear time-invariant difference equations will be considered.

Consider the linear discrete system $\Sigma d$:

$$y(k+1) = Ay(k) + Bu(k), \qquad k = k_o, k_o+1, \ldots$$

where $y(k) \in \mathbb{R}^m$; $u(k) \in \mathbb{R}^p$ and with initial condition $\|y(k_o)\| < k_y$.

Definition (2.21): $\Sigma d$ is said to be externally stable if for any $k_o$, any $y(k_o)$ with $\|y(k_o)\| < k_y$ and any $u(.)$ such that $\|u(k)\| \leq \delta$ and for all $k \in [-\infty, \infty]$ there is a constant $\varepsilon(k_o, y(k_o), \delta) > 0$ such that $\|y(k)\| \leq \varepsilon$ for all $k \geq k_o$.

In other words if every bounded input produces a bounded output we have external stability.

<u>Theorem (2.11)</u> : $\Sigma d$ is externally stable if $\sum_{i=0}^{\infty}\|G_i\| = \beta < \infty$ where $G_i = A^{i-1}B$.

<u>Proof</u> : $\Sigma d$ can be written as the following $\Sigma I/O$:
$y(k) = \sum_{i=0}^{\infty} G_i u(k-i)$, where $G_i = A^{i-1}B$ and $y(k_o) = 0$.
Now $\|y(k)\| = \|\sum_{i=0}^{\infty} G_i u(k-i)\|$ and
$\|y(k)\| \leqq \sum_{i=0}^{\infty}\|G_i\| \, \|u(k-i)\| \leqq \sum_{i=0}^{\infty}\|G_i\|\delta$.
$\|y(k)\|$ remains bounded for all $k \geqq k_o$ if
$\sum_{i=0}^{\infty}\|G_i\| = \beta < \infty$. In that case we have $\|y(k)\| \leqq \beta\delta \leqq$
$\leqq \varepsilon < \infty$ where $\varepsilon(\beta,\delta)$.

From the foregoing it can be seen that $\varepsilon$ depends on $\sup\|u(i)\|$ and $\sum_{i=0}^{\infty}\|G_i\| = \beta$ which may be of interest for deriving external stability conditions. Suppose $\bar{\varepsilon} = \|\bar{y}\|$ to be a limit norm of a reference output $\bar{y}$ not to be exceeded by the output norm $\|y(k)\|$ for all k. If $\sum_{i=0}^{\infty}\|G_i\| = \beta$ and $\delta = \sup_{-\infty \leqq i \leqq \infty} \|u(i)\|$ then $\|y(k)\| \leqq \beta\delta \leqq \varepsilon$ implies the inequality $\beta\delta \leqq \bar{\varepsilon}$, which may be a useful inequality for measuring the sequence of maximum inputs ($\delta$) to be allowed, such that $\|y(k)\| \leqq \bar{\varepsilon}$.

<u>Example (2.15)</u>:

Consider the scalar system $y(k) = \sum_{i=0}^{\infty} g_i u(k-i)$, where $g_i = a^{i-1}b$ with $0 < |a| < 1$ and with a limit output norm $\bar{\varepsilon} = |\bar{y}|$. Define the infinite sequences $u \triangleq (u(k), u(k-1), ..)$ and $g \triangleq (g_o, g_1, ...)$ and suppose $\delta = \sup_{-\infty < i < \infty} |u(i)|$. Because $0 < |a| < 1$ we have $\sum_{i=0}^{\infty}|g_i| < \infty$ and

$$|y(k)| \leqq \sum_{i=0}^{\infty}|g_i|\,|u(k-i)| \leqq \|g\|_1 \, \|u\|_\infty \leqq \|g\|_1\delta \leqq \varepsilon$$ using Hölders inequality, where $\|g\|_1$ denotes the $l_1$-norm and $\|u\|_\infty$ the $l_\infty$-norm. Because $\|g\|_1 = \sum_{i=0}^{\infty}|g_i| = |b| + |b||a| + |b||a^2| + \ldots = \beta$ we have

$\beta = |b|/(1-|a|)$. The inequality is $\beta\delta \leqq \bar{\varepsilon}$ or $\delta \leqq \bar{\varepsilon}(1-|a|)/|b|$. It can be seen that the maximum allowable input $\delta$ is increasing with decreasing $|a|$ and $|b|$ and increasing $\bar{\varepsilon}$, which is to be expected.

<u>Remark</u>: Because there are many ways to define matrix norms, and because the norm of a matrix depends on the norm of the input, any norm will do.

# III. Feature Space Modelling

## 3.1. Introduction.

It is rather remarkable that the stochastic linear state space model and Jöreskog's general linear structural model, extensively used in social sciences, are - to a certain extent - equivalent in structure, see e.g. Jöreskog (1977). Jöreskog's model is, however, static and structural, whereas the stochastic linear state space model is (time) dynamic, but not structural. By structural we mean that there exists a relationship between output variables (or output factors). In section 3.2 a general model is formulated, called the linear structural feature space (LSF) model, which essentially features the main characteristics of the two models. It is a linear, dynamic, structural model, which consists of two equations: a structural linear dynamic process equation in the feature space and a linear output or measurement equation. The reduced form version of the (LSF) model, denoted by (LRF) model can be seen as a linear stochastic state space model with stochastic inputs, see for details Otter (1981a).

In this chapter it is shown that models, related to (data-oriented) techniques such as factor analysis, regression covariance modelling, canonical variables and state space realization are special cases of the (LSF) model or the (LRF) model. In chapter VI it is shown that in a variety of cases postulated economic models or models implicitly assumed in certain techniques (e.g. exponential smoothing) appear to be special cases of the (LSF) or (LRF) model.

## 3.2. A Linear Stochastic Dynamic Model with Feature Space.

Consider the following model, called the linear structural feature space (LSF) model:

process equation:

$$\begin{bmatrix} \tilde{A}_{0,1}(k) & \tilde{A}_{0,2}(k) \\ 0 & I \end{bmatrix} \begin{bmatrix} \underline{x}_y(k+1) \\ \underline{x}_u(k+1) \end{bmatrix} = \begin{bmatrix} \tilde{A}_{1,1}(k) & \tilde{A}_{1,2}(k) \\ 0 & \tilde{A}_{1,3}(k) \end{bmatrix} \begin{bmatrix} \underline{x}_y(k) \\ \underline{x}_u(k) \end{bmatrix} +$$

$$+ \begin{bmatrix} \tilde{B}_1(k) \\ \tilde{B}_2(k) \end{bmatrix} u_1(k) + \begin{bmatrix} \underline{\tilde{w}}_1(k) \\ \underline{\tilde{w}}_2(k) \end{bmatrix}$$

or

$$\tilde{A}_o(k)\underline{x}(k+1) = \tilde{A}_1(k)\underline{x}(k) + \tilde{B}(k)u_1(k) + \underline{\tilde{w}}(k)$$

$$\text{initial condition: } \underline{x}(0) \sim N(\mu_x(0), \Sigma_x(0))$$

output equation:

$$\begin{bmatrix} \underline{y}(k) \\ \underline{u}(k) \end{bmatrix} = \begin{bmatrix} C_y(k) & 0 \\ 0 & C_u(k) \end{bmatrix} \begin{bmatrix} \underline{x}_y(k) \\ \underline{x}_u(k) \end{bmatrix} + \begin{bmatrix} D_1(k) \\ D_2(k) \end{bmatrix} u_2(k) + \begin{bmatrix} \underline{v}_1(k) \\ \underline{v}_2(k) \end{bmatrix}$$

or

$$\underline{Y}(k) = C(k)\underline{x}(k) + D(k)u_2(k) + \underline{v}(k), \qquad k = 1,2,...$$

where $\underline{x}_y(k)$ is a $n_1$-dimensional Gaussian vector called the output feature vector, which may be unobservable; $\underline{x}_u(k)$ is a $n_2$-dimensional Gaussian vector called the input feature vector, which may be unobservable; $u_1(k)$ is a p-dimensional deterministic input vector; $\underline{\tilde{w}}_1(k)$ and $\underline{\tilde{w}}_2(k)$ are white noise vectors called process noise with (time-varying) covariances respectively $\text{cov}\{\underline{\tilde{w}}_1(k)\underline{\tilde{w}}_1'(j)\} = \Sigma_{\tilde{w}_1}(k)\delta_{kj}$ and $\text{cov}\{\underline{\tilde{w}}_2(k)\underline{\tilde{w}}_2'(j)\} = \Sigma_{\tilde{w}_2}(k)\delta_{kj}$ and where it is assumed that $\text{cov}\{\underline{\tilde{w}}_1(k)\underline{\tilde{w}}_2'(j)\} = 0$ for all k and j; $\underline{y}(k)$ is a $m_1$-dimensional observable Gaussian output vector; $\underline{u}(k)$ is a $m_2$-dimensional observable Gaussian input vector; $u_2(k)$ is a q-dimensional deterministic input vector; $\underline{v}_1(k)$ and $\underline{v}_2(k)$ are white noise vectors called measurement noise with covariances respectively $\text{cov}\{\underline{v}_1(k)\underline{v}_1'(j)\} = \Sigma_{v_1}(k)\delta_{kj}$ and $\text{cov}\{\underline{v}_2(k)\underline{v}_2'(j)\} = \Sigma_{v_2}(k)\delta_{kj}$ and $\text{cov}\{\underline{v}_1(k)\underline{v}_2'(j)\} = 0$ for all k and j. It is further assumed that $\text{cov}\{\underline{x}(k)\underline{\tilde{w}}'(j)\} = 0$ for all k and j; $\text{cov}\{\underline{x}(k)\underline{v}'(j)\} = 0$ for all k and and $\text{cov}\{\underline{\tilde{w}}(k)\underline{v}'(j)\} = 0$ for all k and j. The (parameter) matrices $\tilde{A}_0(k)$, $\tilde{A}_1(k)$, $\tilde{B}(k)$, $C(k)$ and $D(k)$ may be known or unknown. The reduced form version of the (LSF) model called (LRF) model is given by the following equations

process equation:

$$\begin{bmatrix} \underline{x}_y(k+1) \\ \underline{x}_u(k+1) \end{bmatrix} = \begin{bmatrix} A_1(k) & A_2(k) \\ 0 & A_3(k) \end{bmatrix} \begin{bmatrix} \underline{x}_y(k) \\ \underline{x}_u(k) \end{bmatrix} + \begin{bmatrix} B_1(k) \\ B_2(k) \end{bmatrix} u_1(k) + \begin{bmatrix} \underline{w}_1(k) \\ \underline{w}_2(k) \end{bmatrix}$$

or

$$\underline{x}(k+1) = A(k)\underline{x}(k) + B(k)u_1(k) + \underline{w}(k),$$

$$\text{initial condition: } \underline{x}(0) \sim N(\mu_x(0), \Sigma_x(0))$$

output equation:

$$\begin{bmatrix} \underline{y}(k) \\ \underline{u}(k) \end{bmatrix} = \begin{bmatrix} C_y(k) & 0 \\ 0 & C_u(k) \end{bmatrix} \begin{bmatrix} \underline{x}_y(k) \\ \underline{x}_u(k) \end{bmatrix} + \begin{bmatrix} D_1(k) \\ D_2(k) \end{bmatrix} u_2(k) + \begin{bmatrix} \underline{v}_1(k) \\ \underline{v}_2(k) \end{bmatrix}$$

or

$$\underline{Y}(k) = C(k)\underline{x}(k) + D(k)u_2(k) + \underline{v}(k),$$

where $A_1(k) = \tilde{A}_{0,1}^{-1}(k)\tilde{A}_{1,1}(k)$; $A_2(k) = \tilde{A}_{0,1}(k)[\tilde{A}_{1,2}(k)-\tilde{A}_{0,2}(k)\tilde{A}_{1,3}(k)]$; $A_3(k) = \tilde{A}_{1,3}(k)$; $B_1(k) = \tilde{A}_{0,1}^{-1}(k)[\tilde{B}_1(k)-\tilde{A}_{0,1}(k)\tilde{A}_{0,2}(k)\tilde{B}_2(k)]$; $B_2(k) = \tilde{B}_2(k)$; $\underline{w}_1(k) = \tilde{A}_{0,1}^{-1}(k)\underline{\tilde{w}}_1(k) - \tilde{A}_{0,1}^{-1}(k)\tilde{A}_{0,2}(k)\underline{\tilde{w}}_2(k)$ and $\underline{w}_2(k) = \underline{\tilde{w}}_2(k)$.

Remark 1: We speak of a stationary (LSF) model respectively a stationary (LRF) model if the parameter and covariance matrices are time-invariant, i.e. $\tilde{A}_{0,1}(k) = \tilde{A}_0$; $\tilde{A}_1(k) = \tilde{A}_1$; $\tilde{B}(k) = \tilde{B}$, $C(k) = C$, $D(k) = D$; $A(k) = A$, $B(k) = B$, $\Sigma_{\tilde{w}}(k) = \Sigma_w$ and $\Sigma_v(k) = \Sigma_v$.

Remark 2: The (LRF) model is in *structure* equivalent to a linear stochastic state space model as discussed in chapter II. The differences between the (LRF) model and the state space model are that (i) the output vector of the (LRF) model, $\underline{Y}(k)$ consists of the output vector $\underline{y}(k)$ and the input vector $\underline{u}(k)$ and (ii) the feature output vector $\underline{x}_y(k)$ is a linear function of the (unobservable) feature input vector $\underline{x}_u(k)$ whereas in the state space model the state vector is a linear function of deterministic observable input. See for details Otter (1981a).

Remark 3: When the feature vector $\underline{x}(k)$ is unobservable, under certain conditions $\underline{x}(k)$ can be recursively estimated from the observable output vector $Y(k)$, $k = 1,2,\ldots$ . This recursive estimation is known as Kalman filtering to be discussed in chapter IV. In chapter V a general estimation method called the prediction error method will be discussed in order to estimate the unknown parameters of the feature space models.

Remark 4: The (LSF) or (LRF) model may be dynamic in *space* or *time* e.g. regions, persons, etc.

## 3.3. Models with Factor Space.

Let $\underline{y}(i) = \overline{\underline{y}}(i)+\underline{v}_1(i)$, $i = 1,\ldots,n$ be p-dimensional independent Gaussian output vectors with zero mean and covariance $\text{cov}\{\underline{y}(i)\underline{y}'(j)\} = E\{(\overline{\underline{y}}(i)+\underline{v}_1(i))(\overline{\underline{y}}(j)+\underline{v}_1(j))'\} = E\{\overline{\underline{y}}(i)\overline{\underline{y}}'(j)\} + E\{\underline{v}_1(i)v_1'(j)\} = (\overline{\Sigma}_y+\Sigma_{v_1})\delta_{ij}$. $\overline{\Sigma}_y$ denotes the covariance of the 'true' vector $\overline{\underline{y}}(i)$ assumed to be positive semidefinite with rank r and $\underline{v}_1(i)$ is measurement noise. $\overline{\Sigma}_y$ can be factorized as $\overline{\Sigma}_y = PP'$ with $P = (\sqrt{\lambda_1}c_1,\ldots,\sqrt{\lambda_r}c_r)$ where $c_i$ is the i-th normalized eigenvector with eigenvalue $\lambda_i$, $i = 1,\ldots,r$. The factorization permits the following representation

$$\overline{\underline{y}}(i) = P\underline{f}_y(i)$$

where the unobservable vector $\underline{f}_y(i) \in \mathbb{R}^r$ is called the factor vector with $E\{\underline{f}_y(i)\} = 0$ and $E\{\underline{f}_y(i)\underline{f}_y(j)\} = I\delta_{ij}$. In fact $\underline{f}_y(i)$ is standard white noise. The output vector $\underline{y}(i)$ can be written as the following model

process equation:

$$\underline{f}_y(i) = \underline{w}_1(i)$$

output equation:

$$\underline{y}(i) = P\underline{f}_y(i) + \underline{v}_1(i), \qquad i = 1,\ldots,n$$

where $\underline{w}_1(i)$ is standard white noise.

Let $\underline{u}(i) = \overline{\underline{u}}(i) + \underline{v}_2(i)$, $i = 1,\ldots,n$ be q-dimensional independent

Gaussian vectors with zero mean and covariance $\text{cov}\{(\underline{\bar{u}}(i)+\underline{v}_2(i))(\underline{\bar{u}}(j)+\underline{v}_2(j))'\} = (\bar{\Sigma}_u+\Sigma_{v_2})\delta_{ij}$, where the rank of the positive semidefinite matrix $\bar{\Sigma}_u$ equals s. Let the factorization of $\bar{\Sigma}_u$ be $\bar{\Sigma}_u = QQ'$ where $Q = (\sqrt{\mu_1}d_1,\ldots,\sqrt{\mu_s}d_s)$ where $d_i$ is the i-th normalized eigenvector with eigenvalue $\mu_i$. Then applying the same analysis as before and combining with the factor output model we have

process equation:

$$\begin{bmatrix} \underline{f}_y(i) \\ \underline{f}_u(i) \end{bmatrix} = \begin{bmatrix} \underline{w}_1(i) \\ \underline{w}_2(i) \end{bmatrix}$$

or

$$\underline{f}(i) = \underline{w}(i)$$

output equation:

$$\begin{bmatrix} \underline{y}(i) \\ \underline{u}(i) \end{bmatrix} = \begin{bmatrix} P & 0 \\ 0 & Q \end{bmatrix} \begin{bmatrix} \underline{f}_y(i) \\ \underline{f}_u(i) \end{bmatrix} + \begin{bmatrix} \underline{v}_1(i) \\ \underline{v}_2(i) \end{bmatrix}$$

or

$$\underline{Y}(i) = C\underline{f}(i) + \underline{v}(i).$$

The covariance of the process noise $\underline{w}(i)$ is

$$\text{cov}\{\underline{w}(i)\underline{w}'(j)\} = \Sigma_w = \begin{bmatrix} I & \Phi_{yu} \\ \Phi_{uy} & I \end{bmatrix}\delta_{ij},$$

where $\Phi_{yu}$ denotes the covariance between $\underline{f}_y(i)$ and $\underline{f}_u(i)$. Jöreskog (1977) assumes the following linear structural relation between the factors $\underline{f}_y(i)$ and $\underline{f}_u(i)$

$$B\underline{f}_y(i) = \Gamma\underline{f}_u(i) + \underline{\varepsilon}(i),$$

where it is assumed that $B^{-1}$ exists and $\underline{\varepsilon}(i)$ is white noise with $\text{cov}\{\underline{\varepsilon}(i)\underline{\varepsilon}'(j)\} = \Sigma_\varepsilon\delta_{ij}$ and uncorrelated with $\underline{f}_u(i)$. Note that in this case $\underline{f}_y(i)$ is not standard white noise. The Jöreskog model can be written as

process equation:

$$\begin{bmatrix} B & -\Gamma \\ 0 & I \end{bmatrix} \begin{bmatrix} \underline{f}_y(i) \\ \underline{f}_u(i) \end{bmatrix} = \begin{bmatrix} \underline{\varepsilon}(i) \\ \underline{w}_2(i) \end{bmatrix}$$

or

$$A\underline{f}(i) = \underline{\tilde{w}}(i)$$

output equation:

$$\begin{bmatrix} \underline{y}(i) \\ \underline{u}(i) \end{bmatrix} = \begin{bmatrix} P & 0 \\ 0 & Q \end{bmatrix} \begin{bmatrix} \underline{f}_y(i) \\ \underline{f}_u(i) \end{bmatrix} + \begin{bmatrix} \underline{v}_1(i) \\ \underline{v}_2(i) \end{bmatrix}$$

or

$$\underline{Y}(i) = C\underline{f}(i) + \underline{v}(i).$$

It is easily seen that the Jöreskog model is a static stationary (LSF) model with $\tilde{A}_o \equiv 0$; $\underline{x}(k) = \underline{f}(k)$; $\tilde{A}_1 = -A$; $\tilde{B} \equiv 0$ and $D \equiv 0$.

Model Determination from a Sample.

Let there be n independent outcomes of the input and output vector, u(i) and y(i), i = 1,...,n and let the sample covariance be

$$S = (1/n)\sum_{i=1}^{n} Y(i)Y'(i) = \begin{bmatrix} S_y & S_{yu} \\ S_{uy} & S_u \end{bmatrix}$$

where it is assumed that $S^{-1}$ exists which implies that $n \geqq (p+q)$.
In order to determine the dimensions of the output and input factor spaces, factorize $S_y$ as $C'S_yC = \hat{\Lambda}_y$ where $\hat{\Lambda}_y = \mathrm{diag}(\hat{\lambda}_1,\ldots,\hat{\lambda}_p)$ and where the estimated eigenvalues $\hat{\lambda}_1 > \hat{\lambda}_2 > \ldots > \hat{\lambda}_p$ and factorize $S_u$ as $D'S_uD = \hat{\Lambda}_u$ where $\hat{\Lambda}_u = \mathrm{diag}(\hat{\mu}_1,\ldots,\hat{\mu}_q)$, where the estimated eigenvalues $\hat{\mu}_1 > \hat{\mu}_2 > \ldots > \hat{\mu}_q$.
It is shown by Anderson (1958, section 14.5) that under the assumption that $\mathrm{plim}(S) = \Sigma$

$$n \sum_{i=r+1}^{p} \hat{\underline{\lambda}}_i \xrightarrow{L} \chi^2_{(p-r)(p-r)}$$

if the first r population eigenvalues $\lambda_1 > \ldots > \lambda_r$ are distinct (and stay distinct as $n \to \infty$) and the last (p-r) population eigenvalues are zero. Thus $n.\sum_{i=r+1}^{p}\hat{\lambda}_i$ can be used as a test statistic. Another procedure is to select the dimension according to the number of eigenvalues greater than or equal to one. By covariance modelling we have

$$\Sigma = E\{\underline{Y}(i)\underline{Y}'(i)\} = \begin{bmatrix} P & 0 \\ 0 & Q \end{bmatrix} \begin{bmatrix} B^{-1}\Gamma\Gamma^{-1}B'^{-1}+B^{-1}\Sigma_\varepsilon B'^{-1} & ,B^{-1}\Gamma \\ \Gamma'B'^{-1} & ,I \end{bmatrix} \begin{bmatrix} P' & 0 \\ 0 & Q' \end{bmatrix} +$$

$$+ \begin{bmatrix} \Sigma_{v_1} & 0 \\ 0 & \Sigma_{v_2} \end{bmatrix}$$

where it is assumed that $E\{\underline{f}(i)\underline{v}'(i)\} = 0$. Because $\underline{Y}(i)$ are independent drawings, the log-likelihood of the n-observations $Y_n = (Y'(i),\ldots,Y'(n))'$ is given by

$$\log p(Y_n;\theta) = -(np/2)\log 2\pi - \tfrac{1}{2}\sum_{i=1}^{n}[Y'(i)\Sigma^{-1}Y(i)+\log|\Sigma|]$$

where $\theta$ denotes the parameter vector. Maximizing the log-likelihood with respect to the unknown parameters is minimizing the function

$L = (1/n)\sum^{n}[Y'(i)\Sigma^{-1}Y(i)+\log|\Sigma|] = (1/n)\sum^{n}(tr(Y(i)Y'(i)\Sigma^{-1}) + \log|\Sigma| =$
$= tr(S\Sigma^{-1}) + \log|\Sigma|$ or the alternative function used by Jöreskog

$$F = \tfrac{1}{2}[\log|\Sigma| + tr(S\Sigma^{-1}) + \log|S| - (p+q)].$$

Let $H_o$ be the null hypothesis of the model under the given specification and $H_1$ be the alternative hypothesis that $\Sigma$ is any other positive definite matrix, then - for large samples - under the null hypothesis

$$(n-1)F_o \sim \chi^2_{\frac{1}{2}(p+q)(p+q+1)-t}$$

where $F_o$ is the minimum value of F and t is the number of unknown parameters. In chapter V it will be shown that the above minimization procedure is a special case of a general estimation method called the prediction error method by treating the observations Y(i) as 'prediction errors'. The unknown factors $\underline{f}(i)$ can be estimated by the Kalman filtering procedure, to be discussed in chapter IV.

## 3.4. Models with Canonical Space.

A brief outline of the technique of canonical correlation is as follows, see for references e.g. Anderson (1958), Dhrymes (1970) or Rijken van Olst (1981).

Consider n independent Gaussian (output) vectors $\underline{y}(i) \in \mathbb{R}^p$ and n independent Gaussian (input) vectors $\underline{u}(i) \in \mathbb{R}^q$, i = 1,...,n where $q \geqq p$ with

$$\underline{Y}(i) = \begin{bmatrix} \underline{y}(i) \\ \underline{u}(i) \end{bmatrix} \sim N_{p+q}\left[\begin{bmatrix} 0 \\ 0 \end{bmatrix}, \begin{bmatrix} \Sigma_y & \Sigma_{yu} \\ \Sigma_{uy} & \Sigma_u \end{bmatrix}\right], \qquad i = 1,\dots,n.$$

It is assumed that the covariance of $\underline{Y}(i)$ is positive definite and that $\Sigma_y^{-1}$ and $\Sigma_u^{-1}$ exist. Applying the canonical correlation procedure we have a linear transformation

$$\begin{bmatrix} \underline{\eta}(i) \\ \underline{\xi}(i) \end{bmatrix} = \begin{bmatrix} P & 0 \\ 0 & Q \end{bmatrix} \begin{bmatrix} \underline{y}(i) \\ \underline{u}(i) \end{bmatrix} = T\underline{Y}(i)$$

such that

$$\begin{bmatrix} \underline{\eta}(i) \\ \underline{\xi}(i) \end{bmatrix} \sim N_{(p+q)}\left[\begin{bmatrix} 0 \\ 0 \end{bmatrix}, \begin{bmatrix} I & \tilde{\Lambda} \\ \tilde{\Lambda}' & I \end{bmatrix}\right]$$

where

$$\tilde{\Lambda} = \begin{bmatrix} \Lambda & 0 \\ 0 & 0 \end{bmatrix}$$

and the (s×s) matrix $\Lambda = \text{diag}(\rho_1,\dots,\rho_s)$ with $s \leqq p$ and $\rho_1 > \rho_2 > \dots$ $\dots > \rho_s$. $P^{-1}$ and $Q^{-1}$ exist. The positive j-th canonical correlation coefficient is $\rho_j = \text{cov}\{\underline{\eta}_j(i)\underline{\xi}_j(i)\}$ where $\underline{\eta}_j(i)$ and $\underline{\xi}_j(i)$ are respectively the j-th coefficient of $\underline{\eta}(i)$ and $\underline{\xi}(i)$.

The above transformation leads to the following model with canonical space

process equation:

$$\begin{bmatrix} I & -\tilde{\Lambda} \\ 0 & I \end{bmatrix} \begin{bmatrix} \underline{\eta}(i) \\ \underline{\xi}(i) \end{bmatrix} = \begin{bmatrix} \underline{\varepsilon}(i) \\ \underline{\tilde{w}}(i) \end{bmatrix}$$

or

$$\underline{\eta}(i) = \tilde{\Lambda}\underline{\xi}(i) + \underline{\varepsilon}(i)$$

output equation:

$$\begin{bmatrix} \underline{y}(i) \\ \underline{u}(i) \end{bmatrix} = \begin{bmatrix} P^{-1} & 0 \\ 0 & Q^{-1} \end{bmatrix} \begin{bmatrix} \underline{\eta}(i) \\ \underline{\xi}(i) \end{bmatrix}$$

where $\underline{\varepsilon}(i)$ is white noise uncorrelated with $\tilde{w}(i)$ and covariance $\Sigma_\varepsilon = I - \tilde{\Lambda}\tilde{\Lambda}'$, and $\tilde{w}(i)$ is standard white noise. An alternative description of the model is

process equation:

$$\underline{\eta}_1(i) = \Lambda\underline{\xi}_1(i) + \underline{\tilde{\varepsilon}}(i)$$

or

$$\begin{bmatrix} I & -\Lambda \\ 0 & I \end{bmatrix} \begin{bmatrix} \underline{\eta}_1(i) \\ \underline{\xi}_1(i) \end{bmatrix} = \begin{bmatrix} \underline{\tilde{\varepsilon}}_1(i) \\ \underline{\tilde{w}}_1(i) \end{bmatrix}$$

output equation:

$$\begin{bmatrix} \underline{y}(i) \\ \underline{u}(i) \end{bmatrix} = \begin{bmatrix} P_1^{-1} & 0 \\ 0 & Q_1^{-1} \end{bmatrix} \begin{bmatrix} \underline{\eta}_1(i) \\ \underline{\xi}_1(i) \end{bmatrix} + \begin{bmatrix} \underline{v}_1(i) \\ \underline{v}_2(i) \end{bmatrix}$$

where $\underline{\eta}_1(i) \in \mathbb{R}^s$; $\underline{\xi}_1(i) \in \mathbb{R}^s$, $\underline{\tilde{\varepsilon}}(i)$ is white noise uncorrelated with $\underline{\xi}_1(i)$; $\tilde{w}_1(i)$ is white noise; $P_1^{-1}$ consists of the first s columns of $P^{-1}$; $Q_1^{-1}$ consists of the first s columns of $Q^{-1}$; $\underline{v}_1(i) = P_2^{-1}\underline{\eta}_2(i)$ is white noise uncorrelated with $\underline{\eta}_1(i)$, where $\underline{\eta}_2(i)$ denotes the vector composed of the last (p-s) elements of $\underline{\eta}(i)$ and $\underline{v}_2(i) = Q_2^{-1}\underline{\xi}_2(i)$ is white noise uncorrelated with $\underline{\xi}_1(i)$, where $\underline{\xi}_2(i)$ denotes the vector composed of the last (q-s) elements of $\underline{\xi}(i)$. It is easily seen that the above models are special static feature space models with as feature vector the vector of canonical variables $\underline{\eta}(i)$ and $\underline{\xi}(i)$.

Model Determination from a Sample.

Let $\hat{\Sigma}$ be a consistent ML-estimate of $\Sigma = E\{\underline{Y}(i)\underline{Y}'(i)\}$, i = 1,...,N.

$$\hat{\Sigma} = N^{-1}\begin{bmatrix} \overset{N}{\Sigma} y(i)y'(i) & \overset{N}{\Sigma} y(i)u'(i) \\ \overset{N}{\Sigma} u(i)y'(i) & \overset{N}{\Sigma} u(i)u'(i) \end{bmatrix} = \begin{bmatrix} \hat{\Sigma}_y & \hat{\Sigma}_{yu} \\ \hat{\Sigma}_{uy} & \hat{\Sigma}_u \end{bmatrix},$$

based on N independent observations of the input and output vector where it is assumed that $\hat{\Sigma}^{-1}$ exists. Apply the one-to-one transformation

$$\begin{bmatrix} \hat{P} & 0 \\ 0 & \hat{Q} \end{bmatrix}\begin{bmatrix} \hat{\Sigma}_y & \hat{\Sigma}_{yu} \\ \hat{\Sigma}_{uy} & \hat{\Sigma}_u \end{bmatrix}\begin{bmatrix} \hat{P}' & 0 \\ 0 & \hat{Q}' \end{bmatrix} = \begin{bmatrix} I & \hat{\tilde{\Lambda}}_p \\ \hat{\tilde{\Lambda}}'_p & I \end{bmatrix}$$

where $\hat{\tilde{\Lambda}}_p = (\hat{\Lambda}_p\ 0)$ with $\hat{\Lambda}_p = \text{diag}(r_1,\ldots,r_p)$ where $r_1 > r_2 > \ldots > r_p$. According to Anderson (1958) the estimated canonical correlation coefficient are ML-estimates.

The null hypothesis that $\rho_{s+1} = \rho_{s+2} = \ldots = \rho_p = 0$ can be tested with the test statistic

$$\underline{w} \triangleq -[N-\tfrac{1}{2}(p+q+1)]\log_e \prod_{i=s+1}^{p}(1-r_i^2).$$

Under the null hypothesis: $\underline{w} \sim \chi^2_{(p-s)(q-s)}$. See for details Rijken van Olst (1981). An estimated model with canonical space is then (if the null hypothesis is not rejected)

process equation:

$$\underline{\eta}_1(i) = \hat{\Lambda}_s \underline{\xi}_1(i) + \underline{\varepsilon}(i)$$

output equation:

$$\begin{bmatrix} \underline{y}(i) \\ \underline{u}(i) \end{bmatrix} = \begin{bmatrix} \hat{P}_1^{-1} & 0 \\ 0 & \hat{Q}_1^{-1} \end{bmatrix}\begin{bmatrix} \underline{\eta}_1(i) \\ \underline{\xi}_1(i) \end{bmatrix} + \begin{bmatrix} \underline{v}_1(i) \\ \underline{v}_2(i) \end{bmatrix}$$

where $\hat{\Lambda}_s = \text{diag}(r_1,\ldots,r_s)$, $\underline{\varepsilon}(i)$ is white noise with estimated covariance $\hat{\Sigma}_\varepsilon = I - \hat{\Lambda}_s^2$; $P_1^{-1}$ is a (p×s) matrix which consists of the first s columns of $\hat{P}^{-1}$; $\hat{Q}_1^{-1}$ is a (q×s) matrix which consists of the first s columns of $\hat{Q}^{-1}$; $\underline{v}_1(i)$ is white noise with estimated covariance $\hat{\Sigma}_{v_1} = \hat{\Sigma}_y - \hat{P}_1^{-1}\hat{P}_1'^{-1}$ and $\underline{v}_2(i)$ is white noise with estimated covariance $\hat{\Sigma}_{v_2} = \hat{\Sigma}_u - \hat{Q}_1^{-1}\hat{Q}_1'^{-1}$.

## 3.5. Singular Value Decomposition and Canonical Correlation

In section 3.4 we have seen that, by applying the canonical correlation procedure, a p×q covariance matrix is transformed into a diagonal matrix with as diagonal entries the canonical correlation coefficients. The procedure can be related to the so-called singular value decomposition, which recently has been emphasized especially in numerical linear algebra. The singular values form, together with the eigenvalues a class of invariants.

Consider a real p×q matrix M with $p \leqq q$ and $r(M) = r \leqq p$.

Definition (3.1) : A decomposition of M into $M = U\Sigma V'$ with p×p matrix U orthogonal, i.e. $U'U = UU' = I$ and q×q matrix V orthogonal, i.e. $V'V = VV' = I$ and

$$\Sigma = \left[\begin{array}{ccc|c} \sigma_1 & & & 0 \\ & \ddots & & \\ & & \sigma_r & \\ \hline & 0 & & 0 \end{array}\right] \begin{array}{l} r \\ \\ \\ p-r \end{array}$$
$$\qquad\qquad r \qquad\qquad q-r$$

with singular values $\sigma_1 \geqq \sigma_2 \geqq \dots \geqq \sigma_r > 0$ is called a *singular value decomposition* (SVD) of M.

It can be shown that every matrix M admits a SVD.
From the SVD we have that $M'MV = V\Sigma'U'U\Sigma V'V = V\Sigma'\Sigma$ and hence the columns of V are the right eigen vectors of M'M and $U'MM' = U'U\Sigma V'V\Sigma'U' = \Sigma\Sigma'U'$ and hence the rows of U are the left eigenvectors of MM'.

On important property of the SVD is the so-called least-squares property which plays a role in model reduction and Hankel norm approximation to be discussed in section 3.6. Consider the problem of approximating a given p×q matrix M with rank r by a lower rank matrix $M_k = U\Sigma_k V'$ with rank $k < r$ where

$$\Sigma_k \triangleq \left[\begin{array}{ccc|c} \sigma_1 & & & 0 \\ & \ddots & & \\ & & \sigma_k & \\ \hline & 0 & & 0 \end{array}\right] \begin{array}{l} k \\ \\ \\ p-k \end{array}$$
$$\qquad\qquad k \qquad\qquad q-k$$

Then we have with $\|M\| = \max_{x \neq 0} \|Mx\|/\|x\|$ the following theorem.

Theorem (3.1) : $\underset{M_k}{\text{minimum}} \|M-M_k\| = \|M-U\Sigma_k V'\| = \sigma_{k+1}$

Proof : The last equality follows from $\|M-U\Sigma_k V'\| =$ $= \|U\Sigma V'-U\Sigma_k V'\| = \|\Sigma-\Sigma_k\| = \sigma_{k+1}$. To see the first equality observe that

$$\|M-M_k\| = \max_{x \neq 0} \|(M-M_k)x\|/\|x\| \geqq \max_{\substack{x \neq 0 \\ x \in \Pi(M_k)}} \|Mx\|/\|x\|$$

where $\Pi(M_k)$ is the null space of $M_k$. If $r(M_k) = k$ then $\dim(\Pi(M_k)) = q-k$. Now it can be shown that

$$\sigma_{k+1} = \underset{\substack{L:\ \text{lin.subspace } \mathbb{R}^q \\ \dim(L) = q-k}}{\text{minimum}} \ \max_{0 \neq x \in L} \|Mx\|/\|x\| =$$

$$= \underset{0 \neq x \in \text{span}(v_{k+1},\ldots,v_q)}{\text{maximum}} \|Mx\|/\|x\|$$

where $V = (v_1,\ldots,v_k,v_{k+1},\ldots,v_q)$. From this it follows that $\min\|M-M_k\| = \sigma_{k+1}$.

Note that $M_k = U\Sigma_k V'$ is not the only rank k matrix which minimizes $\|M-M_k\|$. To see this consider any k×k matrix P with $\|P\| \leqq \sigma_{k+1}$, e.g. $P = \text{diag}(p_1,\ldots,p_k)$ with $\max_j |p_j| \leqq |\sigma_{k+1}|$ then $M_k' = U(\Sigma_k+\tilde{P})V'$ also has $\|M-M_k'\| = \sigma_{k+1}$ with

$$\tilde{P} \triangleq \begin{bmatrix} P & 0 \\ 0 & 0 \end{bmatrix}.$$

The minimization of $\|M-M_k'\|$ over the matrices $M_k'$ with rank k is not unique. However a minimizer can be found.

The canonical correlation procedure can be related to the SVD as follows. From section 3.4 we know that the covariance of the output $\Sigma_y$; the covariance of the input $\Sigma_u$ and the covariance of the input and output $\Sigma_{yu}$ are transformed into $P\Sigma_y P' = I$; $Q\Sigma_u Q' = I$ and $P\Sigma_{yu}Q' = \tilde{\Lambda}$. Because $\Sigma_y$ and $\Sigma_u$ are positive definite symmetric matrices we have $\Sigma_y = C\Lambda_y C'$ where $\Lambda_y = \text{diag}(\lambda_1,\ldots,\lambda_p)$ with $\lambda_i$, $i = 1,\ldots,p$ as eigenvalues of $\Sigma_y$ and C orthogonal, i.e. $C'C = CC' = I$. From this we have that $\Sigma_y = C\Lambda_y^{\frac{1}{2}}\Lambda_y^{\frac{1}{2}}C'$ and $\Lambda_y^{-\frac{1}{2}}C'\Sigma_y C\Lambda_y^{-\frac{1}{2}} = I$. Define $P \triangleq \Lambda_y^{-\frac{1}{2}}C'$ then P consists of the normalized eigenvectors and is orthogonal, i.e. $P'P = PP' = I$. By the same reasoning we have that Q consists of the normalized eigenvectors of $\Sigma_u$ and is orthogonal i.e. $Q'Q = QQ' = I$. From this we have $P'P\Sigma_{yu}Q'Q = \Sigma_{yu} = P'\tilde{\Lambda}Q$ which is a SVD of the covariance matrix $\Sigma_{yu}$ with $U = P'$; $\tilde{\Lambda} = \Sigma$ and $V' = Q$.

## 3.6. Models with State Space: Balanced Realizations and Model Reduction.

From section 2.1 we have that a linear stationary input-output model can be written as

$$y(k) = \sum_{i=0}^{\infty} G_i u(k-i)$$

where $y(k) \in \mathbb{R}^p$ is the output vector and $u(k) \in \mathbb{R}^q$ is the input-vector. It is assumed that $p \leqq q$. From this relation we have the future outputs

$$\begin{bmatrix} y(k+1) \\ y(k+2) \\ \\ \vdots \end{bmatrix} = \begin{bmatrix} G_1 & G_2 & G_3 & \cdots \\ G_2 & G_3 & \cdots\cdots & \\ G_3 & \cdots\cdots\cdots & & \\ \vdots & \vdots & & \end{bmatrix} \begin{bmatrix} u(k) \\ u(k-1) \\ \\ \vdots \end{bmatrix} + \begin{bmatrix} G_0 & 0 & 0 & \cdots \\ G_1 & G_0 & 0 & \cdots \\ G_2 & G_1 & G_0 & \cdots \\ \vdots & \vdots & \vdots & \vdots \end{bmatrix} \begin{bmatrix} u(k+1) \\ u(k+2) \\ \\ \vdots \end{bmatrix}$$

or

$$Y^+ = Hu^- + Tu^+$$

where H is the Hankel matrix and T a Toeplitz matrix. If $r(H) = n < \infty$ then the relation between past inputs and future outputs is described by an n-dimensional memory vector called the state-vector. By the realization algorithm described in section 2.3 a state-space model (realization) can be obtained. However the realization is not unique, see theorem 2.6. In the sequel a particular realization is discussed called the *balanced* realization, which can be used for model reduction, that is the process of associating a lower order model with a given state-space realization (a model with a lower dimensional state-vector). Model reduction is important because the impulse response function $\{G_i\}$ are often obtained from noisy observations which makes it difficult to determine the rank of the Hankel matrix.

Consider the following given state space model $\Sigma(A,B,C,D)$ with $x(k) \in \mathbb{R}^n$,

$$x(k+1) = Ax(k) + Bu(k)$$

$$y(k) = Cx(k) + Du(k)$$

Suppose A to be stable, i.e. $|\sigma(A)| < 1$, the pair (A,B) reachable and the pair (A,C) observable. When the above last two conditions apply it is said that the triple (A,B,C) is *minimal*. The so-called *reachability Gramian* W is given by

$$\min_{\substack{u \\ 0 \rightarrow x_0}} \sum_{k=-\infty}^{-1} \|u(k)\|^2 = x_0' W^{-1} x_0$$

where $W = \sum_{k=0}^{\infty} A^k BB'(A')^k$ is the unique solution of the Lyapunov equation $W - AWA' = BB'$ with $W = W' > 0$. The intuitive interpretation of $x_o' W^{-1} x_0$ is that its represents the minimum amount of control 'energy' required to drive the state vector from 0 to $x_0$. Thus $x_0' W^{-1} x_0$ 'large' means that the state-vector is difficult to excite compared to $x_0' W^{-1} x_0$ 'small'. The so-called *observability Gramian* M is given by

$$\sum_{k=0}^{\infty} \|y(k)\|^2 = x_0' M x_0$$

where $M = \sum_{k=0}^{\infty} (A')^k C'CA^k$ is the unique solution of the Lyapunov equation $M - A'MA = C'C$ with $M = M' > 0$. The intuitive interpretation of $x_0' M x_0$ is that it gives the amount of observation 'energy' available in the initial state $x_0$. Thus $x_0' M x_0$ 'large' means that $x_0$ is easy to observe compared with $x_0' M x_0$ 'small'.

Definition (3.2) : The realization $\Sigma(A,B,C,D)$ is said to be balanced if $W = M$.

The intuitive reasoning of balancing is to neglect states which are difficult to excite and which are difficult to observe (they contribute little to the observation 'energy'). However a state may be difficult to excite but easy to observe or easy to excite and difficult to observe. Therefore balancing is a compromise between the two.

In section 2.3 it is shown that a system $\Sigma(TAT^{-1}, TB, CT^{-1}, D)$ generates the same input-output behaviour as $\Sigma(A,B,C,D)$. The transformed reachability and observability Gramians are respectively $W_T = TWT'$ and $M_T = (T^{-1})'MT^{-1}$.

Theorem (3.2) : If $\Sigma(A,B,C,D)$ is minimal with A stable then there exists a transformation matrix T such that $M_T = W_T = \Sigma$ with $\Sigma = \text{diag}(\sigma_1,\dots,\sigma_n)$ where $\sigma_1 \geqq \sigma_2 \geqq \dots \geqq \sigma_n > 0$ are the singular values.

Proof : Because $W = W' > 0$ and $M = M' > 0$ there exists a regular matrix S such that $M = S'S$. Now $SWS' = (SWS')' > 0$ and hence there exists an orthonormal matrix U such that $SWS' = U\Sigma^2U'$ with $\Sigma^2 = \text{diag}(\sigma_1^2,\dots,\sigma_n^2)$ and $\sigma_1 \geqq \sigma_2 \geqq \dots \geqq \sigma_n > 0$. The transformation matrix $T = \Sigma^{-\frac{1}{2}}U'S$. The transformed Gramians are $W_T = TWT' = \Sigma^{-\frac{1}{2}}U'SWS'U\Sigma^{-\frac{1}{2}} = \Sigma$ and $M_T = (T^{-1}\ MT^{-1} =$ $= \Sigma^{\frac{1}{2}}U'(S')^{-1}(S'S)S^{-1}U\Sigma^{\frac{1}{2}} = \Sigma$ thus both Gramians are equal and diagonal and $\Sigma(TAT^{-1},TB,CT^{-1},D)$ is balanced.

The balanced realization procedure is now as follows. Let H be the Hankel matrix with $r(H) = n < \infty$, then there exists a realization and because $G_i = CA^{i-1}B$, $i = 1,2,\dots$

$$H = \begin{bmatrix} G_1 & G_2 & G_3 & \dots \\ G_2 & G_3 & \dots\dots & \\ G_3 & \dots\dots\dots & & \\ \vdots & \vdots & & \end{bmatrix} = \begin{bmatrix} C \\ CA \\ CA^2 \\ \vdots \end{bmatrix} (B \ AB \ A^2B \ \dots) = \mathcal{O}\mathcal{C}$$

where $\mathcal{O}$ and $\mathcal{C}$ are the (extended) observability and controllability matrices. The SVD of H is given by

$$H = U\Sigma V'$$

with $U'U = I$; $VV' = I$ and $\Sigma = \text{diag}(\sigma_1,\dots,\sigma_n)$ with $\sigma_1 \geqq \sigma_2 \geqq \dots \geqq \sigma_n > 0$ as singular values. Let $\mathcal{O} = U\Sigma^{\frac{1}{2}}$ and $\mathcal{C} = \Sigma^{\frac{1}{2}}V'$ then $H = \mathcal{O}\mathcal{C}$. Let "$\uparrow$" be the shift-up operator then

$$\mathcal{O}A = \begin{bmatrix} CA \\ CA^2 \\ \vdots \end{bmatrix} = \mathcal{O}^{\uparrow}$$

The *balanced realization* $\Sigma_B(A,B,C,D)$ is given by: $A = \mathcal{O}^+\mathcal{O}^\uparrow$ ; B = first q columns of $\mathcal{C}$; C = first p rows of $\mathcal{O}$ and $D = G_0$. Here $\mathcal{O}^+$ denotes the pseudo-inverse e.g. $(\mathcal{O}'\mathcal{O})^{-1}\mathcal{O}'$.
The observability Gramian $\mathcal{O}'\mathcal{O} = \Sigma$ and controllability Gramian $\mathcal{C}\mathcal{C}' = \Sigma$.
The balanced realization is stable and unique.

Model Reduction and Approximation

One of the crucial steps in the realization procedure is to determine the rank of the Hankel matrix. Due to observations errors the rank of the Hankel matrix may lead to a high dimensionality of the state-vector. Problem is to approximate a high-dimensional realization by a lower order system. Recent results are based on a article of Adamjan, Arov and Klein (1971), see e.g. Kung and Lin (1981), Moore (1981) and especially Glover (1984). A detailed analysis is beyond the scope of this book and only a sketch of model reduction is presented.
Let $F(z) = C(zI-A)^{-1}B$ be the transfer function (without D) of $\Sigma(A,B,C,D)$ with A stable then the *Hankel norm* of F(z) is defined as

$$\|F(z)\|_H \triangleq \overline{\sigma}(H)$$

where $\overline{\sigma}(H)$ is the greatest singular value of the Hankel matrix H. Now given the Hankel matrix with rank n the problem is to find a Hankel matrix $\tilde{H}$ with given $r(\tilde{H}) = k$ such that $\|H-\tilde{H}\|_H = \overline{\sigma}(H-\tilde{H})$ is minimum. The SVD of H is given by $H = U\Sigma V'$ with $U'U = I$ and $U = (u_1,u_2,\ldots,u_n)$; $V'V = I$ and $V = (v_1,\ldots,v_n)$ and $\Sigma = \mathrm{diag}(\sigma_1,\ldots,\sigma_n)$ with $\sigma_1 \geq \sigma_2 \geq \ldots$ $\ldots \geq \sigma_n > 0$. An approximant which minimizes the Hankel norm is given by $L_R \triangleq U_1\Sigma_k V_1'$ with $\Sigma_k \triangleq \mathrm{diag}(\sigma_1,\ldots,\sigma_k)$; $U_1 = (u_1,\ldots,u_k)$ and $V_1 = (v_1,\ldots,v_k)$, see section 3.5 theorem 3.1. The Hankel norm $\|H-L_R\| = \sigma_{k+1}$. However $L_R$ is in general not a Hankel matrix and therefore does not represent a dynamic system of order k. However the following decomposition still holds; $L_R = \mathcal{O}\mathcal{C}$ with $\mathcal{O} = U_1\Sigma_k^{\frac{1}{2}}$ and $\mathcal{C} = \Sigma_k^{\frac{1}{2}}V'_1$. Applying the balanced realization procedure given before leads to the so-called

Principal Hankel Component (PHC) approximation:

$A_k = \mathcal{O}^+\mathcal{O}^\uparrow = \Sigma_k^{-\frac{1}{2}}U_1'U_1^\uparrow\Sigma_k^{\frac{1}{2}}$; $B_k$ = first q columns of $\mathcal{C}$; $C_k$ = first p rows of $\mathcal{O}$ and $D_k = G_0$.

It must be remembered however that $\mathcal{O}$ and $\mathcal{C}$ are not 'true' observability and controllability matrices and that the PHC-approximation is a least-squares approximation. A correct approach is given in Glover (1984) but only for continuous systems.

A relative simple approximation procedure which is equivalent to the above approximation is by considering the balanced realization $\Sigma_b(A,B,C,D)$:

$$\begin{bmatrix} x_1(k+1) \\ x_2(k+1) \end{bmatrix} = \begin{bmatrix} A_{11} & A_{12} \\ A_{21} & A_{22} \end{bmatrix} \begin{bmatrix} x_1(k) \\ x_2(k) \end{bmatrix} + \begin{bmatrix} B_1 \\ B_2 \end{bmatrix} u(k)$$

$$y(k) = (C_1 \quad C_2) \begin{bmatrix} x_1(k) \\ x_2(k) \end{bmatrix} + Du(k)$$

with $x_1(k) \in \mathbb{R}^s$ and $x_2(k) \in \mathbb{R}^{k-s}$. The s-th order approximation, suggested by the singular values $\sigma_{s+1}, \sigma_{k+2}, \ldots, \sigma_n$ 'close' to zero, is given by considering only the first s components of the state-vector which are 'easy' to excite and 'easy' to observe, leading to the lower-order model:

$$x_1(k+1) = A_{11}x_1(k) + B_1u(k)$$

$$\tilde{y}(k) = C_1x_1(k) + Du(k)$$

It can be shown Pernabo and Silverman (1982) that $A_{11}$ is stable.

<u>Model Determination from a Sample</u>

Suppose we have (2r+1) observations $u(-r),\ldots,u(0),\ldots,u(r)$ and (r+1) noisy observations $y(0),\ldots,y(r)$ such that $N = (r+1)/2$ is an integer. From the stochastic input-output description

$$\underline{y}(k) = \sum_{i=0}^{\infty} G_i u(k-i) + \underline{v}(k)$$

with $\underline{v}(k)$ white-noise we have the regression model

$$\begin{bmatrix} \underline{y}'(r) \\ \underline{y}'(r-1) \\ \vdots \\ \underline{y}'(0) \end{bmatrix} = \begin{bmatrix} u'(r) & & u'(0) \\ u'(r-1) & \ldots & u'(-1) \\ \vdots & & \vdots \\ u'(0) & \ldots & u'(-r) \end{bmatrix} \begin{bmatrix} G_0' \\ G_1' \\ \vdots \\ G_r' \end{bmatrix} + \text{'rest'}$$

or

$$\underline{Y} = UG + \text{'rest'}$$

with least-squares estimate $\hat{G} = (U'U)^{-1}U'Y$. A least-squares estimate of the finite dimensional Hankel matrix with $N = (r+1)/2$ is

$$H_N = \begin{bmatrix} \hat{G}_1 & \hat{G}_2 \cdots & \hat{G}_N \\ \hat{G}_2 & \cdots\cdots & \hat{G}_{N+1} \\ \vdots & & \vdots \\ \hat{G}_N & \cdots\cdots & \hat{G}_{2N-1=r} \end{bmatrix}$$

Due to the approximation of the true input-output description and the noise it is to be expected that $r(H_N) = pN$ (it is assumed that $p \leqq q$), so the system may be of high order especially with r large.

Let the SVD of $H_N$ be $H_N = U\Sigma V'$ with $U'U = I_{pN}$; $V'V = I_{qN}$ and

$$\Sigma = \left[\begin{array}{ccc|c} \sigma_1 & & & \\ & \ddots & & 0 \\ & & \sigma_{pN} & \\ \hline & 0 & & 0 \end{array}\right]$$

$$\qquad\quad pN \qquad\qquad qN-pN$$

where $\sigma_1 \geqq \sigma_2 \geqq \ldots \geqq \sigma_{pN} > 0$ are the singular values. If the 'true' system is of dimension $k \ll pN$ it is to be expected that $\sigma_{k+1}, \sigma_{k+2}, \ldots$ $\ldots, \sigma_{pN}$ are close to zero. Let $\Sigma_1 = \text{diag}(\sigma_1,\ldots,\sigma_k)$; $U = (U_1 \;\; U_2)$ with $U_1 = (u_1,\ldots,u_k)$ and $V = (V_1 \;\; V_2)$ with $V_1 = (v_1,\ldots,v_k)$ then a PHC-approximation is $\Sigma(A_k,B_k,C_k,D)$ with $A_k = \Sigma_1^{-\frac{1}{2}}U_1'U_1^{\uparrow}\Sigma_1^{\frac{1}{2}}$; $B_k$ = first q columns of $\mathcal{C} = \Sigma_1^{\frac{1}{2}}V_1$; $C_k$ = first p rows of $\mathcal{O} = U_1\Sigma_1^{\frac{1}{2}}$ and $D = \hat{G}_0$.

<u>Remark</u>: Because the singular values may be interpreted as canonical correlation coefficients the null hypothesis $\sigma_{k+1} = \sigma_{k+2} = \ldots \sigma_{pH} = 0$ can be tested with the test statistic described in section 3.4.

## 3.7. State Space Representation of Multivariate Time-Series

Consider the generalized Wold decomposition

$$\underline{y}(k) = \sum_{i=0}^{\infty} G_i \underline{\varepsilon}(k-i) = G(z)\underline{\varepsilon}(k)$$

where $\underline{y}(k)$ is a p-dimensional Gaussian vector with zero mean; $G(z) = G_0 + G_1 z + G_2 z^2 + \ldots$ is a stable rational transfer function in the lag operator z and $\underline{\varepsilon}(k)$ is a p-dimensional standard white noise vector. It is also assumed that $G'(z^{-1})$ is stable.

From the above model we have the following relation between future outputs and past inputs.

$$\begin{bmatrix} \underline{y}(k+1) \\ \underline{y}(k+2) \\ \\ \vdots \end{bmatrix} = \begin{bmatrix} G_1 & G_2 & \cdots \\ G_2 & G_3 & \cdots \\ G_3 & \cdots\cdots & \\ \vdots & \vdots & \end{bmatrix} \begin{bmatrix} \underline{\varepsilon}(k) \\ \underline{\varepsilon}(k-1) \\ \\ \vdots \end{bmatrix} + \begin{bmatrix} G_0 & 0 & \cdots \\ G_1 & G_0 & \cdots \\ G_2 & G_1 & \cdots \\ \vdots & \vdots & \end{bmatrix} \begin{bmatrix} \underline{\varepsilon}(k+1) \\ \underline{\varepsilon}(k+2) \\ \\ \vdots \end{bmatrix}$$

or

$$\underline{Y}^+ = H\underline{\varepsilon}^- + T\underline{\varepsilon}^+$$

where H is a Hankel matrix and T is a Toeplitz matrix. The past outputs are given by

$$\begin{bmatrix} \underline{y}(k) \\ \underline{y}(k-1) \\ \\ \vdots \end{bmatrix} = \begin{bmatrix} G_0 & G_1 & G_2 & \cdots \\ 0 & G_0 & G_1 & \cdots \\ 0 & 0 & G_0 & \cdots \\ \vdots & \vdots & \vdots & \end{bmatrix} \begin{bmatrix} \underline{\varepsilon}(k) \\ \underline{\varepsilon}(k-1) \\ \\ \vdots \end{bmatrix}$$

or

$$\underline{Y}^- = T'\underline{\varepsilon}^-$$

The covariance between the future and past outputs is given by

$$\text{cov}\{\underline{Y}^+\underline{Y}'^-\} = R_H = HT$$

where the generalized Hankel $R_H$ is

$$R_H \triangleq \begin{bmatrix} R_1 & R_2 & R_3 & \cdots \\ R_2 & R_3 & \cdots & \\ R_3 & R_4 & \cdots & \\ \vdots & \vdots & & \end{bmatrix}$$

where $R_i \triangleq E\{\underline{y}(k+i)\underline{y}'(k)\}$, $i = 0,1,2,\ldots$ .
If rank(H) = $n < \infty$ then there exists a finite dimensional relation between future outputs and past outputs. Suppose rank(T) exceeds the rank of H then rank($R_H$) $\leqq$ n thus rank($R_H$) is finite dimensional. Conversely if rank($R_H$) = n then rank(H) = n and a realization exists. Define

$$R_H^{N,N} \triangleq E\left[\begin{bmatrix} \underline{y}(k+1) \\ \vdots \\ \underline{y}(k+N) \end{bmatrix}\left[(\underline{y}'(k),\ldots,\underline{y}'(k-N+1)\right]\right] = \begin{bmatrix} R_1 & R_2 & \cdots & R_N \\ R_2 & R_3 & \cdots & \\ \vdots & & & \\ R_N & \cdots\cdots & & R_{2N-1} \end{bmatrix}$$

with rank($R_H^{N,N}$) = n. Using the canonical correlation technique we can factorize the covariance $R_H^{N,N}$ as

$$PR_H^{N,N}Q = \tilde{\Lambda} = \begin{bmatrix} \Lambda & 0 \\ 0 & 0 \end{bmatrix}$$

where $\Lambda = \text{diag}(\rho_1,\ldots,\rho_n)$ with positive correlation coefficients $\rho_1 > \rho_2 > \ldots > \rho_n$, that is, there exists n independent relations between future and past outputs. Let $\underline{v}(k) \in \mathbb{R}^{pN}$ be the transformed future outputs, i.e. $\underline{v}(k) = PY^N(k+1)$, where $Y^N(k+1) \triangleq (\underline{y}'(k+1),\underline{y}'(k+2),\ldots$ $\ldots,\underline{y}'(k+N))'$ and $\underline{u}(k) \in \mathbb{R}^{pN}$ be transformed past outputs, i.e. $\underline{u}(k) = Q\underline{Y}_N(k)$, where $\underline{Y}_N(k) \triangleq (\underline{y}'(k),\underline{y}'(k-1),\ldots,\underline{y}'(k-N+1))'$. According to section (3.4) we have the following canonical model:

process equation:

$$\begin{bmatrix} \underline{v}_1(k) \\ \underline{v}_2(k) \end{bmatrix} = \begin{bmatrix} \Lambda & 0 \\ 0 & 0 \end{bmatrix} \begin{bmatrix} \underline{u}_1(k) \\ \underline{u}_2(k) \end{bmatrix} + \begin{bmatrix} \underline{w}_1(k) \\ \underline{w}_2(k) \end{bmatrix}$$

or

$$\underline{v}(k) = \tilde{\Lambda}\underline{u}(k) + \underline{w}(k)$$

output equation:

$$\begin{bmatrix} Y^N(k+1) \\ Y_N(k) \end{bmatrix} = \begin{bmatrix} P^{-1} & 0 \\ 0 & Q^{-1} \end{bmatrix} \begin{bmatrix} \underline{v}(k) \\ \underline{u}(k) \end{bmatrix}$$

where $\underline{w}_1(k)$ and $\underline{w}_2(k)$ are white noise processes with covariances respectively $\Sigma_{w_1} = I - \Lambda^2$ and $\Sigma_{w_2} = I$, uncorrelated with $\underline{u}_1(k)$ and $\underline{u}_2(k)$ and $\mathrm{cov}\{\underline{w}_1(k)\underline{w}_2'(k)\} = 0$.
An alternative version of the above model is

process equation:

$$\underline{v}_1(k) = \Lambda\underline{u}_1(k) + \underline{w}_1(k)$$

output equation:

$$\begin{bmatrix} \underline{Y}^N(k+1) \\ \underline{Y}_N(k) \end{bmatrix} = \begin{bmatrix} P_1^{-1} & 0 \\ 0 & Q_1^{-1} \end{bmatrix} \begin{bmatrix} \underline{v}_1(k) \\ \underline{u}_1(k) \end{bmatrix} + \begin{bmatrix} \underline{\varepsilon}_1(k) \\ \underline{\varepsilon}_2(k) \end{bmatrix}$$

with $\Sigma_{w_1} = I - \Lambda^2$; $P_1^{-1}$ is a (pN×n) matrix which consists of the first n columns of $P^{-1}$ and $Q_1^{-1}$ is a (pN×n) matrix which consists of the first n columns of $Q^{-1}$; $\underline{\varepsilon}_1(k) = P_2^{-1}\underline{v}_2(k)$ is white noise uncorrelated with $\underline{v}_1(k)$ and $\underline{\varepsilon}_2(k) = Q_2^{-1}\underline{u}_2(k)$ is white noise uncorrelated with $\underline{u}_1(k)$. Both models are stationary (LRF) models with as feature vector, a vector of canonical variables. The above representation may be suitable for prediction purposes.
A (MSE) predictor is given by

$$\underline{Y}_p^N(k+1) = P_1^{-1}\Lambda\underline{u}_1(k),$$

where $\underline{u}_1(k) = Q_1 Y_n(k)$. $Q_1$ is a (n×pN) matrix which consists of the first n rows of Q.

A more dynamic representation is the following, see for a more detailed study Akaike (1975). Because $\underline{u}(k) = Q\underline{Y}_N(k)$ and the process is stationary we have also $\underline{u}(k+1) = QY_N(k+1)$ where $Y_N(k+1) = (y'(k+1), y'(k), \ldots, y'(k-N+2))'$ is a mixed vector of a future output $y(k+1)$ and past outputs; $\underline{u}(k)$ and $\underline{v}(k)$ are orthonormal basis for the future outputs $y(k+1), \ldots, y(k+N)$ and past inputs $y(k), \ldots, y(k-N+1)$. Because $\underline{u}(k+1) = QY_N(k+1)$ we have $Y_N(k+1) = Q^{-1}\underline{u}(k+1)$ and $\underline{y}(k+1) = \tilde{Q}^{-1}\underline{u}(k+1)$ where $\tilde{Q}^{-1}$ is a (p×pN) matrix which consists of the first p rows of $Q^{-1}$. We have also that $\underline{v}(k) = PY^N(k+1)$ and $Y^N(k+1) = P^{-1}\underline{v}(k)$ and hence $\underline{y}(k+1) = \tilde{P}^{-1}\underline{v}(k)$ where $\tilde{P}^{-1}$ is a (p×pN) matrix which consists of the first p rows of $P^{-1}$. From the two relations we have that

$$\underline{y}(k+1) = \tilde{Q}^{-1}\underline{u}(k+1) = \tilde{P}^{-1}\underline{v}(k) = \tilde{P}^{-1}[\tilde{\Lambda}\underline{u}(k)+\underline{w}(k)]$$

and hence

$$\underline{u}(k+1) = \tilde{Q}^{\#}\tilde{P}^{-1}[\tilde{\Lambda}\underline{u}(k)+\underline{w}(k)]$$

or

$$\begin{bmatrix} \underline{u}_1(k+1) \\ \underline{u}_2(k+1) \end{bmatrix} = \begin{bmatrix} H_{11} & H_{12} \\ H_{21} & H_{22} \end{bmatrix} \begin{bmatrix} \Lambda & 0 \\ 0 & 0 \end{bmatrix} \begin{bmatrix} \underline{u}_1(k) \\ \underline{u}_2(k) \end{bmatrix} + \begin{bmatrix} \underline{w}_1(k) \\ \underline{w}_2(k) \end{bmatrix}$$

$$= \begin{bmatrix} F_1 & 0 \\ F_2 & 0 \end{bmatrix} \begin{bmatrix} \underline{u}_1(k) \\ \underline{u}_2(k) \end{bmatrix} + \begin{bmatrix} \tilde{\underline{w}}_1(k) \\ \tilde{\underline{w}}_2(k) \end{bmatrix}$$

where $\tilde{Q}^{\#}$ denotes a left inverse of $\tilde{Q}^{-1}$; $F_1 = H_{11}\Lambda$ and $F_2 = H_{21}\Lambda$. $H_{11}$ is an (n×n) matrix which consists of the first n rows and first n columns of $\tilde{Q}^{\#}\tilde{P}^{-1}$ and $H_{21}$ is a ((pN−n)×n) matrix which consists of the last (pN−n) rows of $\tilde{Q}^{\#}\tilde{P}^{-1}$ and first n columns of $\tilde{Q}^{\#}\tilde{P}^{-1}$.
Because the canonical variables of $\underline{u}(k+1)$ are uncorrelated $\text{cov}\{\underline{u}_1(k+1)\underline{u}_2'(k+1)\} = 0$. Now $\underline{u}(k)$ and $\underline{w}(k)$ are uncorrelated which implies that either $F_1 = 0$ or $F_2 = 0$. From the above relation $\underline{u}(k+1) = \tilde{Q}^{\#}\tilde{P}^{-1}\underline{v}(k)$ and the first n components of $\underline{v}(k)$ are linearly related to $\underline{u}_1(k)$, thus the first n components of $\underline{u}(k+1)$ are linearly related to $\underline{u}_1(k+1)$ which implies that not all elements of $F_1$ are zero. From this it follows that $F_2 = 0$. The dynamic relation becomes

$$\begin{bmatrix} \underline{u}_1(k+1) \\ \underline{u}_2(k+1) \end{bmatrix} = \begin{bmatrix} F_1 & 0 \\ 0 & 0 \end{bmatrix} \begin{bmatrix} \underline{u}_1(k) \\ \underline{u}_2(k) \end{bmatrix} + \begin{bmatrix} \underline{\tilde{w}}_1(k) \\ \underline{\tilde{w}}_2(k) \end{bmatrix}$$

or

$$\underline{u}(k+1) = \tilde{F}\underline{u}(k) + \underline{\tilde{w}}(k)$$

For (k+2) the relation is

$$\underline{u}(k+2) = \tilde{F}\underline{u}(k+1) + \tilde{w}(k+1)$$

Now $\underline{u}(k+1)$ is a linear combination of $\underline{u}_1(k)$ and $\tilde{w}(k)$ where $\underline{\tilde{w}}(k)$ and $\underline{u}_1(k)$ are uncorrelated and $\underline{u}(k+2)$ is a linear combination of $\underline{u}_1(k+1)$ and $\tilde{w}(k+1)$ where $\underline{\tilde{w}}(k+1)$ and $\underline{u}_1(k+1)$ are uncorrelated. From this it follows that $\underline{\tilde{w}}(k+1)$ and $\underline{\tilde{w}}(k)$ are uncorrelated and hence the $\text{cov}\{\underline{\tilde{w}}(k+1)\underline{\tilde{w}}'(k)\} = 0$ thus $\{\underline{\tilde{w}}(k)\}$ is a white noise process.

The *dynamic* state space model can be written as

process equation:

$$\underline{u}_1(k+1) = F_1\underline{u}_1(k) + \underline{\tilde{w}}_1(k)$$

output equation:

$$\underline{y}(k) = \tilde{Q}_1^{-1}\underline{u}_1(k) + \underline{\varepsilon}(k),$$

where $\underline{u}_1(k) \in \mathbb{R}^n$ is the Gaussian state vector which consists of n canonical variables with $\text{cov}\{\underline{u}_1(k)\underline{u}_1'(k)\} = I$; $\underline{\tilde{w}}_1(k)$ is white noise with $\text{cov}\{\tilde{w}_1(k)\tilde{w}_1'(k)\} = I - F_1F_1'$ and uncorrelated with $\underline{u}_1(k)$; $\tilde{Q}_1^{-1}$ is a matrix which consists of the first p rows and first n columns of $Q^{-1}$, $\underline{\varepsilon}(k)$ is a white noise process with $\text{cov}\{\underline{\varepsilon}(k)\underline{\varepsilon}'(k)\} = R_0 - \tilde{Q}_1^{-1}\tilde{Q}_1'^{-1}$ and uncorrelated with $\underline{u}_1(k)$ and $\underline{\tilde{w}}_1(k)$. $F_1 = H_{11}\Lambda$ where $H_{11}$ is a (n×n) matrix which consists of the first n rows and n columns of $\widetilde{Q^{\#}P}^{-1}$ and $\Lambda = \text{diag}(\rho_1,\ldots,\rho_n)$.

The above representation may be suitable for prediction. A (MSE) predictor is given by

$$\underline{y}^p(k+1) = \tilde{Q}_1^{-1}\underline{u}_1^p(k+1) = \tilde{Q}_1^{-1}F_1\underline{u}_1(k).$$

State Space Representation from a Sample.

Let

$$S_i \triangleq \frac{1}{(2N+p-i)} \sum_{j=0}^{2N+p-i} y(j+i)y'(j), \; i = 0,1,\ldots,2N-1$$

be ML-estimates of $R_i$, $i = 0,\ldots,2N-1$ based on (2N+p) observations $y(0),\ldots,y(2N+p)$ where N is an integer and it is assumed that $S_i^{-1}$, $i = 0,\ldots,2N-1$ exists. The estimated finite generalized (Np×Np) Hankel matrix is

$$\hat{R}_H^{N,N} = \begin{bmatrix} R_1 & R_2 & \cdots & R_N \\ \vdots & & & \vdots \\ R_N & & & R_{2N-1} \end{bmatrix}$$

By means of the canonical correlation technique the covariance matrix $\hat{R}_H^{N,N}$ (namely the covariance between future and past outputs) can be factorized as

$$\hat{P}\hat{R}_H^{N,N}\hat{Q} = \hat{\tilde{\Lambda}}$$

where $\hat{\tilde{\Lambda}} = \Lambda$ with $\hat{\Lambda} = \mathrm{diag}(r_1,\ldots,r_{Np})$ where $r_1 > r_2 > \ldots > r_{Np}$ are the estimated positive canonical correlation coefficients and $\hat{P}^{-1}$ and $\hat{Q}^{-1}$ exist.

Assume that the null hypothesis $\rho_{n+1} = \rho_{n+2} = \ldots = \rho_{Np} = 0$ - to be tested by the statistic

$$w = [2N+p-\tfrac{1}{2}(2Np+1)]\log_e \prod_{i=n+1}^{Np} (1-r_i^2)$$

which under the null hypothesis is distributed as $\chi^2_{(Np-n)(Np-n)}$ - can not be rejected then the dimension of the state space is n.

A possible estimated model would be

process equation:

$$\underline{v}_1(k) = \hat{\Lambda}_n u_1(k) + \underline{w}(k)$$

output equation

$$\underline{Y}^N(k+1) = \hat{P}^{-1} \underline{v}_1(k) + \underline{\varepsilon}(k)$$

where $\underline{v}_1(k) \in \mathbb{R}^n$ is a vector which consists of the first n canonical variables of $v(k) = \hat{P}Y^N(k+1)$, where $Y^N(k+1) = (y'(k+1),\ldots,y'(k+N))'$; $\hat{\Lambda}_n = \mathrm{diag}(r_1,\ldots,r_n)$; $u_1(k) \in \mathbb{R}^n$ is a vector which consists of the first n canonical variables of $u(k) = \hat{Q}Y_N(k)$ where $Y_N(k) = (y'(k),\ldots$ $\ldots,y'(k-N+1))'$; $\underline{w}(k)$ is white noise with covariance $\hat{\Sigma}_w = I - \hat{\Lambda}_n\hat{\Lambda}_n'$; $\hat{P}_1^{-1}$ is a matrix which consists of the first n columns of $\hat{P}^{-1}$ and $\underline{\varepsilon}(k)$ is white noise with covariance $\hat{\Sigma}_\varepsilon = \hat{P}_2^{-1}\hat{P}_2'^{-1}$ where $\hat{P}_2^{-1}$ is a matrix which consists of the last (Np-n) columns of $\hat{P}^{-1}$.

A *dynamic* estimated state space representation of the time-series is given by

process equation:

$$\underline{u}_1(k+1) = \hat{F}_1\underline{u}_1(k) + \underline{w}(k)$$

output equation:

$$\underline{y}(k) = \hat{\tilde{Q}}^{-1}\underline{u}_1(k) + \underline{\varepsilon}(k)$$

where the state vector $u_1(k) \in \mathbb{R}^n$ is a vector which consists of the first n canonical variables of $u(k) = QY_N(k)$ with $\mathrm{cov}\{\underline{u}_1(k)\underline{u}_1'(k)\} = I$; $\hat{F}_1 = \hat{H}_{11}\hat{\Lambda}$ where $\hat{\Lambda} = \mathrm{diag}(r_1,\ldots,r_n)$; $\hat{H}_{11}$ is a (n×n) matrix which consists of the first n rows and n colums of $(\hat{\tilde{Q}}^{\#}\tilde{P}^{-1})$. $\hat{\tilde{Q}}^{\#}$ is the left inverse of $\hat{\tilde{Q}}^{-1}$, a (p×Np) matrix of the first p rows of $\hat{Q}^{-1}$ and $\hat{\tilde{P}}^{-1}$ is a (p×Np) matrix which consists of the first p rows of $\hat{P}^{-1}$. The estimated covariance of the white noise $\underline{w}(k)$ is $\hat{\Sigma}_w = I - \hat{F}_1\hat{F}_1'$; $\hat{\tilde{Q}}^{-1}$ is a (p×n) matrix which consists of the first p rows and first n columns $\hat{Q}^{-1}$.
The estimated covariance of the white noise $\underline{\varepsilon}(k)$ is $\hat{\Sigma}_\varepsilon = S_o - \hat{\tilde{Q}}_1^{-1}\hat{\tilde{Q}}_1'^{-1}$.
A (MSE) predictor based on the estimated model is given by

$$\hat{\underline{y}}^p(k+1) = \hat{\tilde{Q}}_1^{-1}\hat{F}_1\underline{u}_1(k)$$

where $\underline{u}_1(k)$ is the vector of the first n canonical variables of $\underline{u}(k) = \hat{Q}Y_N(k)$ where $Y_N(k) = (\underline{y}'(k),\ldots,\underline{y}'(k-N))'$.

For an extensive study of time series analysis and system theory we refer to Aoki (1983).

## 3.8. Regression Models with Parameter Space.

Consider the linear regression equation

$$\underline{y}(k) = x(k)\beta + \underline{\varepsilon}(k), \qquad k = 1,2,...$$

where the output vector $\underline{y}(k) \in \mathbb{R}^{p}$ is Gaussian; the matrix $x(k) \in \mathbb{R}^{p\times m}$ is a matrix of input variables; $\beta \in \mathbb{R}^{m}$ is the parameter vector and $\underline{\varepsilon}(k)$ is a white noise vector with covariance $\Sigma$. The parameter vector and regression equation can be rewritten as the following non-stationary (LRF) model

process equation:

$$\beta(k+1) = \beta(k)$$

output equation:

$$\underline{y}(k) = x(k)\beta(k) + \underline{\varepsilon}(k),$$

where the parameter vector $\beta(k)$ is the feature vector. The (LRF) model permits regression models with time-varying parameters, e.g.

process equation:

$$\underline{\beta}(k+1) = A\underline{\beta}(k) + Bu_1(k) + \underline{w}(k)$$

output equation:

$$\underline{y}(k) = x(k)\underline{\beta}(k) + \underline{\varepsilon}(k),$$

where $\underline{w}(k)$ is a white noise vector and $u_1(k)$ is a deterministic input. By Kalman filtering the unknown parameter vector $\beta(k)$ can be estimated from the output $y(k)$, which will be discussed in the next chapter.

# IV. Discrete Kalman Filtering

## 4.1. Derivation of the Filter.

In this chapter we deal with the problem of 'reconstructing' the unknown sequence $\{x(i)\}$, $i = 1,2,\ldots$ of feature vectors in the (LRF) model from the input and output observations, which is known as Kalman filtering.

From the previous chapter it is known that the (LRF) model:

process equation:

$$\underline{x}(k+1) = A(k)\underline{x}(k) + B(k)u_1(k) + \underline{w}(k), \tag{3.1}$$

$$\text{initial condition } \underline{x}(0) \sim N(\mu_{x(0)}, \Sigma_x(0))$$

output equation:

$$\underline{y}(k) = C(k)\underline{x}(k) + D(k)u_2(k) + \underline{v}(k), \tag{3.2}$$

where $\underline{x}(k) \in \mathbb{R}^n$ is the unobservable feature vector; $\underline{y}(k) \in \mathbb{R}^p$ is an observable 'output' vector; $u_1(k) \in \mathbb{R}^s$ and $u_2(k) \in \mathbb{R}^m$ are observable input vectors and $\{(\underline{w}'(k)\underline{v}'(k))'\}$, $k = 0,1,2,\ldots$ is a sequence of white noise vectors with time-varying covariances:

$$E\left[\begin{bmatrix}\underline{w}(k)\\ \underline{v}(k)\end{bmatrix}\left[\underline{w}'(s)\underline{v}'(s)\right]\right] = \begin{bmatrix}\Sigma_w(k) & \Sigma_{wv}(k)\\ \Sigma_{vw}(k) & \Sigma_v(k)\end{bmatrix}\delta_{ks}$$

It is assumed that (i) the dimension of the feature vector is known, (ii) the time-varying parameters of $A(k)$, $B(k)$, $C(k)$, $D(k)$, $\Sigma_w(k)$, $\Sigma_v(k)$ $\Sigma_{wv}(k)$ are known, (In chapter V a general estimation method the so-called prediction error estimation method will be discussed in order to estimate the time-invariant parameters of $A$, $B$, $C$ $D$, $\Sigma_w$, $\Sigma_v$ and $\Sigma_{wv}$.) (iii) the pair $(A(k),C(k))$ is completely stochastically reconstructable; the pair $(A(k),\sqrt{\Sigma_w}(k))$ is completely stochastically controllable.

In the sequel we derive the Kalman filter in a non-rigorous way. See for a thorough treatment e.g. Jazwinski (1970) or Sage and Melsa (1971). Let

$\hat{\underline{x}}(j|k)$ be an estimator for x(j), based linearly on the sequence of observations $\{y(i),u_1(i),u_2(i)\}$, i = 1,2,...,k. The estimator is called a *predictor* if j > k; a *smoother* if j < k and a (Kalman) *estimator* if j = k. For notational convenience we write $\hat{\underline{x}}(k|k) = \hat{\underline{x}}(k)$. Let $\tilde{\underline{x}}(j|k) \triangleq \underline{x}(j) - \hat{\underline{x}}(j|k)$ be the error with error covariance $\Sigma_{\tilde{x}}(j|k)$. The statistical problem formulation is the following; construct a 'best' (to be defined) recursive (linear) estimator, based linearly on the observation sequence $\{\underline{y}(i),u_1(i),u_2(i)\}$ and a prior initial estimate. Best in the sense that $E\{\tilde{\underline{x}}(j|k)'\tilde{\underline{x}}(j|k)\}$ is minimum (minimum error variance estimator). For the moment two further assumptions are made: (i) the input sequences $\{u_1(k) = 0\}$ and $\{u_2(k) = 0\}$ for all k, which is not an essential restriction for the derivation of the estimator and (ii) the measurement noise and process noise are uncorrelated, i.e. $\Sigma_{wv}(k) = 0$ for all k.
Consider the linear predictor

$$\hat{\underline{x}}(k+1|k) = A(k)\hat{\underline{x}}(k). \tag{3.3}$$

Subtracting equation (3.3) from the process equation (3.1) gives

$$\tilde{\underline{x}}(k+1|k) = A(k)\tilde{\underline{x}}(k) + \underline{w}(k) \tag{3.4}$$

with error covariance matrix

$$\Sigma_{\tilde{x}}(k+1|k) = A(k)\Sigma_{\tilde{x}}(k)A'(k) + \Sigma_w(k) \tag{3.5}$$

$\Sigma_{\tilde{x}}(k+1|k)$ is minimum if $\Sigma_{\tilde{x}}(k)$ is minimum; minimum in the sense that every other error covariance matrix exceeds $\Sigma_{\tilde{x}}(k)$ by a positive semi-definite matrix. $\Sigma_{\tilde{x}}(k)$ is minimized as follows.
Consider the following recursive linear estimator

$$\hat{\underline{x}}(k+1) = A(k)\hat{\underline{x}}(k) + K(k+1)[\underline{y}(k+1)-C(k+1)\hat{\underline{x}}(k+1|k)] \tag{3.6}$$

This equation itself is a (LRF) model with as feature vector the observable estimator $\hat{\underline{x}}(k)$ and as input the prediction error or innovation $\underline{r}(k+1) \triangleq \underline{y}(k+1) - C(k+1)\hat{\underline{x}}(k+1|k)$. The unknown matrix K(k+1) is called the gain matrix and has to be determined in such a way that $\Sigma_{\tilde{x}}(k+1)$ is minimum. From equation (3.6) and output equation (3.2) we have that

$$\hat{\underline{x}}(k+1) = A(k)\hat{\underline{x}}(k) + K(k+1)[C(k+1)A(k)\tilde{\underline{x}}(k)+C(k+1)\underline{w}(k)+\underline{v}(k+1)] \tag{3.7}$$

Subtracting equation (3.7) from the process equation (3.1) gives

$$\underline{\tilde{x}}(k+1) = [I-K(k+1)C(k+1)][A(k)\underline{\tilde{x}}(k)+\underline{w}(k)] - K(k+1)\underline{v}(k+1) \qquad (3.8)$$

Further we have that

$$\Sigma_{\tilde{x}}(k+1) = E\{(\underline{\tilde{x}}(k+1)-E\{\underline{\tilde{x}}(k+1)\})(\underline{\tilde{x}}(k+1)-E\{\underline{\tilde{x}}(k+1)\})'\}$$

$$= E\{\underline{\tilde{x}}(k+1)\underline{\tilde{x}}'(k+1)\} - E\{\underline{\tilde{x}}(k+1)\}E\{\underline{\tilde{x}}'(k+1)\}$$

and hence

$$E\{\underline{\tilde{x}}'(k+1)\underline{\tilde{x}}(k+1)\} = E\{\underline{\tilde{x}}'(k+1)\}E\{\underline{\tilde{x}}(k+1)\} + tr(\Sigma_{\tilde{x}}(k+1)).$$

$E\{\underline{\tilde{x}}'(k+1)\underline{\tilde{x}}(k+1)\}$ can be minimized by letting $E\{\underline{\tilde{x}}'(k+1)\} = 0$ which can be done by choosing an unbiased estimator. This in turn is achieved by choosing as prior estimate $\hat{x}(0) = \mu_x(0)$. By taking $\hat{x}(0) = \mu_x(0)$ we have

$$E\{\underline{\tilde{x}}(0)\} = E\{\underline{x}(0)\} - E\{\hat{x}(0)\} = \mu_x(0) - \mu_x(0) = 0,$$

$$E\{\underline{\tilde{x}}(1)\} = E\{\underline{x}(1)\} - E\{\underline{\hat{x}}(1)\} = A(0)\mu_x(0) - A(0)\mu_x(0) = 0,$$

etc. From the error difference equation (3.8) we have with $R(k+1) \triangleq [I-K(k+1)C(k+1)]$

$$\Sigma_{\tilde{x}}(k+1) = R(k+1)[A(k)\Sigma_{\tilde{x}}(k)A'(k)+\Sigma_w(k)]R'(k+1) +$$

$$+ K(k+1)\Sigma_v(k+1)K'(k+1)$$

$$= R(k+1)\Sigma_{\tilde{x}}(k+1|k)R'(k+1) + K(k+1)\Sigma_v(k+1)K'(k+1) \qquad (3.9)$$

which is a matrix equation quadratic in the unknown gain matrix K(k+1). Now $tr(\Sigma_{\tilde{x}}(k+1))$ is minimum if $\Sigma_{\tilde{x}}(k+1)$ is minimum, that is if $\Sigma_{\tilde{x}}(k)$ is minimum. Assume $\Sigma_{\tilde{x}}(0)$ is minimum which is the case if we choose as prior estimate $\Sigma_{\tilde{x}}(0) = \Sigma_x(0)$, then $\Sigma_{\tilde{x}}(k+1)$, $k = 0,1,2,\ldots$ is minimum by choosing K(k+1) such that $\Sigma_{\tilde{x}}(k+1)$ is minimum. Differentiating the error difference equation (3.9) with respect to K(k+1) yields the following equation

$$K(k+1) = \Sigma_{\tilde{x}}(k+1|k)C(k+1)[C(k+1)\Sigma_{\tilde{x}}(k+1|k)C'(k+1)+$$

$$+\Sigma_v(k+1)]^{-1}, \qquad k = 0,1,2,\ldots \qquad (3.10)$$

Substitution of the right hand side of equation (3.10) into the error covariance difference equation (3.9) gives after some calculation

$$\Sigma_{\tilde{x}}(k+1) = [I-K(k+1)C(k+1)]\Sigma_{\tilde{x}}(k+1|k).$$

Summarizing the relevant equations, which is known as the discrete Kalman filter we have, with observable vectors $u_1(k)$ and $u_2(k)$

The discrete Kalman Filter (with uncorrelated process and measurement noise)

*Initial estimates:*

$$\hat{x}(0) = \mu_x(0), \quad \Sigma_{\tilde{x}}(0) = \Sigma_x(0)$$

*One-step ahead predictor:*

$$\underline{\hat{x}}(k+1|k) = A(k)\underline{\hat{x}}(k) + B(k)u_1(k)$$

*A-priori error covariance:*

$$\Sigma_{\tilde{x}}(k+1|k) = A(k)\Sigma_{\tilde{x}}(k)A'(k) + \Sigma_w(k)$$

*Filter gain algorithm:*

$$K(k+1) = \Sigma_{\tilde{x}}(k+1|k)C'(k+1)[C(k+1)\Sigma_{\tilde{x}}(k+1|k)C'(k+1)+\Sigma_v(k+1)]^{-1}$$

*Filter algorithm:*

$$\underline{\hat{x}}(k+1) = \underline{\hat{x}}(k+1|k) + K(k+1)[\underline{y}(k+1)-C(k+1)\underline{\hat{x}}(k+1|k)-D(k+1)u_2(k+1]$$

*A-posteriori error covariance algorithm:*

$$\Sigma_{\tilde{x}}(k+1) = [I-K(k+1)C(k+1)]\Sigma_{\tilde{x}}(k+1|k).$$

In the foregoing it is assumed that $\Sigma_{wv}(k) = 0$ for all k. When $\Sigma_{wv}(k) \neq 0$ we have the following Kalman filter, see e.g. Kwakernaak (1972, page 550).

The Discrete Kalman Filter (with correlated process and measurement noise)

*Initial Estimates:*

$$\hat{x}(0) = \mu_x(0), \quad \Sigma_{\tilde{x}}(0) = \Sigma_x(0)$$

*One-period ahead predictor:*

$$\hat{\underline{x}}(k+1|k) = A(k)\hat{\underline{x}}(k) + B(k)u_1(k)$$

*A-priori error covariance algorithm:*

$$\Sigma_{\tilde{x}}(k+1|k) = A(k)\Sigma_{\tilde{x}}(k)A'(k) + \Sigma_w(k)$$

*Filter gain algorithm:*

$$K(k+1) = [\Sigma_{\tilde{x}}(k+1|k)C'(k+1)+\Sigma_{wv}(k)][C(k+1)\Sigma_{\tilde{x}}(k+1|k)C'(k+1)+$$

$$+C(k+1)\Sigma_{wv}(k)+\Sigma_{vw}(k)C'(k+1)+\Sigma_v(k-1)]^{-1}$$

*Filter algorithm:*

$$\hat{\underline{x}}(k+1) = \hat{\underline{x}}(k+1|k) - K(k+1)[\underline{y}(k+1)-C(k+1)\hat{\underline{x}}(k+1|k)-D(k+1)u_2(k+1)]$$

*A posteriori error covariance matrix*

$$\Sigma_{\tilde{x}}(k+1) = [I-K(k+1)C(k+1)]\Sigma_{\tilde{x}}(k+1|k) - K(k+1)\Sigma_{vw}(k).$$

Statistical Properties of the Kalman Estimator.

The Kalman estimator is the best *linear* unbiased estimator for every distribution of the noise vectors $\underline{w}(k)$, $\underline{v}(k)$ and initial distribution of $\underline{x}(0)$. Best in the sense that the error covariance of any other *linear* estimator exceeds the error covariance of the Kalman estimator by a positive semidefinite matrix. It is the best of all linear and nonlinear estimators if the noise sequence $\{\underline{w}'(k)\underline{v}'(k)\}$ and initial distribution of $\underline{x}(0)$ are assumed to be Gaussian, see for details Sage and Melsa (1971). In that case the filter generates the conditional mean and conditional covariance of the feature vector $\underline{x}(k)$, given the observations $\{y(j),u_1(j),u_2(j),\ j = 1,2,\dots,k\}$. See for a further discussion the next section.

## 4.2. The Kalman Filter applied to the Classical Linear Regression Model with Constant Parameters.

In subsection 2.1 we formulate the classical linear regression equation which is rewritten in subsection 2.2 as a special (LRF) model

In subsection 2.3 the Kalman filter is applied to the special (LRF) model and the recursive estimation algorithms are written out explicitly.

*2.1 The Linear Regression Equation and Model in Time-Series Situations.*

Consider the following equation:

$$\underline{y}(t) = \sum_{i=1}^{n} \beta_i h_i(t) + \underline{v}(t), \qquad t = 1,2,... \tag{2.1.1}$$

expressing that a stochastic variable $\underline{y}$ of which measurements are available at times t = 1,2,... can be 'explained' by means of n known 'fitting' functions $h_1,...,h_n$. The 'weights' $\beta_1,...,\beta_n$ are unknown non-stochastic constant parameters. The errors $\underline{v}(1),\underline{v}(2),...$ are independent normally distributed random variables with mean zero and variance $\sigma^2 < \infty$. We can rewrite (2.1.1) in vector notation as follows

$$\underline{y}(t) = h(t)\beta + \underline{v}(t), \tag{2.1.2}$$

where $h(t) = (h_1(t),h_2(t),...,h_n(t))$ and $\beta' = (\beta_1,\beta_2,...,\beta_n)$. In economic studies $h_i(t)$ is often a measurement of a variable or a known function of that measurement, which partially 'causes' $\underline{y}(t)$. In economic terms $h_i(t)$ is an exogenous variable. This includes the case $h_i(t) \equiv 1$.

Suppose we have T observations y(1),y(2),...,y(T) on $\underline{y}$ together with T known vectors of values of fitting functions, arranged in the following model, called the standard linear regression model

$$\underline{Y}(T) = H(T)\beta + \underline{V}(T) \tag{2.1.3}$$

where $\underline{Y}(T)' = (\underline{y}(1),\underline{y}(2),...,\underline{y}(T))$, $H'(T) = (h'(1),h'(2),...,h'(T))$ and $\underline{V}'(T) = (\underline{v}(1),\underline{v}(2),...,\underline{v}(T))$. The covariance matrix of $\underline{V}(T) = \sigma^2 I_{(T)}$, where $I_{(T)}$ represents the unit matrix of order T.

We are interested in estimating the unknown parameter vector β. Of course the least squares method would do (provided that $T \geqq n$) but we investigate the possibility of applying the Kalman estimation procedure. Because the filter is applied to the (LRF) model, we have to reformulate equation (2.1.2) as a special (LRF) model. This is done in the next subsection.

*2.2 The Linear Regression Equation reformulated as a Special Feature Space Model.*

The parameter vector $\beta$ is unknown and has to be estimated, so it is natural to consider the parameter vector to be the feature vector. We know that $\beta$ is a time invariant non-stochastic vector, and satisfies therefore the trivial difference equation:

process equation:

$$\beta(t+1) = \beta(t) \tag{2.2.1}$$

output equation:

$$\underline{y}(t) = h(t)\beta(t) + \underline{v}(t). \tag{2.2.2}$$

Now (2.2.1) and (2.2.2) form a simple (LRF) model with (2.2.1) as the process equation.

*2.3 The Kalman Filter Specialized to the (LRF) Model in Subsection 2.2.*

Before we can start the procedure we have to known certain parameters. For the model in subsection 2.2 we must give a value for $\hat{\beta}(0)$, the initial estimate of the parameter vector $\beta$ and a value for $\Sigma_{\tilde{\beta}}(0)$, the corresponding 'error covariance' matrix, where $\tilde{\beta}(0) = \beta - \hat{\beta}(0)$ denotes the error of $\hat{\beta}(0)$. Furthermore we have to know $\sigma^2$, the variance of the errors.

What values can be chosen for $\hat{\beta}(0)$, $\Sigma_{\tilde{\beta}}(0)$ and $\sigma^2$ in practice? The 'error covariance' matrix $\Sigma_{\tilde{\beta}}(0)$ can be used as a measure of uncertainty with respect to the values we have chosen for $\hat{\beta}(0)$ and $\sigma^2$. The more uncertain we feel about these values, the larger we take the values for the (diagonal) elements of $\Sigma_{\tilde{\beta}}(0)$. In fact we proceed in a Bayesian-like manner. In section 4.3 we examine the Bayesian character of the filter in more detail.

We select for $\hat{\beta}(0)$, $\Sigma_{\tilde{\beta}}(0)$ and $\tilde{\sigma}^2$ respectively the values $\mu$, $\Sigma \neq 0$ and $\sigma^2 \neq 0$. As stated above, it is assumed that we have T observations on $\underline{y}$ and T vectors of fitting functions. The filter algorithm becomes for $t = 0$

$$\underline{\hat{\beta}}(1) = \mu + K(1)\{\underline{y}(1) - h(1)\mu\}, \tag{2.3.1}$$

where

$$K(1) = \Sigma h'(1)(h(1)\Sigma h'(1)+\tilde{\sigma}^2)^{-1},$$

The a-posteriori 'error covariance' algorithm yields:

$$\Sigma_{\tilde{\beta}}(1) = \{I_{(n)}-K(1)h(1)\}\Sigma. \qquad (2.3.2)$$

Continuing in this way for t = 1,2,... we have for t = T-1:

$$\underline{\hat{\beta}}(T) = \underline{\hat{\beta}}(T-1) + K(T)\{\underline{y}(T)-h(T)\underline{\hat{\beta}}(T-1)\}, \qquad (2.3.3)$$

where

$$K(T) = \Sigma_{\tilde{\beta}}(T-1)h'(T)\{h(T)\Sigma_{\tilde{\beta}}(T-1)h'(T)+\tilde{\sigma}^2\}^{-1}$$

and

$$\Sigma_{\tilde{\beta}}(T) = \{I_{(n)}-K(T)h(T)\}\Sigma_{\tilde{\beta}}(T-1) \qquad (2.3.4)$$

In section 4.3 we show how (2.3.3) and (2.3.4) can be written in a non-recursive form. It turns out that the resulting Kalman estimator $\underline{\hat{\beta}}(T)$ is the weighted average of $\mu$, the value of the initial estimate $\hat{\beta}(0)$ and the least squares estimator.

## 4.3. The Kalman Filter Considered to be a Bayesian Estimation Procedure and some (Asymptotic) Properties.

In the following subsections we show for a certain regression model, the equivalence of the Kalman estimator, and a corresponding Bayes estimator. A relationship is established between the Kalman and least squares estimator, and is used to derive some (asymptotic) properties of the Kalman estimator. The section ends with a comparison of the two estimators.

### *3.1 A Bayesian Estimation Procedure*

Recall model (2.1.2):

$$\underline{y}(t) = h(t)\beta + \underline{v}(t), \qquad t = 1,2,...$$

If we want to apply a Bayesian approach then an a-priori distribution of the parameter vector has to be specified. We use the assumption of normality and postulate the following model:

$$\underline{y}(t) = h(t)\underline{B} + \underline{v}(t), \qquad t = 1,2,\ldots \tag{3.1.1}$$

where $\underline{B} \sim N_n(\mu,\Sigma)$. It is assumed that $-\infty < \mu_h < \infty$, $h = 1,2,\ldots,n$ and $0 < |\Sigma| < \infty$. The specification of the distribution of the errors $\underline{v}(1),\underline{v}(2),\ldots$ remains the same.

Suppose at time t=1 that y(1) and h(1) are known. Then

$$\begin{bmatrix} \underline{B} \\ \underline{y}(1) \end{bmatrix} \sim N_{n+1}\left[\begin{bmatrix} \mu \\ h(1)\mu \end{bmatrix}, \begin{bmatrix} \Sigma & \Sigma h'(1) \\ h(1)\Sigma & h(1)\Sigma h'(1)+\sigma^2 \end{bmatrix}\right]$$

and the a-posteriori or conditional distribution of $\underline{B}$, given $\underline{y}(1) = y(1)$ for the value h(1) of the fitting functions vector, is n-dimensional normal with mean

$$\mu + \Sigma h'(1)\{y(1)-h(1)\mu\}/\{h(1)\Sigma h'(1)+\sigma^2\},$$

and covariance matrix

$$\Sigma - \Sigma h'(1)h(1)\Sigma/\{h(1)\Sigma h'(1)+\sigma^2\},$$

see for instance Anderson (1958). If we assume any 'squared error' cost function the mean of the a-posteriori distribution is an optimal estimator, in the sense that the Bayes risk is minimal, see Sage and Melsa (1971). In practice, $\sigma^2$ will be unknown, but in order to apply the theory we shall have to choose a value say $\tilde{\sigma}^2$ for $\sigma^2$. Notice that for t=1 the Kalman filtering equations (2.3.1) and (2.3.2) generate the mean and the covariance matrix of the a-posteriori distribution of $\underline{B}$.

We can repeat the procedure for $t = 2,3,\ldots,T$, by using the a-posteriori distribution of $\underline{B}$ at time t as the a-priori distribution at time t+1. It can be shown that the Kalman filter coincides with the above procedure.

The a-posteriori distribution of $\underline{B}$ at time T, according to the above mentioned recursive scheme, can equally well be obtained directly. The a-posteriori of $\underline{B}$ given $\underline{Y}(T) = Y(T)$ for the value H(T) of the fitting functions (see section 2.1) is normal with mean

$$\mu + \Sigma H'(T)\{H(T)\Sigma H'(T)+\tilde{\sigma}^2 I_{(T)}\}^{-1}\{Y(T)-H(T)\mu\} \tag{3.1.2}$$

and covariance matrix

$$\Sigma - \Sigma H'(T)\{H(T)\Sigma H'(T)+\tilde{\sigma}^2 I_{(T)}\}^{-1}H(T)\Sigma. \tag{3.1.3}$$

Hence (3.1.2) is the Kalman estimate for $\underline{B}$ based on the first T observations. Now we try to relate the Kalman estimator to the classical least squares estimator

$$\dot{\underline{B}}(T) = \{H'(T)H(T)\}^{-1}H'(T)\underline{Y}(T),$$

where the existence of $\{H'(T)H(T)\}^{-1}$ is assumed; i.e. the (LRF) model is completely reconstructable, see theorem (2.3). $\dot{\underline{B}}(T)$ is a sufficient statistic provided that $\sigma^2$ is known. We already postulated $\sigma^2 = \tilde{\sigma}^2$. Least squares theory learns that the conditional distribution of $\dot{\underline{B}}(T)$, given the true value B, and the error variance $\tilde{\sigma}^2$, is $N_n(B,\tilde{\sigma}^2\{H'(T)H(T)\}^{-1})$. We postulated $\underline{B} \sim N_n(\mu,\Sigma)$ and hence

$$\begin{bmatrix} \underline{B} \\ \dot{\underline{\beta}}(T) \end{bmatrix} \sim N_{2n}\left[\begin{bmatrix} \mu \\ \mu \end{bmatrix}, \begin{bmatrix} \Sigma & \Sigma \\ \Sigma & \Sigma+\tilde{\sigma}^2\{H'(T)H(T)\}^{-1} \end{bmatrix}\right]$$

$\dot{\underline{\beta}}(T)$ is sufficient and the a-posteriori distribution of $\underline{B}$ given $\underline{Y}(T) = Y(T)$ coincides with the a-posteriori distribution of $\underline{B}$ given the corresponding outcome of $\dot{\underline{\beta}}(T) = \dot{\beta}(T)$ and hence is normal with mean

$$\mu + \Sigma[\Sigma+\tilde{\sigma}^2\{H'(T)H(T)\}^{-1}]^{-1}\{\dot{\beta}(T)-\mu\} \tag{3.1.4}$$

and covariance matrix

$$\Sigma - \Sigma[\Sigma+\tilde{\sigma}^2\{H'(T)H(T)\}^{-1}]^{-1}\Sigma. \tag{3.1.5}$$

Thus (3.1.4) is an alternative expression for (3.1.2) and (3.1.5) is an alternative expression for (3.1.3). An alternative expression for the Kalman estimator $\hat{\underline{\beta}}(T)$ is thus given by (3.1.4). The Kalman estimator is the weighted sum of the a-priori mean $\mu$ and the least squares estimator $\dot{\underline{\beta}}(T)$ with weighting matrices respectively

$$D(T) = I_{(n)} - \Sigma[\Sigma+\tilde{\sigma}^2\{H'(T)H(T)\}^{-1}]^{-1}$$

and

$$E(T) = \Sigma[\Sigma+\tilde{\sigma}^2\{H'(T)H(T)\}^{-1}]^{-1}.$$

*3.2 Some (Asymptotic) Properties of the Kalman Estimator*

From (3.1.4) we know that

$$\hat{\underline{\beta}}(T) = D(T)\mu + E(T)\dot{\underline{\beta}}(T) = \dot{\underline{\beta}}(T) + D(T)\{\mu-\dot{\underline{\beta}}(T)\}. \qquad (3.2.1)$$

Taking expectations for a given vector $\beta$ of unknown parameters we have

$$E\{\hat{\underline{\beta}}(T)\} - \beta = D(T)(\mu-\beta),$$

because the least squares estimator $\dot{\underline{\beta}}(T)$ is unbiased. It can be shown that

$$D(T) = \{I_{(n)}+\tilde{\sigma}^2\Sigma H'(T)H(T)\}^{-1},$$

so the bias can be written as

$$E\{\hat{\underline{\beta}}(T)\} - \beta = \{I_{(n)}+\tilde{\sigma}^2\Sigma H'(T)H(T)\}^{-1}(\mu-\beta). \qquad (3.2.2)$$

From (3.2.2) it can be seen that the bias decreases with increasing covariance matrix $\Sigma$ and also with increasing values of T. It may be seen that the elements of $\Sigma$ have to be taken substantially larger than $\tilde{\sigma}^2$, because otherwise a considerable bias may occur especially for small values of T. The bias is zero if the initial estimate $\hat{\beta}(0) = \mu$ equals $\beta$ and tends to zero if $\tilde{\sigma}^2$ tends to zero, or if $\Sigma^{-1}$ tends to zero. In the last case the Kalman estimator tends to the least squares estimator, as will be shown in subsection 3.3. The Kalman estimator is in general biased.

Now we examine some asymptotic properties of $\hat{\underline{\beta}}(T)$, namely its consistency and the limiting distribution of $T^{\frac{1}{2}}\{\hat{\underline{\beta}}(T)-\beta\}$ as T approaches infinity. Multiplying (3.2.1) by $T^{\frac{1}{2}}$ and taking probability limits we have

$$\text{plim}[T^{\frac{1}{2}}\{\hat{\underline{\beta}}(T)-\dot{\underline{\beta}}(T)\}] = \lim T^{\frac{1}{2}}D(T)\mu - \lim T^{\frac{1}{2}}D(T)\text{plim}\dot{\underline{\beta}}(T) = 0,$$

provided that $T^{\frac{1}{2}}D(T)$ tends to zero if $T \to \infty$. A standard and sufficient condition is that for $T \to \infty$, $\lim\{T^{-1}H'(T)H(T)\} = Q$, where Q is a $(n \times n)$ positive definite matrix. After a few calculations it can be shown that the sequence TD(T), T = n,n+1,... is bounded so $\lim T^{\frac{1}{2}}D(T) = 0$. Further we know that $\underline{\dot{\beta}}(T)$ is a consistent estimator ($\text{plim}\{\underline{\dot{\beta}}(T)-\beta\} = 0$) and hence

$$\text{plim}[T^{\frac{1}{2}}\{\underline{\hat{\beta}}(T)-\underline{\dot{\beta}}(T)\}] = \text{plim}[T^{\frac{1}{2}}[\{\underline{\hat{\beta}}(T)-\beta\}-\{\underline{\dot{\beta}}(T)-\beta\}]] = 0,$$

which implies $\text{plim}(\underline{\hat{\beta}}(T)-\beta) = 0$. We may conclude that $\underline{\hat{\beta}}(T)$ is a consistent estimator.

Finally we turn to the limiting distribution of $T^{\frac{1}{2}}\{\underline{\hat{\beta}}(T)-\beta\}$. It is known, see for example Theil (1971), that under the assumption $\lim\{T^{-1}H'(T)H(T)\} = Q$, the random vector $T^{\frac{1}{2}}\{\underline{\dot{\beta}}(T)-\beta\}$ has a normal limiting distribution with zero mean and covariance matrix $\tilde{\sigma}^2Q^{-1}$. From asymptotic distribution theory it is known that, if the sequence of differences of two random vector converges in probability to zero and if one random vector has a limiting distribution, then the other random vector has the same limiting distribution. We have shown that

$$T^{\frac{1}{2}}\{\underline{\hat{\beta}}(T)-\beta\} - T^{\frac{1}{2}}\{\underline{\dot{\beta}}(T)-\beta\}$$

converges in probability to zero. Thus the limiting distribution of $T^{\frac{1}{2}}\{\underline{\hat{\beta}}(T)-\beta\}$ is also normal with zero mean and covariance matrix $\sigma^2Q^{-1}$.

### *3.3 The Kalman and Least Squares Estimator Compared*

We have seen in subsection 3.1 that the least squares estimator is given by

$$\underline{\dot{\beta}}(T) = \{H'(T)H(T)\}^{-1}H'(T)\underline{Y}(T) \qquad (3.3.1)$$

with the following error covariance matrix

$$\Sigma_{\dot{\beta}}(T) = \tilde{\sigma}^2\{H'(T)H(T)\}^{-1}. \qquad (3.3.2)$$

In order to compare the above equations with the non-recursive expressions for the Kalman estimator and its 'error-covariance' matrix, which are given respectively by equations (3.1.2) and (3.1.3), we rewrite these equations as follows:

$$\underline{\hat{\beta}}(T) = \{H'(T)H(T)+\tilde{\sigma}^2\Sigma^{-1}\}^{-1}\{H'(T)\underline{Y}(T)+\tilde{\sigma}^2\Sigma^{-1}\mu\}, \qquad (3.3.3)$$

$$\Sigma_{\tilde{\beta}}(T) = \tilde{\sigma}^2\{H'(T)H(T)+\tilde{\sigma}^2\Sigma^{-1}\}^{-1}. \qquad (3.3.4)$$

From (3.3.2) and (3.3.4) we see that the Kalman estimator has a smaller

error covariance matrix than the least squares estimator $\dot{\underline{\beta}}(T)$. The estimator $\hat{\underline{\beta}}(T)$ is biased, whereas $\dot{\underline{\beta}}(T)$ is unbiased. From equation (3.3.3) it can be seen that the Kalman estimator reduces to the least squares estimator if $\tilde{\sigma}^2 = 0$ or if $\Sigma^{-1} = 0$.
In practice it means that the larger we choose the starting error covariance matrix $\Sigma$, with relative small values $\mu$ and $\tilde{\sigma}^2$, the more the Kalman estimator reduces to the least squares estimator.

## 4.4. Stability of the Discrete Kalman Filter and its Steady State.

In the sequel some lemma's and theorems from Jazwinski (1970) are summarized for the (LRF) model without input sequences $\{u_1(k)\}$ and $\{u_2(k)\}$.

Lemma : If the (LRF) model is uniformly completely stochastically controllable and reconstructable and if $\Sigma_{\tilde{x}}(0) > 0$ then $\Sigma_{\tilde{x}}(k)$ is uniformly bounded from above and uniformly bounded from below if $k \geqq N$. (N is a positive integer used in theorems 2.4 and 2.5 in chapter II).

Proof : See Jazwinski (1970).

Theorem (4.1) : If the (LRF) model is uniformly completely stochastically controllable and reconstructable then the discrete Kalman estimator is exponentially stable.

Proof : See Jazwinski (1970).

Theorem (4.2) : If the (LRF) model is uniformly completely stochastically reconstructable and controllable and $\Sigma^1_{\tilde{x}}(k)$ and $\Sigma^2_{\tilde{x}}(k)$ are any two solutions with initial conditions $\Sigma^1_{\tilde{x}}(0) \geqq 0$ and $\Sigma^2_{\tilde{x}}(0) \geqq 0$ then $\|\delta\Sigma_{\tilde{x}}(k)\| \to 0$ for $k \to \infty$ where $\delta\Sigma_{\tilde{x}}(k) \triangleq \Sigma^1_{\tilde{x}}(k) - \Sigma^2_{\tilde{x}}(k)$ and $\|.\|$ denotes the Euclidean norm.

According to Jazwinski, theorem (4.2) has two important consequences:
(i) the initial estimate $\Sigma_{\tilde{x}}(0)$ is 'forgotten' as more and more data are processed; This is important for $\Sigma_{\tilde{x}}(0)$ is often poorly known. The Kalman

filter is *robust* with respect to initial estimates (ii) the computation of $\Sigma_{\tilde{x}}(k)$ is stable. Numerical errors in $\Sigma_{\tilde{x}}(k)$ are also 'forgotten'.

Steady State Kalman Filtering.

Consider the stationary (LRF) model, without deterministic input

$$\underline{x}(k+1) = A\underline{x}(k) + \underline{w}(k)$$
$$\underline{y}(k) = C\underline{x}(k) + \underline{v}(k)$$

where $\text{cov}\{\underline{w}(k)\underline{w}'(s)\} = \Sigma_w \delta_{ks}$ and $\text{cov}\{\underline{v}(k)\underline{v}'(s)\} = \Sigma_v \delta_{ks}$. Assume that the pair (A,C) is uniformly completely stochastically reconstructable and the pair $(A,\sqrt{\Sigma_w})$ is uniformly completely stochastically controllable, then, following Bertsekas (1976), the filter algorithm tends to the following equation

$$\hat{x}(k+1|k) = A\hat{x}(k|k-1) + A\Sigma C'(C\Sigma C'+\Sigma_v)^{-1}(y(k)-C\hat{x}(k|k-1))$$

where $\Sigma$ is the positive definite solution of the algebraic *Riccati* equation (ARE)

$$\Sigma = A[\Sigma-\Sigma C'(C\Sigma C'+\Sigma_v)^{-1}C\Sigma]A' + \Sigma_w.$$

In that case it is said that the filter is in its *steady state*.

Example (4.1), taken from Eykhoff (1974)

Consider the scalar time invariant (LRF) model

$$\underline{x}(k+1) = a\underline{x}(k) + \underline{w}(k), \text{ initial condition } \underline{x}(0) \sim N(x_o,\sigma_x^2(0)),\ k \geqq 0,$$
$$\underline{y}(k) = \underline{x}(k) + \underline{v}(k)$$

The sequence $\{(\underline{w}(k)\underline{v}(k)\}$ k = 0,1,2,... is white noise with

$$\text{cov}\left[\begin{bmatrix}\underline{w}(k)\\ \underline{v}(k)\end{bmatrix}(\underline{w}(s)\underline{v}(s))\right] = \begin{bmatrix}V & 0\\ 0 & N\end{bmatrix}\delta_{ks}$$

The Kalman filter is given by the equations

*Initial estimates:*

$$\hat{x}(0) = x_0;\quad \Sigma_{\tilde{x}}(0) = \sigma_x^2(0) = P(0)$$

*A-priori error covariance algorithm:*

$$Q(k+1) = a^2P(k) + V$$

*Filter gain algorithm:*

$$K(k+1) = Q(k+1)/(Q(k+1)+N)$$

*Filter algorithm:*

$$\hat{x}(k+1) = a\hat{x}(k) + K(k+1)[y(k+1-a\hat{x}(k)]$$

*A-posteriori error covariance algorithm:*

$$P(k+1) = Q(k+1) - Q^2(k+1)/(Q(k+1)+N) = NQ(k+1)/(Q(k+1)+N)$$

The filter equation can be rewritten as

$$\hat{x}(k+1) = \alpha(k+1)a\hat{x}(k) + \beta(k+1)y(k+1)$$

with $\alpha(k+1) \triangleq N/(Q(k+1)+N)$ and $\beta(k+1) \triangleq Q(k+1)/(Q(k+1)+N)$ which implies $\alpha(k+1) + \beta(k+1) = 1$. Consider two cases

A: no prior knowledge about $x(0)$: $\hat{x}(0) = 0$; $P(0) = \infty$; $N = V$; $a = \sqrt{0.5} \approx 0.7$

B: exact prior knowlegde : $\hat{x}(0) = x_0$, $P(0) = 0$; $N = V$; $a = \sqrt{0.5} \approx 0.7$.

The evaluation of Q(k), K(k) and P(k) for the two cases are shown in the table below.

| Case A | | | | Case B | | |
|---|---|---|---|---|---|---|
| Q(k) | K(k) | P(k) | k | Q(k) | K(k) | P(k) |
| | | ∞ | 0 | | | 0 |
| ∞ | 1 | N | 1 | N | 0.5 | 0.5N |
| 1.5N | 0.6 | 0.6N | 2 | 1.25N | 0.555 | 0.555N |
| 1.3N | 0.565 | 0.565N | 3 | 1.278N | 0.56 | 0.56N |
| 1.283N | 0.56 | . | 4 | 1.28N | 0.56 | . |
| 1.28N | 0.56 | . | 5 | . | . | . |

After a few steps K(k) reaches the so-called steady state solution $\overline{K} = 0.56$. The following picture shows the a-posteriori covariance of the estimates:

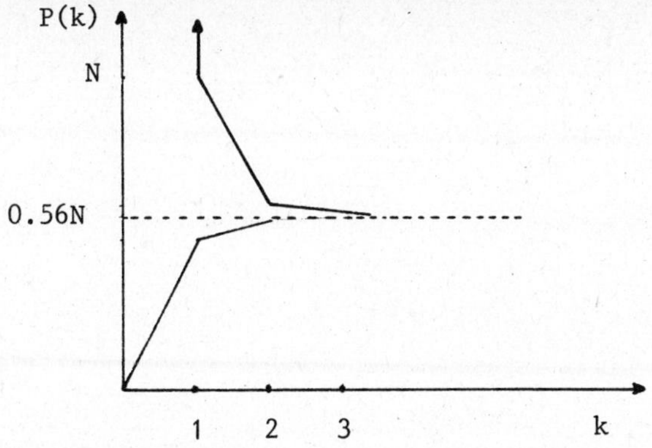


The condition for stationarity is given by $P(k+1) = P(k) = \overline{P}$ which implies that $Q(k)$ and $K(k)$ are also time-invariant, say $\overline{Q}$ and $\overline{K}$ . The time-invariant solution of the above equation is

$$N\overline{Q}(\overline{Q}+N)^{-1} = \overline{P}$$

$$N(a^2\overline{P}+V)(a^2\overline{P}+V+N)^{-1} = \overline{P}$$

which is rewritten as the following (Riccati) equation

$$\overline{P}^2 + (N-V-a^2N)\overline{P} - NV = 0.$$

For the two cases discussed we have

$$\overline{P}^2 - 0{,}5N\overline{P} - N^2 = 0$$

with positive root $\overline{P} = 0.56N$ (the positive definite solution of the Riccati equation).

## 4.5. Prediction Errors (Innovations).

In the previous sections we have seen that the Kalman estimator is a linear function of the prediction errors $\underline{r}(k+1) = \underline{y}(k+1) - C(k+1)\hat{\underline{x}}(k+1\ k) - D(k+1)u_2(k+1)$, $k = 0,1,2,\ldots$ . If the model is correctly specified, the sequence of prediction errors is a white noise sequence, as will be shown in the sequel. The white noise characteristics of the prediction errors can be used for a model check. The prediction errors are also used in a general estimation method called the prediction error estimation to be discussed in the next chapter. Because the Kalman filter generates prediction errors it is a useful tool for the prediction error estimation method.

Assume that the (LRF) model is correctly specified with the usual Gaussian assumptions on the noise vectors and initial distribution of $\underline{x}(0)$, then the sequence of prediction errors $\{\underline{r}(j)\}$, $j = 1,2,\ldots$ is a white noise sequence with mean

$$E\{\underline{r}(j)\} = E\{\underline{y}(j)\} - C(j)E\{\hat{\underline{x}}(j|j-1)\} - D(j)u_2(j)$$

$$= C(j)E\{\tilde{\underline{x}}(j|j-1)\} = 0,$$

because $E\{\tilde{\underline{x}}(j-1)\} = 0$, and time-varying covariance

$$\Sigma_r(j) = C(j)\Sigma_{\tilde{x}}(j|j-1)C'(j) + \Sigma_v(j).$$

The independence of the prediction errors is geometrically illustrated for $k = 1,2$ and $3$, given the observations $y(1), y(2)$ and $y(3)$ and no external input $u_1(k)$ and $u_2(k)$, $k = 0,1,2,3$. We have $r(1) = y(1) - C(1)\hat{x}(1|0)$; $r(2) = y(2) - C(2)\hat{x}(2|1)$ and $r(3) = y(3) - C(3)\hat{x}(3|2)$. The linear predictions $\hat{x}(2|1)$ and $\hat{x}(3|2)$ depend on the observation(s) $y(1)$ and $\{y(2), y(1)\}$ respectively. Now $\{r(i)\}$ is minimum because $\hat{x}(i|i-1)$ is a minimum error prediction. $C(2)\hat{x}(2|1)$ is a linear combination of $\hat{x}(1|0)$ and $r(1)$ and hence a vector in a vector space spanned by $\hat{x}(1|0)$ and $r(1)$. The projection of $y(2)$ on this space is $C(2)\hat{x}(2|1)$; $r(2)$ is orthogonal to this space and hence $r(2) \perp r(1)$. $C(3)\hat{x}(3|2)$ is a vector in the vector space spanned by $\hat{x}(2|1)$ and $r(2)$. The projection of $y(3)$ on this space is $C(3)\hat{x}(3|2)$; $r(3)$ is orthogonal to this space and hence $r(3) \perp r(2) \perp r(1)$. In picture

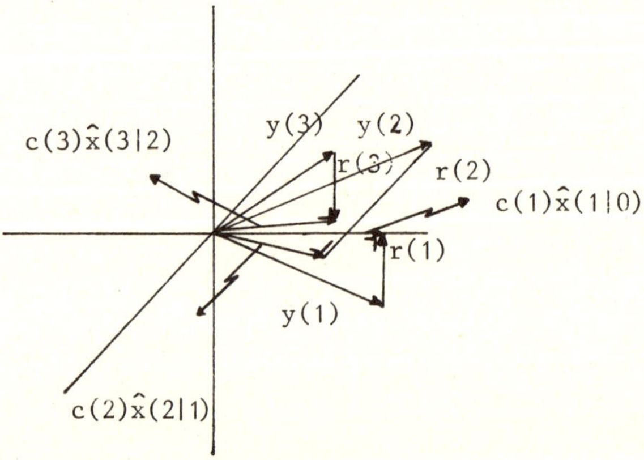

## 4.6. Divergence of the Filter.

As already stated the Kalman filter relies heavily on the correct specification of the (LRF) model. According to Sage and Melsa (1971) the actual error may become unbounded, even if the error covariance $\Sigma_{\tilde{x}}(k)$ in the filter is vanishingly small. This phenomenon, referred to as *divergence* of the filter can seriously affect the applicability of the filter.

An example will be given, taken from Sage and Melsa (1971), to show that, applying the filter to an incorrectly specified model, results in increasing prediction errors, which are not theoretically predicted by the error covariance $\Sigma_{\tilde{x}}(k)$. Let the 'true' process equation be

$$x(k) = x(k-1) + \alpha$$

where the feature variable $x(k) \in \mathbb{R}$ and $\alpha$ is a constant.
The assumed process equation is

$$\bar{x}(k) = \bar{x}(k-1).$$

The output equation is

$$\underline{y}(k) = \bar{x}(k) + \underline{v}(k)$$

where $\underline{v}(k)$ is standard white noise. Let $\hat{x}(0) = 0$ and $\Sigma_{\tilde{x}}(0) = \Sigma_x(0) = \infty$, so no initial knowledge about the initial feature variable $x(0)$ is assumed. Applying the filter we have after N observations

$$\hat{x}(N) = x(0) + 2^{-1}(N+1)\alpha + N^{-1}\sum_{i=1}^{N} v(i)$$

and the error variance given by the filter is

$$\bar{\sigma}^2\hat{\tilde{x}}(N) = 1/N$$

indicating that for $N \to \infty$ the estimate would converge to its true value. This is not true, which can be shown by computing the *actual* error variance. The actual state after N periods of the feature variable is

$$x(N) = x(0) + \alpha N$$

so that the actual estimation error is

$$\tilde{x}(N) = 2^{-1}(N-1)\alpha - N^{-1}\sum_{i=1}^{N} v(i)$$

and the actual mean squared error variance is

$$\sigma^2_{\tilde{x}}(N) = 4^{-1}(N-1)^2\alpha^2 + N^{-1} = E\{\tilde{\underline{x}}(N)\}^2 + \bar{\sigma}^2_{\tilde{x}}(N)$$

From this equation it can be seen that the actual mean-squared error becomes unbounded as N increases and hence the estimate diverges from the true value of the feature variable. The reason why the estimate diverges is that the gain $K(N) = 1/N$ approaches zero 'too rapidly', *decoupling* the estimate from the observations. To overcome this divergence several modifications of the gain matrix are suggested. The basic concept of these approaches is to limit the decrease of the gain to avoid decoupling. The suggested procedures canbe placed into three broad classes:

(i) Direct increase of the gain

(ii) Limiting the error covariance

(iii) Artificial increase of the process noise covariance, which is closely related to the single exponential smoothing technique, to be discussed in chapter VI. See for details of the procedures Sage and Melsa.

Because the divergence occurs as a result of misspecification and wrongly assumed parameters, the problem is basically one of modelspecification and parameter estimation. A general estimation method called the prediction error estimation is presented in the next Chapter and it is shown that the non-linear ML-parameter estimates of the (LSF) and (LRF) model are 'special' prediction error estimates, if the prediction error covariance is taken as criterion for the validity of the model. Because the divergence of the filter may give rise to increasing prediction errors, adjustment of the assumed parameters, by means of the prediction error method with the prediction error covariance as criterion, may serve as a 'feed-back' mechanism for the filter, preventing in this way decoupling.

However, before discussing the estimation methods we have to deal with the so-called parameter identifiability problem that is the problem that no two (or more) parameter values may lead to the same distribution function of the observed variables. If the parameters are not identifiable, then certain estimators such as the ML-estimators may not be used.

# V. Parameter Identifiability, Prediction-Error Estimation and Model Check

## 5.1. Parameter Identifiability.

The parameter identifiability concepts used in system theory and econometrics differ. In system theory the parameter identifiability definition is formulated in terms of the consistency of parameter estimates, see e.g. Tse and Anton (1972) or Ljung (1976), whereas in econometrics the parameter identifiability is related to a unique association of a distribution function to a given parameter vector. In the sequel we discuss the latter and summarize the definitions and results as given by Bowden (1973) and Rothenberg (1971).

Consider a probability space $(\Omega, A, P_\theta)$ where $\Omega$ is some non-empty set, A is a $\sigma$-algebra of subsets of $\Omega$ and $P_\theta$ is a family of probability measures defined on $\Omega$, with parameter vector $\theta \in \Theta \subset \mathbb{R}^m$, where $\Theta$ is an open set. Consider the random vector $\underline{y}$ with realizations $y \in A \subset \mathbb{R}^p$ with probability density function $p(.;\theta)$.

Assumption 1: The set A of y values for which $p(y;\theta)$ is strictly positive is the same for all $\theta$ in $\Theta$.

Assumption 2: The function p is smooth in $\theta$. Specifically, we assume that for all $\theta \in \Theta$ and for all y in A the functions $p(y;\theta)$ and $\log p(y;\theta)$ are continuously differentiable with respect to $\theta$.

Assumption 3: The elements of Fisher's information matrix

$$R(\theta) \triangleq [r_{ij}] = E_{\underline{y}|\theta}\left[\frac{\partial \log p(y;\theta)}{\partial \theta_i} \frac{\partial \log p(y;\theta)}{\partial \theta_j}\right]$$

exist and are continuous on $\Theta$.

Definition (5.1) : Two parameter points $\theta_1$ and $\theta_2$ are said to be observationally equivalent if with probability one $p(.;\theta_1) = p(.;\theta_2)$.

Definition (5.2) : A parameter point $\theta_o$ is said to be *globally* identifiable if there exists no other $\theta \in \Theta$ such that with probability one $p(.;\theta_o) = p(.;\theta)$. A parameter point $\theta_o$ is said to be *locally* identifiable if there exists an open neighbourhood $\tilde{\Theta} \in \Theta$ of $\theta_o$ such that with probability one, no point in $\tilde{\Theta}$ is observationally equivalent with $\theta_o$.

In the sequel we associate parameter identifiability with Kullback's information criterion. Following Kullback (1959) define the logarithm of the likelihood ratio $\log(p(y;\theta_o)/p(y;\theta))$ as the information in $\underline{y} = y$ for discriminating in favour of $p(y;\theta_o)$ against $p(y;\theta)$. The mean information is given by

$$I(\theta_o,\theta) = \int_{-\infty}^{\infty} \log\left(\frac{p(y;\theta_o)}{p(y;\theta)}\right) p(y;\theta_o)dy$$

or the alternative function used by Bowden

$$H(\theta,\theta_o) = \int_{-\infty}^{\infty} \log\left(\frac{p(y;\theta)}{p(y;\theta_o)}\right) p(y;\theta_o)dy.$$

It can be shown that if $p(.;\theta)$ is different from $p(.;\theta_o)$ and if $H(\theta,\theta_o)$ is finite then $H(\theta,\theta_o) < 0$. Otherwise $H(\theta,\theta_o) = 0$.

<u>Theorem (5.1a)</u> : The parameter point $\theta_o$ is *globally* identifiable if and only if the equation $H(\theta,\theta_o) = 0$ has as solution in $\Theta$ only $\theta = \theta_o$. The parameter point $\theta_o$ is locally identifiable if and only if $\theta_o$ is the only solution in some open neighbourhood $\tilde{\Theta} \subset \Theta$ of $\theta_o$.

As stated by Bowden parameter identifiability is closely connected with the maximum of $H(\theta,\theta_o)$. If this maximum is global and attained only at $\theta = \theta_o$, then $\theta_o$ is globally identifiable. A sufficient condition for $\theta_o$ to be globally identifiable is that $H(\theta,\theta_o)$ is strictly concave in $\Theta$ and $\Theta$ itself is convex. If the maximum is unique in an open neighbourhood of $\theta_o$ local identifiability holds. A sufficient condition for a unique local maximum is that $H'(\theta_o,\theta_o) = 0$ and $H''(\theta_o,\theta_o)$ is negative definite where $H'(\theta_o,\theta_o) \triangleq \left.\frac{\partial H(\theta,\theta_o)}{\partial\theta}\right|_{\theta=\theta_o}$ and $H''(\theta_o,\theta_o) \triangleq \left.\frac{\partial^2 H(\theta,\theta_o)}{\partial\theta\partial\theta'}\right|_{\theta=\theta_o}$.

It is shown by Bowden that the condition of $H''(\theta_o,\theta_o)$ to be negative definite corresponds to the condition that the Fisher information matrix $R(\theta_o)$ is non-singular, i.e. has full rank.

Theorem (5.1b) : The parameter point $\theta_o$ is locally identifiable if and only if the Fisher information matrix $R(\theta_o)$ is non-singular.

Constraints on the Parameter Set

Assume the parameter vector $\theta \in \Theta$ is known to satisfy a set of constraints

$$\psi_i(\theta) = 0, \qquad i = 1,\ldots,k$$

where $\psi_i(\theta)$ is differentiable with respect to $\theta$. Let $\Theta'$ be the intersection of $\Theta$ and the solution set of $\psi_i(\theta) = 0$, $i = 1,\ldots,k$. Denote the Jacobian by

$$\Psi(\theta) = [\psi_{ij}(\theta)] = \frac{\partial\psi_i}{\partial\theta_j} .$$

Define a $(m+k) \times m$ matrix by

$$M(\theta) \triangleq \begin{bmatrix} R(\theta) \\ \Psi(\theta) \end{bmatrix}$$

then we have

Theorem (5.2) : Suppose $\theta_o$ to be an interior point of $\Theta'$, Then a sufficient condition for $\theta_o$ to be locally identifiable is that $M(\theta_o)$ has rank m.

Proof : See Rothenberg (1971).

## 5.2. Stochastic Reconstructability and Parameter Identifiability.

Consider the following (LRF) model:

$$x(k+1) = Ax(k)$$

$$\underline{y}(k) = Cx(k) + \underline{v}(k)$$

where $x(k) \in \mathbb{R}^m$ is an unobservable feature vector with initial value $x(0)$ to be determined and $y(k) \in \mathbb{R}^p$ is an observable output vector. The noise sequence $\{\underline{v}(k)\}$ is assumed to be white noise with $\text{cov}\{\underline{v}(k)\underline{v}'(s)\} = \Sigma_v\delta_{ks}$ and A and C are *known*.

The model for N+1 observations y(i), i = 0,...,N is

$$\begin{bmatrix} \underline{y}(0) \\ \\ \vdots \\ \underline{y}(N) \end{bmatrix} = \begin{bmatrix} C \\ CA \\ \vdots \\ CA^{N-1} \end{bmatrix} x(0) + \begin{bmatrix} \underline{v}(0) \\ \\ \vdots \\ \underline{v}(N) \end{bmatrix}$$

or

$$\underline{Y}(N) = \tilde{A}x(0) + \underline{V}.$$

The log-likelihood is given by

$$\log p(Y(N);x(0)) = (Np/2)\log 2\pi + (N/2)\log \det\Sigma -$$

$$- \tfrac{1}{2}[Y(N)-\tilde{A}x(0)]'\Sigma^{-1}[Y(N)-\tilde{A}x(0)]$$

where

$$\Sigma = \begin{bmatrix} \Sigma_v & 0 & \dots & 0 \\ 0 & \Sigma_v & \dots & \\ \vdots & \vdots & & \vdots \\ 0 & \dots\dots & & \Sigma_v \end{bmatrix}$$

By considering the unknown initial feature vector x(0) to be the parameter, then x(0) is identifiable (or in system terms x(0) is stochastically reconstructable) from the observations {y(0),...,y(N)} if the Fisher information matrix

$$R(x(0)) = -E_{\underline{Y}(N)|x(0)}\left[\frac{\partial^2 \log p(Y(N);x(0))}{\partial x(0)\partial x(0)'}\right] = \tilde{A}'\Sigma^{-1}\tilde{A} =$$

$$= \sum_{j=1}^{N} (CA^{j-1})'\Sigma_v^{-1}(CA^{j-1})$$

is non-singular, which is exactly the condition for stochastic reconstructability, see chapter II, theorem (2.5). Note that according to definition (2.12) a better term would be stochastic observability.

Example (5.1):

Consider the (LRF) model (regression model)

process equation:

$$\beta(k+1) = \beta(k) = \dots = \beta_o$$

output equation:

$$\underline{y}(k) = x(k)\beta(k) + \underline{v}(k), \; k = 1,2,\dots,T$$

where the feature vector is the unknown parameter vector $\beta_o \in \mathbb{R}^n$. The output vector $y(k) \in \mathbb{R}$ and $x(k) \in \mathbb{R}^n$ is a deterministic input row vector.

After T observations the model can be written as

process equation:

$$\beta(k+1) = \beta(k) = \dots = \beta_o$$

output equation:

$$\underline{y} = X\beta_o + \underline{V}$$

with $\underline{y} \triangleq (\underline{y}(1),\dots,\underline{y}(T))'$; $X \triangleq (x'(1),\dots,x'(T))'$ and $\underline{V} \triangleq (\underline{v}(1),\dots,v(T))'$. Suppose $\underline{V}$ to be a Gaussian random vector with zero expectation and $\text{cov}\{\underline{VV}'\} = \Omega_o$. Denote by $\theta$ the set of coefficients $\beta$ and $\Omega$, where it is assumed that $\Omega^{-1}$ exists. The expression for $H(\theta,\theta_o)$ is

$$H(\theta,\theta_o) = \tfrac{1}{2}\left(\log\left(\frac{\det \Omega_o}{\det \Omega}\right) + T - E_{\underline{y}|\beta_o}\{[X(\beta_o-\beta)+\underline{V}]'\Omega^{-1}[X(\beta_o-\beta)+\underline{V}]\}\right)$$

$$= \tfrac{1}{2}\left(\log\left(\frac{\det \Omega_o}{\det \Omega}\right) + T - \text{tr}(\Omega^{-1}\Omega_o) - (\beta_o-\beta)'X'\Omega^{-1}X(\beta_o-\beta)\right)$$

Now

$$\frac{\partial H(\theta,\theta_o)}{\partial \beta} = -(X'\Omega^{-1}X)(\beta_o-\beta)$$

This equation equals zero for $\beta \neq \beta_o$ only if $(X'\Omega^{-1}X)$ has not full rank (i.e. if X has no full column rank). If $(X'\Omega^{-1}X)$ is invertible then $\beta_o$ is identifiable. Note that this condition is exactly the condition for stochastic reconstructability of $\beta_o$. As shown by Bowden $\Omega_o$ is still identifiable even if $\beta_o$ is not identifiable, because with $-(X'\Omega^{-1}X)(\beta_o-\beta) = 0$ in the expression for $H(\theta,\theta_o)$, $H(\theta,\theta_o)$ is an expression in $\Omega$ alone. Thus if X has no full column rank $\beta_o$ is not identifiable (or stochastically reconstructable) but $\Omega_o$ is identifiable.

## 5.3. Prediction Error Estimation.

Consider the following general (prediction) model

$$\underline{y}(k) = f(z^{(k-1)},k,\theta) + \underline{\varepsilon}(k,\theta), \qquad k = 1,2,\ldots$$

where $y(k) \in \mathbb{R}^p$ denotes the output observation vector; $z^{(k-1)}$ is a vector consisting of previous values of the output vector, i.e. $y^{(k-1)} = (y'(k-1),\ldots,y'(0))'$ and current and previous values of an input vector $u(k) \in \mathbb{R}^m$, i.e. $u^{(k)} = (u'(k),u'(k-1),\ldots,u'(0))'$; $\theta \in \Theta$ is the parameter vector, where it is assumed that $\Theta$ is some open set in $\mathbb{R}^n$. Let the prediction model be given by

$$\hat{y}(k|\theta) = f(z^{(k-1)},k,\theta)$$

then the prediction error $\underline{\varepsilon}(k,\theta) = \underline{y}(k) - \hat{y}(k|\theta)$. Let $l(\varepsilon(k,\theta),\theta,k)$ be some scalar measure, i.e. $l(.,.,.)$: $\mathbb{R}^p \times \mathbb{R}^n \times R \to \mathbb{R}$. A criterion for the validity of the prediction model after N observations of the output vector is given by

$$V_N(\theta,z^{(N)}) \triangleq N^{-1}\sum_{k=1}^{N} l(\varepsilon(k,\theta),\theta,k).$$

It is stressed that $\theta$ is a *constant* for the N observations. Let an estimate $\hat{\theta}(N)$ be such that $V_N(\hat{\theta}(N),z^{(N)})$ is minimum.

### Asymptotic Properties of $\hat{\theta}(N)$.

The following conditions are imposed:

C1: The deterministic input sequence $\{u(k)\}$ is 'persistently exciting' of order 2p-1. The definition of 'persistently exciting' is the following. Assume $\{u(k)\}$ is such that

$$\lim_{N\to\infty} N^{-1}\sum_{k=1}^{N} u(k)u'(k-j) = r(j) \text{ exists for all } j,\ 0 \leq j \leq p.$$

Form the (p×p) block matrix $R_p$, whose i, k-th block entry is r(i-k). The sequence $\{u(k)\}$ is said to be 'persistently exciting' of order p if $R_p$ is non-singular. According to Kok and Van Wijk (1978) we have that if $\{u(k)\}$ is persistently exciting of order 2p-1, the impulse response matrix $G_i$, i = 0,1,... can be determined uniquely from the input-output statistics. Loosely speaking it means that the input sequence must be 'rich' enough to excite all modes of the system.

C2: The limit

$$\overline{V}(\theta) = \lim_{N \to \infty} E_{\underline{z}^{(N)}|\theta} \{V_N(\theta, \underline{z}^{(N)})\}$$

exists. The function $\overline{V}(\theta)$ is the expected value of the criterion corresponding to a certain fixed value of the parameter $\theta$. According to Ljung and Söderström (1983, section 3.3.3) we have the following

Theorem (5.3) : Under weak regularity conditions $\hat{\theta}(N)$ converges with probability one to $\theta^*$ such that $\overline{V}(\theta^*)$ is a minimum of $\overline{V}(\theta)$ as N tends to infinity. It means that a model with as estimate $\hat{\theta}(N)$ gives the 'best' description of the data, 'best' measured in terms of the expected value of the criterion. Moreover if $\hat{\theta}(N)$ converges to $\theta^*$ such that

$$\overline{V}''(\theta^*) \triangleq \left. \frac{\partial^2 \overline{V}(\theta)}{\partial\theta\partial\theta'} \right|_{\theta=\theta^*}$$

is invertible then

$$\sqrt{N}(\underline{\hat{\theta}}(N) - \theta^*) \overset{L}{\rightarrow} N(0,P)$$

where

$$P = [\overline{V}''(\theta^*)]^{-1} \lim_{N \to \infty} N E_{\underline{z}^{(N)}|\theta^*} \{V_N'(\theta^*)[V_N'(\theta^*)]^T\}[\overline{V}''(\theta^*)]^{-1}$$

where $V_N'(\theta^*) \triangleq \left. \frac{\partial V_N(\theta)}{\partial\theta} \right|_{\theta=\theta^*}$ and T denotes the matrix transposition.

Example (5.2):

Consider the linear regression model

$$\underline{y}(k) = u'(k)\beta + \underline{\varepsilon}(k,\beta), \qquad k = 1,2,\ldots,N$$

where $y(k) \in \mathbb{R}$ is the output vector; $u(k) \in \mathbb{R}^m$ is the input vector and $\beta \in \mathbb{R}^m$ is the parameter vector. Let the prediction model be $\hat{y}(k|\beta) = u'(k)\beta$ then the prediction error $\underline{\varepsilon}(k,\beta) = \underline{y}(k) - \hat{y}(k|\beta)$. Let the criterion for N observations be $\underline{V}_N(\beta) = N^{-1} \sum_{k=1}^{N} \underline{\varepsilon}^2(k,\beta)$. In matrix notation we have for N observations the linear model

$$\begin{bmatrix} \underline{y}(1) \\ \vdots \\ \underline{y}(N) \end{bmatrix} = \begin{bmatrix} u'(1) \\ \vdots \\ u'(N) \end{bmatrix} \beta + \begin{bmatrix} \underline{\varepsilon}(1,\beta) \\ \vdots \\ \underline{\varepsilon}(N,\beta) \end{bmatrix}$$

or

$$\underline{Y}_N = U_N\beta + \underline{\varepsilon}_N(\beta).$$

The criterion

$$\underline{V}_N(\beta) = N^{-1}\underline{\varepsilon}_N'(\beta)\underline{\varepsilon}_N(\beta) = N^{-1}(\underline{Y}_N - U_N\beta)'(\underline{Y}_N - U_N\beta).$$

Suppose

$$\overline{V}(\beta) = \lim_{N\to\infty} E_{\underline{Y}_N|\beta}\{\underline{V}_N(\beta)\} = \lim_{N\to\infty} E_{\underline{Y}_N|\beta} N^{-1}\{\underline{Y}_N'\underline{Y}_N - 2\underline{Y}_N'U_N\beta + \beta'U_N'U_N\beta\}$$

exists which means that $\lim_{N\to\infty} E_{\underline{Y}_N|\beta}\{N^{-1}\underline{Y}_N'\underline{Y}_N\} = S$, $\lim_{N\to\infty} E_{\underline{Y}_N|\beta}\{N^{-1}\underline{Y}_N'U_N\} = R$ and $\lim_{N\to\infty} N^{-1}U_N'U_N = Q$ are bounded.

Suppose the 'true' model to be

$$\underline{y}(k) = u'(k)\beta_o + \tilde{\underline{\varepsilon}}(k)$$

where $\{\tilde{\underline{\varepsilon}}(k)\}$ is white noise with $\mathrm{cov}\{\tilde{\underline{\varepsilon}}(k)\tilde{\underline{\varepsilon}}(s)\} = \sigma^2\delta_{ks}$. It is easily seen that $\overline{V}(\beta_o) = \min_{\beta} \overline{V}(\beta) = \sigma^2$. Let the estimate $\hat{\beta}(N)$ (the ordinary least squares estimate) be such that $\hat{\beta}(N)$ minimizes $V_N(\beta)$ then according to theorem (5.3) $\hat{\beta}(N)$ converges w.p. one to $\beta_o$. Moreover

$$\sqrt{N}(\hat{\underline{\beta}}(N) - \beta_o) \xrightarrow{L} N(0,P)$$

where $P = 4^{-1}Q^{-1}4\sigma^2QQ^{-1} = \sigma^2Q^{-1}$ because $\left.\frac{\partial^2\overline{V}(\beta)}{\partial\beta\partial\beta'}\right|_{\beta=\beta_o} = 2^{-1}Q$ and

$$\lim_{N\to\infty} N E_{\underline{Y}_N|\beta_o}\{N^{-2}4(U_N'\underline{Y}_N - U_N'U_N\beta_o)(U_N'\underline{Y}_N - U_N'U_N\beta_o)'\} =$$

$$\lim_{N\to\infty} N E_{\underline{Y}_N|\beta_o}\{N^{-2}4(U_N'(U_N\beta_o + \tilde{\underline{\varepsilon}}_N) - U_N'U_N\beta_o)(\text{———})'\} =$$

$$\lim_{N\to\infty} E_{\underline{Y}_N|\beta_o}\{N^{-1}4U_N'\tilde{\underline{\varepsilon}}_N\tilde{\underline{\varepsilon}}_N'U_N\} = 4\sigma^2Q.$$

Prediction Error and Maximum Likelihood (ML) Estimation.

Let in the general model

$$\underline{y}(k) = f(z^{(k-1)},k,\theta) + \underline{\varepsilon}(k,\theta)$$

the sequence $\{\underline{\varepsilon}(k,\theta)\}$ be *independent* random vectors with p.d.f. $p_{\underline{\varepsilon}(k,\theta)}(.)$ with bounded second and higher moments. The p.d.f. may depend upon k and $\theta$. It is further assumed that the sequence of inputs $\{u(k)\}$ is purely exogenous and not depending upon $\theta$ and the prediction errors, c.g. u(k) is not generated by some feed-back law. The conditional density function

$$p(y(k)|z^{(k-1)},\theta) = [p_{\underline{\varepsilon}(k,\theta)}(y(k)-f(z^{(k-1)},k,\theta))]J$$

$$= p_{\underline{\varepsilon}(k,\theta)}(\varepsilon(k,\theta))$$

where the Jacobian $J = |\det[\partial\varepsilon(k,\theta)/\partial y(k)]| = 1$

The log-likelihood for N observations $y^{(N)} = (y'(1),\ldots,y'(N))'$ is given by Bayes' rule as

$$\log p(y^{(N)};u^{(N)},\theta) = \sum_{k=1}^{N}\log p(y(k)|z^{(k-1)},\theta) =$$

$$= \sum_{k=1}^{N}\log p_{\underline{\varepsilon}(k,\theta)}(\varepsilon(k,\theta)).$$

If we choose for the measure $l(\varepsilon(k,\theta),\theta,k) = -\log p_{\underline{\varepsilon}(k,\theta)}(\varepsilon(k,\theta))$, the p.d.f. of the prediction errors is then

$$\log p(y^{(N)};u^{(N)},\theta) = -NV_N(\theta,z^{(N)}).$$

From theorem (5.3) we have that if $\overline{V}(\theta_o) = \min_{\theta} \overline{V}(\theta)$ where $\overline{V}(\theta) =$ $= \lim_{\underline{y}^{(N)}|\theta} \{\underline{V}_N(\theta,z^{(N)})\}$ then the ML estimate $\hat{\theta}_{ML}(N) = \min_{\theta} NV_N(\theta)$ converges w.p. one to $\theta_o$. Moreover

$$\sqrt{N}(\underline{\hat{\theta}}_{ML}(N)-\theta_o) \overset{L}{\rightarrow} N(0,P)$$

where P is the inverse of the Fisher information matrix per sample. This can be seen as follows. Because $V_N(\theta,z^{(N)}) = -N^{-1}\log p(y^{(N)},u^{(N)},\theta)$ we have that

$$\left.\frac{\partial^2\bar{V}(\theta)}{\partial\theta\partial\theta}\right|_{\theta=\theta_o} = -\lim_{N\to\infty} N^{-1} E_{\underline{y}^{(N)}|\theta_o}\left[\left.\frac{\partial^2 \log p(y^{(N)};u^{(N)},\theta)}{\partial\theta\partial\theta}\right|_{\theta=\theta_o}\right]$$

$$= \lim_{N\to\infty} N^{-1} R_N(\theta_o)$$

where $R_N(\theta_o)$ is the Fisher information matrix for N observations.

$$\lim_{N\to\infty} N E_{\underline{y}^{(N)}|\theta_o}\left[N^{-2}\left.\frac{\partial \log p(y^{(N)};u^{(N)},\theta)}{\partial\theta}\right|_{\theta=\theta_o}\right]\left[\left.\frac{\partial \log p(y^{(N)};u^{(N)},\theta)}{\partial\theta}\right|_{\theta=\theta_o}\right]^T$$

$$= \lim_{N\to\infty} N^{-1} R_N(\theta_o)$$

and hence

$$P = (\lim_{N\to\infty} N^{-1} R_N(\theta_0))^{-1}$$

which is the limiting variance of $\sqrt{N}(\hat{\underline{\theta}}(N)-\theta_0)$.

## 5.4. A Non-Linear Minimization Procedure.

As stated by Åström (1979) optimization or minimization problems in parameter estimation can rarely be solved analytically. The criterion $V_N(\theta,z^{(N)})$ may have several local minima and curved ridges which may make minimization difficult. There are many ways of finding a local extremum of a function numerically based on direct search methods or methods based on the evaluation of $V_N(\theta,z^{(N)})$, its gradient $\partial V_N(\theta,z^{(N)})/\partial\theta$, leading to the so-called sensitivity equations and the Hessian $\partial^2 V_N(\theta,z^{(N)})/\partial\theta\partial\theta'$, which is of particular importance, because of its relation to the Fisher information matrix, providing a generic test for (local) parameter identifiability. In the sequel the Newton-Raphson procedure is summarized, which proved to be satisfactory, see e.g. Goodwin and Payne (1977).

Newton-Raphson Procedure.

(i) Make an initial guess for $\theta$, say $\hat{\theta}_k$, with index k=0

(ii) Evaluate $\left.\frac{\partial V_N(\theta,z^{(N)})}{\partial\theta}\right|_{\theta=\hat{\theta}_k}$ and $\left.\frac{\partial^2 V_N(\theta,z^{(N)})}{\partial\theta\partial\theta'}\right|_{\theta=\hat{\theta}_k}$

(iii) Perform a linear search (in order to avoid instability) using a scalar search constant s such that

$$V_N\left[\hat{\theta}_k - s\left[\left.\frac{\partial^2 V_N(\theta,z^{(N)})}{\partial\theta\partial\theta'}\right|_{\theta=\hat{\theta}_k}\right]^{-1} \left.\frac{\partial V_N(\theta,z^{(N)})}{\partial\theta}\right|_{\theta=\hat{\theta}_k}, z^{(N)}\right]$$

is minimized for $s = s_k^*$

(iv) $$\hat{\theta}_{k+1} = \hat{\theta}_k - s_k^*\left[\left.\frac{\partial^2 V_N(\theta,z^{(N)})}{\partial\theta\partial\theta'}\right|_{\theta=\hat{\theta}_k}\right]^{-1} \left.\frac{\partial V_N(\theta,z^{(N)})}{\partial\theta}\right|_{\theta=\hat{\theta}_k}$$

(v) If $V_N(\hat{\theta}_{k+1},z^{(N)}) - V_N(\hat{\theta}_k,z^{(N)})$ is suitably small then $\hat{\theta}(N) = \hat{\theta}_{k+1}$ and stop, otherwise set k = k+1 and return to (ii).

Remark 1: The inverse of the Hessian provides an implicit generic test for local parameter identifiability and is a measure for the accuracy of the parameter estimates.

Remark 2: The above procedure is a 'one-shot' method. See for a treatment of on-line methods and corresponding convergence properties Ljung (1983).

Remark 3: An interesting connection between convergence rate and robustness is found in Tsypkin (1983).

## 5.5. Prediction Error Estimation of the (LSF) and (LRF) model.

From chapter III we have that the (LSF) model is

$$A_{0,(\theta)}\underline{x}(k+1) = A_{1,(\theta)}(k)\underline{x}(k) + \tilde{B}_{(\theta)}(k)u_1(k) + \underline{\tilde{w}}(k)$$

$$\underline{Y}(k) = C_{(\theta)}(k)\underline{x}(k) + D_{(\theta)}(k)u_2(k) + \underline{v}(k),$$

$$k = 1,2,\ldots,N$$

where $x(k) \in \mathbb{R}^{n=n_1+n_2}$ is the unobservable feature vector; $u_1(k) \in \mathbb{R}^p$ is an observable deterministic input vector assumed to be 'persistently exciting' of order 2n-1; $\{\underline{\tilde{w}}(k)\}$ is a white noise sequence with $\mathrm{cov}\{\underline{\tilde{w}}(k)\underline{\tilde{w}}'(k)\} = \Sigma_{(\theta),\tilde{w}}(k)$; $Y(k) \in \mathbb{R}^{m=m_1+m_2}$ is an observable output vector; $u_2(k) \in \mathbb{R}^q$ is an observable deterministic input vector to be 'persistently exciting' of order 2n-1 and $\{\underline{v}(k)\}$ is a white noise sequence with $\mathrm{cov}\{\underline{v}(k)\underline{v}'(k)\} = \Sigma_{(\theta),v}(k)$. The initial feature vector x(0) is assumed to be Gaussian with mean $\mu_{(\theta),x}(0)$ and covariance $\Sigma_{(\theta),x}(0)$ and uncorrelated with $\{\underline{\tilde{w}}(k)\}$ and $\{\underline{v}(k)\}$. It is further assumed that $\{\underline{\tilde{w}}(k)\}$ and $\{\underline{v}(k)\}$ are uncorrelated. The unknown parameters of $A_0(k)$, $A_1(k)$, $\tilde{B}(k)$, $\Sigma_{\tilde{w}}(k)$, C(k), D(k), $\Sigma_v(k)$, $\mu_x(0)$ and $\Sigma_x(0)$ are collected in the S-dimensional parameter vector $\theta \in \Theta$ with as true parameter point $\theta_o$ and where $\Theta$ is some open set in $\mathbb{R}^S$. The (LRF) model is given by

$$\underline{x}(k+1) = A_{(\theta)}(k)\underline{x}(k) + B_{(\theta)}(k)u_1(k) + \underline{w}(k)$$

$$\underline{Y}(k) = C_{(\theta)}(k)\underline{x}(k) + D_{(\theta)}(k)u_2(k) + \underline{v}(k)$$

with $A_{(\theta)}(k) = A^{-1}_{0,(\theta)}(k)A_{1,(\theta)}(k)$; $B_{(\theta)}(k) = A^{-1}_{0,(\theta)}(k)\tilde{B}_{(\theta)}(k)$ and $w(k) = A^{-1}_{0,(\theta)}(k)\underline{\tilde{w}}(k)$ with time-varying covariance $\Sigma_{(\theta),w}(k) = A^{-1}_{0,(\theta)}(k)\Sigma_{(\theta),\tilde{w}}(k)(A^{-1}_{0,(\theta)}(k))'$.

In the sequel the following assumptions are imposed:

C3: The pair $(A_{(\theta)}(k), C_{(\theta)}(k))$ is uniformly completely stochastically reconstructable for all $\theta \in \Theta$.

C4: The pair $(A_{(\theta)}(k), \sqrt{\Sigma_{(\theta),w}}(k))$ is uniformly completely stochastically controllable for all $\theta \in \Theta$.

Because the initial distribution of $\underline{x}(0)$ is Gaussian and the noise processes are Gaussian, the conditional distribution $p(Y^{(j)}|Y^{(j-1)}, u_1^{(j)}, u_2^{(j)}, \theta)$ is deterministic by its conditional mean (prediction)

$$\hat{Y}(j|\theta) = C_{(\theta)}(j)\hat{x}_{(\theta)}(j|j-1) + D_{(\theta)}(j)u_2(j) =$$
$$= f(Y^{(j-1)}, u_1^{(j)}, u_2^{(j)}, \theta)$$

and conditional covariance

$$\Sigma_{(\theta),\hat{Y}}(j|\theta) = C_{(\theta)}(j)\Sigma_{(\theta),\tilde{x}}(j|j-1)C'_{(\theta)}(j) + \Sigma_{(\theta),v}(k)$$

where $\hat{x}_{(\theta)}(j|j-1)$ and $\Sigma_{(\theta),\tilde{x}}(j|j-1)$ are respectively the conditional mean and covariance of $\underline{x}(j)$ generated by the Kalman filter with parameter vector $\theta$ and $Y^{(j-1)} = (Y'(j),\ldots,Y'(1))'$; $u_1^{(j)} = (u_1'(j),\ldots,u_1'(0))'$ and $u_2^{(j)} = (u_2'(j),\ldots,u_2'(1))'$. The sequence of prediction errors $\underline{\varepsilon}(j,\theta) = \underline{Y}(j) - \hat{Y}(j|\theta)$ is Gaussian with covariance

$$\Sigma_\varepsilon(j,\theta) = E\{[C_{(\theta)}(j)\underline{\tilde{x}}_{(\theta)}(j|j-1)+\underline{v}(j)][\text{------}]'\}$$

$$= C_{(\theta)}(j)\Sigma_{(\theta),\tilde{x}}(j|j-1)C'_{(\theta)}(j) + \Sigma_{(\theta),v}(j) = \Sigma_{(\theta),\hat{Y}}(j)$$

The log-likelihood of N observations $Y^{(N)}$ is given by

$$\log p(Y^{(N)}|u_1^{(N)},u_2^{(N)},\theta) = \sum_{j=1}^{N}\log p(Y(j)|Y^{(j-1)},u_1^{(j)},u_2^{(j)},\theta)$$

$$= -(Nm/2)\log 2\pi - \tfrac{1}{2}\sum_{j=1}^{N}[\varepsilon(j,\theta)'\Sigma_\varepsilon^{-1}(j,\theta)\varepsilon(j,\theta) + \log\det\Sigma_\varepsilon(j,\theta)].$$

The ML estimate of $\theta$ can be obtained by maximizing the log-likelihood with respect to $\theta$. In prediction error terms we have the measure $-1(\varepsilon(j,\theta),\theta,j) = \varepsilon'(j,\theta)\Sigma_\varepsilon^{-1}(j,\theta)\varepsilon(j|\theta) + \log\det\Sigma_\varepsilon(j,\theta)$ and the criterion $-NV_N(\theta) = \log p(Y^{(N)}|u_1^{(N)},u_2^{(N)};\theta)$.
From the previous section we have seen that if $\overline{V}(\theta)$ exists and there is some true parameter point $\theta_0$ such that $\overline{V}(\theta_0) = \min \overline{V}(\theta)$ then, w.p. one, the ML estimate $\hat{\theta}(N)$ converges to $\theta_0$. Note that the inverse of the Hessian provides an implicit test for parameter identifiability.

The Stationary (LSF)-Model: Parameter Identifiability and PE-Estimation.

Consider the stationary (LSF)-model with $u_1(k) = u_2(k) = u(k)$,

$$A_0\underline{x}(k+1) = A_1\underline{x}(k) + \overline{B}u(k) + \underline{\overline{w}}(k),\ k = k_0+1,k_0+2,\ldots$$

$$\underline{Y}(k) = C\underline{x}(k) + Du(k) + \underline{v}(k)$$

with $x(k) \in \mathbb{R}^n$; $u(k) \in \mathbb{R}^p$; $Y(k) \in \mathbb{R}^m$ and initial state $x(0) = 0$; $\mathrm{cov}\{\underline{\overline{w}}(k)\underline{\overline{w}}'(s)\} = \Sigma_{\overline{w}}\delta_{ks} = \overline{Q}$ and $\mathrm{cov}\{\underline{v}(k)\underline{v}'(s)\} = \Sigma_v\delta_{ks} = R$. The (LRF)-model is given by

$$\underline{x}(k+1) = A\underline{x}(k) + Bu(k) + \underline{w}(k),\ k = k_0+1,k_0+2,\ldots$$

$$\underline{Y}(k) = C\underline{x}(k) + Du(k) + \underline{v}(k)$$

with $A = A_0^{-1}A_1$; $B = A_0^{-1}\overline{B}$ and $\underline{w}(k) = A_0^{-1}\underline{\overline{w}}(k)$ with covariance $Q = A_0^{-1}\overline{Q}(A_0^{-1})'$

In the sequel the following assumptions are made:

a1: The eigenvalues of A have moduli less than one in absolute value, i.e. $|\sigma(A)| < 1$ (the matrix A is stable).

a2: The (LRF)-model has reached (nearly) its steady-state, i.e. the stochastic process $\{\underline{Y}(k)\}$ is stationary, which implies the stochastic process $\{\underline{x}(k)\}$ to be stationary.

In the steady-state the covariance of $\{x(k)\}$ is given by the Lyapunov equation $P = APA' + Q$ with solution

$$P = \sum_{j=0}^{\infty} A^j Q(A')^j = \sum_{j=0}^{k_0} A^j Q(A')^j + \sum_{k_0+1}^{\infty} A^j Q(A')^j = P(k_0) + \tilde{P}$$

We must choose $k_0$ large such that $\|P-P(k_0)\| < \varepsilon$, where $\varepsilon$ is a small positive number and $\|.\|$ denotes the Euclidean norm.

a3: The sequence $\{u(k)\}$ is deterministic, observable, bounded and independent of $\{\underline{Y}(k)\}$, i.e. no feed-back is present.

a4: The sequence $\{u(k)\}$ is 'persistently exciting' of order 2n-1.

The *transfer* (T)-model of the (LRF)-model is given by

$$\underline{Y}(k) = G(z)u(k) + \underline{\eta}(k)$$

where $G(z) = G_0 + G_1 z^{-1} + G_2 z^{-2} + \ldots$ with $G_0 = D$ and $G_i = CA^{i-1}B$, $i = 1,2,\ldots$ and where $z^{-1}u(k) = u(k-1)$ is the unit delay operator. The sequence $\{\eta(k)\}$ with

$$\eta(k) = C(zI-A)^{-1}w(k) + \underline{v}(k)$$

is a stochastic process with rational *spectral density* function

$$\phi_\eta(z) = C(zI-A)^{-1}Q(z^{-1}I-A')^{-1}C' + R$$

with $z = e^{iw}$, $w \in \mathbb{R}$.

Remark: Whether $z^{-1}$ should be interpreted as a unit delay operator or the inverse of the z-transform variable will be clear from the context. See for a discussion of the relationship between G(z) and the z-transform of the (LRF)-model Goodwin and Payne (1977, p.63).

## Parameter Identifiability

The parameter identifiability problem will be split into two parts.

First the relation between the LRF-model and the transfer model will be considered and then the relation LSF-model and LRF-model.

Let $\alpha \in \Omega \subset \mathbb{R}^q$ be a vector of free parameters of the LRF-model in an open set $\Omega \subset \mathbb{R}^q$ such that $(A,B,C,D,Q,R)(\alpha) : \Omega \to \mathbb{R}^N$ with $N = 2n^2 + np + mn + mp + m^2$.

The following assumptions are imposed:

a5: $|\sigma(A(\alpha))| < 1$ for $\alpha \in B(\alpha_0,\varepsilon)$ where $B(\alpha_0,\varepsilon) \subset \Omega$ is an open ball around $\alpha_0 \in \Omega$.

a6: The pair $(A(\alpha),B(\alpha))$ is reachable, i.e. rank $(B(\alpha),A(\alpha)B(\alpha),\ldots$ $\ldots,A^{n-1}(\alpha)B(\alpha)) = n$ for $\alpha \in B(\alpha_0,\varepsilon)$.

a7: The pair $(A(\alpha),\sqrt{Q(\alpha)})$ is reachable.

a8: The pair $(A(\alpha),C(\alpha))$ is observable, i.e. rank $(C'(\alpha),(C(\alpha)A(\alpha))',\ldots$ $\ldots,(C(\alpha),A^{n-1}(\alpha)')' = n$.

<u>Remark</u>. When assumptions a6 and a8 apply it is said that the triple $(A(\alpha),B(\alpha),C(\alpha))$ is minimal. Consider the LRF-model

$$\underline{x}(k+1) = A(\alpha)\underline{x}(k) + B(\alpha)u(k) + \underline{w}(k)$$

$$\underline{Y}(k) = C(\alpha)\underline{x}(k) + D(\alpha)u(k) + \underline{v}(k)$$

The T-model is given by $\underline{Y}(k) = G(z,\alpha)u(k) + \underline{\eta}(k)$ with transfer function

$$G(z,\alpha) = D(\alpha) + \sum_{j=1}^{\infty} C(\alpha)A^{j-1}(\alpha)B(\alpha)z^{-j}$$

and where the spectral density function of $\underline{\eta}(k)$ is given by

$$\phi_\eta(z,\alpha) = C(\alpha)[zI-A(\alpha)]^{-1}Q(\alpha)(z^{-1}I-A'(\alpha))^{-1}C'(\alpha) + R(\alpha).$$

The conditional p.d.f. of $\underline{Y}(k)$ given $u^{(k)} = (u'(k),u'(k-1),\ldots,u'(k_0))'$ is Gaussian and determined by the pair $(G(z,\alpha),\phi_\eta(z,\alpha))$.

Consider a (coordinate) transformation $T \in GL(n)$ with $GL(n) = \{T \mid \det(T) \neq 0\}$ on $\underline{x}(k)$, i.e. $\tilde{\underline{x}}(k) = T\underline{x}(k)$ then the transformed LRF-model is

$$\tilde{\underline{x}}(k+1) = \tilde{A}(\alpha)\tilde{\underline{x}}(k) + \tilde{B}(\alpha)u(k) + \tilde{\underline{w}}(k)$$

$$\underline{Y}(k) = \tilde{C}(\alpha)\tilde{\underline{x}}(k) + D(\alpha)u(k) + \underline{v}(k)$$

with $\tilde{A}(\alpha) = TA(\alpha)T^{-1}$; $\tilde{B}(\alpha) = TB(\alpha)$; $\tilde{C}(\alpha) = C(\alpha)T^{-1}$ and $\tilde{\underline{w}}(k) = T\underline{w}(k)$.

The transfer function of the transformed LRF-model is

$$\tilde{G}(z,\alpha) = C(\alpha)T^{-1}[zI-TA(\alpha)T^{-1}]^{-1}TB(\alpha) + D(\alpha) = G(z,\alpha)$$

and the spectral density

$$\tilde{\phi}_\eta(z,\alpha) = C(\alpha)T^{-1}(zI-TA(\alpha)T^{-1})^{-1}TQT'(z^{-1}I-(T^{-1})'A'(\alpha)T')^{-1}(T^{-1})'C'(\alpha) + $$

$$+ R(\alpha) = \phi_\eta(z,\alpha),$$

and hence all state space models with a coordinate transformation generate the same conditional p.d.f. It is said that they are T-equivalent; $(A(\alpha),B(\alpha),C(\alpha),D(\alpha),Q(\alpha),R(\alpha)) \overset{T}{\Leftrightarrow} (TA(\alpha)T',TB(\alpha),C(\alpha)T^{-1},D(\alpha),TQ(\alpha)T', R(\alpha))$.

The following theorem provides a rank condition for local parameter identifiability. The theorem is essentially an extension of a theorem given by Glover (1973).

<u>Theorem (5.4)</u> : Let $(A,B,C,D,Q,R)(\alpha)$: $\Omega \rightarrow \mathbb{R}^N$ (with $\Omega$ an open set in $\mathbb{R}^q$) be a c' (continuously differentiable on $\Omega$) parametrization of the LRF-model and suppose $(A(\alpha),B(\alpha), C(\alpha))$ minimal with $\alpha \in B(\alpha_0,\varepsilon)$ for some $\varepsilon > 0$. Then

A: The parametervector $\alpha$ is locally identifiable at $\alpha = \alpha_0$ if and only if $F: GL(n) \times \Omega \rightarrow \mathbb{R}^N$ is locally injective at $T = I$ and $\alpha = \alpha_0$ where $F(T,\alpha) \triangleq (TA(\alpha)T^{-1},TB(\alpha),C(\alpha)T^{-1},TQ(\alpha)T',D(\alpha), R(\alpha))$.

B: If rank $(\frac{\partial F(T,\alpha)}{\partial(T,\alpha)}) = r$ for $\alpha \in B(\alpha_0,\varepsilon)$ then $(A,B,C,D,Q,R)(\alpha)$ is locally identifiable at $\alpha = \alpha_0$ and $T = I$ if and only if $r = n^2 + q$ or equivalently if $\det(X'(\alpha_0)X(\alpha_0)) \neq 0$ where the $N\times(n^2+q)$ matrix

$$X(\alpha) \triangleq \left[\frac{\partial\tilde{F}(I,\alpha)}{\partial t'}, \frac{\partial\tilde{F}(I,\alpha)}{\partial\alpha'}\right] = \left[\begin{array}{c|c} I_n \otimes A'(\alpha)-A(\alpha)\otimes I_n & \\ I_n \otimes B'(\alpha) & \\ -C(\alpha)\otimes I_n & \\ (I_{n^2}+P)(I_n \otimes Q(\alpha)) & M(\alpha) \\ 0_{mp,n^2} & \\ 0_{m^2,n^2} & \end{array}\right]$$

where P is the permutation matrix and the $(N\times 1)$ vector $F(T,\alpha)$ and $(N\times q)$ matrix $M(\alpha)$ are respectively

$$\tilde{F}(T,\alpha) \triangleq \begin{bmatrix} vec(TA(\alpha)T^{-1}) \\ vec(TB(\alpha)) \\ vec(C(\alpha)T^{-1}) \\ vec(TQ(\alpha)T) \\ vec(D(\alpha)) \\ vecR(\alpha) \end{bmatrix} \quad \text{and } M(\alpha) \triangleq \begin{bmatrix} \partial vecA(\alpha)/\partial\alpha' \\ \partial vecB(\alpha)/\partial\alpha' \\ \partial vecC(\alpha)/\partial\alpha' \\ \partial vecQ(\alpha)/\partial\alpha' \\ \partial vecD(\alpha)/\partial\alpha' \\ \partial vecR(\alpha)/\partial\alpha' \end{bmatrix}$$

with $vec(A) \triangleq (a_1',a_2',\ldots,a_n')'$ where $a_j$ is the j-th column of A and $t \triangleq vecT$.

Proof : Part A: If F is not locally injective then for all $\varepsilon > 0$ there exist $(T_\varepsilon,\alpha_\varepsilon)$, $(S_\varepsilon,\beta_\varepsilon) \in B_\varepsilon(I,\alpha_o)$ such that $F(T_\varepsilon,\alpha_\varepsilon) = F(S_\varepsilon,\beta_\varepsilon)$ with $T_\varepsilon,S_\varepsilon \in GL(n)$ and hence $S_\varepsilon^{-1}T_\varepsilon A(\alpha_\varepsilon)T_\varepsilon^{-1}S_\varepsilon = A(\beta_\varepsilon)$; $S_\varepsilon^{-1}T_\varepsilon B(\alpha_\varepsilon) = B(\beta_\varepsilon)$; $C(\alpha_\varepsilon)T_\varepsilon^{-1}S_\varepsilon = C(\beta_\varepsilon)$; $D(\alpha_\varepsilon) = D(\beta_\varepsilon)$; $S_\varepsilon^{-1}T_\varepsilon Q(\alpha_\varepsilon)T_\varepsilon'(S_\varepsilon')^{-1} = Q(\beta_\varepsilon)$ and $R(\alpha_\varepsilon) = R(\beta_\varepsilon)$ which implies $G(z,\alpha_\varepsilon) = G(z,\beta_\varepsilon)$ and $\phi_\eta(z,\alpha_\varepsilon) = \phi_\eta(z,\beta_\varepsilon)$ and hence $p(.|u^{(k)},\alpha_\varepsilon) = p(.|u^{(k)},\beta_\varepsilon)$ for all $u^{(k)}$ thus $\alpha_0$ is not locally identifiable.

Now suppose $\alpha_0$ is not locally identifiable, i.e. $p(.|u^{(k)},\alpha_\varepsilon) = p(.|u^{(k)},\beta_\varepsilon)$ for $\alpha_\varepsilon,\beta_\varepsilon \in B(\alpha_0,\varepsilon)$ and for every $u^{(k)}$ then $G(z,\alpha_\varepsilon) = G(z,\beta_\varepsilon)$ and $\phi_\eta(z,\alpha_\varepsilon) = \phi_\eta(z,\beta_\varepsilon)$ and hence $F(T_\varepsilon,\alpha_\varepsilon) = F(S_\varepsilon,\beta_\varepsilon)$ which implies $F(S_\varepsilon^{-1}T_\varepsilon,\alpha_\varepsilon) = F(I,\beta_\varepsilon)$.

Because $(A(\alpha),B(\alpha),C(\alpha))$ is minimal for $\alpha \in B(\alpha_0,\varepsilon)$ we have as a consequence of the reachability condition

$$rank(W(\alpha)) = rank(B(\alpha),A(\alpha)B(\alpha),\ldots,A^{n-1}(\alpha)B(\alpha)) = n$$

with $W(\alpha) \triangleq (B(\alpha),A(\alpha)B(\alpha),\ldots,A^{n-1}(\alpha)B(\alpha))$. Then $W(\beta_\varepsilon) = S_\varepsilon^{-1}T_\varepsilon W(\alpha_\varepsilon)$ and $W(\beta_\varepsilon)W'(\alpha_\varepsilon) = S_\varepsilon^{-1}T_\varepsilon W(\alpha_\varepsilon)W'(\alpha_\varepsilon)$ and hence

$$S_\varepsilon^{-1}T_\varepsilon = W(\beta_\varepsilon)W'(\alpha_\varepsilon)[W(\alpha_\varepsilon)W'(\alpha_\varepsilon)]^{-1}$$

which implies that $S_\varepsilon^{-1}T_\varepsilon$ is a continuous function of $(\alpha_\varepsilon,\beta_\varepsilon)$. Therefore $\| S_\varepsilon^{-1}T_\varepsilon - I_n \|$ can be made arbitrarily small by taking $\varepsilon$ sufficiently small and hence there does not exist a neighbourhood of $(I,\alpha_0)$ in which F is injective because $F(S_\varepsilon^{-1}T_\varepsilon,\alpha_\varepsilon) = F(I,\beta_\varepsilon)$ thus F is not locally injective.

Part B: We use part A and a standard result on injective maps. Let $\Omega$ be an open set in $\mathbb{R}^n$ and $f: \Omega \to \mathbb{R}^m$ be a $C^k$ map with $k \geqq 1$. Then if $\partial f(x)/\partial x$ has a constant rank r in the neighbourhood of $x_0$ then f is locally injective if and only if $r = n$.

The Jacobian of F or equivalently $\tilde{F}$ is given by the $N\times(n^2+q)$ matrix

$$\left[\frac{\partial\tilde{F}(T,\alpha)}{\partial t'},\frac{\partial\tilde{F}(T,\alpha)}{\partial\alpha'}\right]$$

with

$$\frac{\partial\tilde{F}(T,\alpha)}{\partial t'} = \begin{bmatrix} I_n\otimes(T^{-1})'A(\alpha) - TA(\alpha)T^{-1}\otimes(T^{-1})' \\ I_n\otimes B'(\alpha) \\ -C(\alpha)T^{-1}\otimes(T^{-1})' \\ (I_{n^2}+P)(I_n\otimes TQ) \\ 0_{mp,n^2} \\ 0_{m^2,n^2} \end{bmatrix}$$

where P is the permutation matrix, and $\frac{\partial\tilde{F}(T,\alpha)}{\partial\alpha'} = EM(\alpha)$, where the $N\times q$ matrix $M(\alpha)$ is defined in theorem (5.4) and the $N\times N$ matrix E is given by

$$E \triangleq \begin{bmatrix} T\otimes(T^{-1})' & & & & & \\ & T\otimes I_p & & & \bigcirc & \\ & & I_m\otimes(T^{-1})' & & & \\ & \bigcirc & & T\otimes T & & \\ & & & & I_m\otimes I_p & \\ & & & & & I_m\otimes I_m \end{bmatrix}$$

The Jacobian

$$\left[\frac{\partial\tilde{F}(T,\alpha)}{\partial t'},\frac{\partial\tilde{F}(T,\alpha)}{\partial\alpha'}\right] = E\left[\frac{\partial\tilde{F}(I,\alpha)}{\partial t'} \,\Big|\, M(\alpha)\right]G$$

$$= EX(\alpha)G$$

where the $(n^2+q)\times(n^2\times q)$ matrix G is given by

$$G \triangleq \begin{bmatrix} T^{-1}\otimes I_n & 0 \\ 0 & I_q \end{bmatrix}$$

which implies that the rank of the Jacobian is determined by the rank of the $N\times(n^2+q)$ matrix $X(\alpha)$ and hence by the condition $\det(X'(\alpha_0)X(\alpha_0)) \neq 0$.

Once the parameters of the LRF-model have been identified, i.e. the matrices A,B,C,D,Q and R, the second part of the identifiability problem deals with the relation LSF-model and LRF-model, that is, the relation between the structural matrices $A_0, A_1, \overline{B}$ and $\overline{Q}$ and the reduced form matrices A,B and Q of the process equations. This is a standard econometric problem, see e.g. Rothenberg (1971, theorem 10) and will lead to the so-called rank and order conditions for parameter-identifiability.

Remark: To establish a local one-to-one relation between $A_0, A_1, \overline{B}$ and $\overline{Q}$ and A,B,Q we can apply in a slightly different form theorem (5.4) again. This can be seen as follows. The process equation of the LSF-model is given by

$$A_0\underline{x}(k+1) = A_1\underline{x}(k) + \overline{B}u(k) + \underline{\overline{w}}(k)$$

Pre-multiplying by $T \in GL(n)$ and transforming into the LRF-process equation gives

$$\underline{x}(k+1) = (TA_0)^{-1}TA_1\underline{x}(k) + (TA_0)^{-1}T\overline{B}u(k) + (TA_0)^{-1}T\underline{\overline{w}}(k)$$

$$= A_0^{-1}A_1\underline{x}(k) + A_0^{-1}\overline{B}u(k) + A_0^{-1}\underline{\overline{w}}(k)$$

$$= A\underline{x}(k) + Bu(k) + \underline{w}(k)$$

and hence all structural process equations are T-equivalent in the sense that they have the same reduced form, i.e.

$$(TA_0, TA_1, T\bar{B}, T\bar{Q}T') \overset{T}{\Leftrightarrow} (A_0, A_1, \bar{B}, \bar{Q}).$$

Let $\theta \in \Theta \subset \mathbb{R}^s$ be a vector of free structural parameters of the process equation in the LSF-model and where $\Theta$ is an open set in $\mathbb{R}^s$, with

$$(A_0, A_1, \bar{B}, \bar{Q})(\theta): \Theta \to \mathbb{R}^{N'}$$

with $N' = 3n^2 + np$, then the adjusted function $\bar{F}$: $GL(n) \times \Theta \to \mathbb{R}^{N'}$ is $\bar{F}(T,\theta) \triangleq (TA_0(\theta), TA_1(\theta), T\bar{B}(\theta), T\bar{Q}(\theta)T')$.

Prediction Error Estimation

It is assumed that the structural parameter vector $\theta \in \Theta \subset \mathbb{R}^q$ of the LSF-model

$$A_{0,(\theta)}\underline{x}(k+1) = A_{1,(\theta)}\underline{x}(k) + \bar{B}_{(\theta)}u(k) + \underline{\bar{w}}(k)$$

$$\underline{Y}(k) = C_{(\theta)}\underline{x}(k) + D_{(\theta)}u(k) + \underline{v}(k)$$

with $\text{cov}\{\underline{\bar{w}}(k)\underline{\bar{w}}'(k)\} = \bar{Q}_{(\theta)}$ and $\text{cov}\{\underline{v}(k)\underline{v}'(k)\} = R_{(\theta)}$ is locally identifiable at $\theta_0$, i.e. $p(.|u^{(k)},\theta_\varepsilon) \neq p(.|u^{(k)},\theta_0)$ for $\theta_\varepsilon \in B(\theta_0,\varepsilon) \subset \mathbb{R}^q$ and $\theta_\varepsilon \neq \theta_0$.

Before we can apply theorem (5.3) to establish large sample properties of the prediction-error estimator the LSF-model has to be transformed into a prediction-error(PE)-model. The transfer model is

$$\underline{Y}(k) = G(z,\theta)u(k) + \underline{\eta}(k) = \bar{Y}(k) + \underline{\eta}(k)$$

thus $\underline{Y}(k)$ consists of a deterministic part $\bar{Y}(k)$ and a moving-average process $\{\underline{\eta}(k)\}$ with spectral density function

$$\phi_\eta(z,\theta) = C(\theta)(zI-A(\theta))^{-1}Q(\theta)(z^{-1}I-A'(\theta))^{-1}C'(\theta) + R(\theta)$$

with $A(\theta) = A_0^{-1}(\theta)A_1(\theta)$ and $Q(\theta) = A_0^{-1}(\theta)\bar{Q}(\theta)(A_0^{-1}(\theta))'$.

Following Picci (1982), Aoki (1983) and Goodwin and Payne (1977) there exists a spectral factorization of $\phi_\eta(z,\theta)$ of the form

$$\phi_\eta(z,\theta) = H(z,\theta)\Sigma(\theta)H'(z^{-1},\theta)$$

with $H(z,\theta) = C(\theta)(zI-A(\theta))^{-1}K(\theta) + I$ where

$$K(\theta) = A(\theta)P(\theta)C'(\theta)[C(\theta)P(\theta)C'(\theta)+R(\theta)]^{-1}$$

and $\Sigma(\theta) = C(\theta)P(\theta)C'(\theta) + R(\theta)$.
$P(\theta)$ is the positive definite solution of the Riccati-equation

$$P(\theta) = A(\theta)[P(\theta)-P(\theta)C'(\theta)[C(\theta)P(\theta)C'(\theta)+R(\theta)]^{-1}C(\theta)P(\theta)]A'(\theta) + \\ + Q(\theta).$$

The moving-average process $\{\underline{\eta}(k)\}$ can be represented in feature space form as

$$\underline{x}^*(k+1) = A(\theta)\underline{x}^*(k) + K(\theta)\underline{\varepsilon}(k,\theta)$$

$$\tilde{\underline{\eta}}(k) = C(\theta)\underline{x}^*(k) + \underline{\varepsilon}(k,\theta)$$

such that $\phi_{\eta}(z,\theta) = \phi_{\tilde{\eta}}(z,\theta)$ and where $\{\underline{\varepsilon}(k,\theta)\}$ is an innovation sequence with covariance $\Sigma(\theta)$.
The deterministic part of $\underline{Y}(k)$, $\overline{Y}(k)$ is in features space form

$$\overline{x}(k+1) = A(\theta)\overline{x}(k) + B(\theta)u(k)$$

$$\underline{\overline{Y}}(k) = C(\theta)\overline{x}(k) + D(\theta)u(k)$$

and hence the T-model $\underline{Y}(k) = \overline{Y}(k) + \underline{\eta}(k)$ can be represented with feature vector $\hat{\underline{x}}(k+1) \triangleq \underline{x}^*(k+1) + \overline{x}(k+1)$ as

$$\hat{\underline{x}}(k+1) = A(\theta)\hat{\underline{x}}(k) + B(\theta)u(k) + K(\theta)\underline{\varepsilon}(k,\theta)$$

$$\tilde{\underline{Y}}(k) = C(\theta)\hat{\underline{x}}(k) + D(\theta)u(k) + \underline{\varepsilon}(k,\theta)$$

with $p_{\underline{Y}(k)}(.|u^{(k)},\theta) = p_{\tilde{\underline{Y}}(k)}(.|u^{(k)},\theta)$. The process equation of the above model represents the steady-state Kalman filtering equation, see section (4.4).
The T-model of the model is given by

$$\tilde{\underline{Y}}(k) = G(z,\theta)u(k) + H_1(z,\theta)\underline{\varepsilon}(k,\theta)$$

with $H_1(\theta,z) = C(\theta)(zI-A(\theta))^{-1}K(\theta) + I$. Now $G(z,\theta)$, $H_1(z,\theta)$ and $H_1^{-1}(z,\theta)$ are stable with $\lim_{|z|\to\infty} H_1(z,\theta) = I$.

The T-model of $\underset{\sim}{\tilde{Y}}(k)$ can be rewritten in PEM-form as

$$\underline{\tilde{Y}}(k) = L_1(z,\theta)\underline{\tilde{Y}}(k-1) + L_2(z,\theta)u(k) + \underline{\varepsilon}(k,\theta) =$$

$$= g(\underline{\tilde{Y}}^{(k-1)},u^{(k)},\theta) + \underline{\varepsilon}(k,\theta)$$

with $L_1(z,\theta) = z(I-H_1^{-1}(z,\theta))$ and $L_2(z,\theta) = H_1^{-1}(z,\theta)G(z,\theta)$ and where $\{\underline{\varepsilon}(k,\theta)\}$ is an innovation sequence generated by the steady-state Kalman filter with $E\{\underline{\varepsilon}(k,\theta)|\tilde{Y}^{(k-1)},u^{(k)}\} = 0$ with covariance $\Sigma(\theta)$. The prediction of $\tilde{Y}(k)$ in period (k-1) is, by using the steady-state Kalman filter, given by

$$\hat{\tilde{Y}}(k,\theta) = C(\theta)\hat{x}(k) + D(\theta)u(k) = g(\tilde{Y}^{(k-1)},u^{(k)},\theta)$$

In the sequel we use a special measure $l(k,\theta,\varepsilon(k,\theta))$ in order to derive non-linear ML-estimates for the unknown parameter vector $\theta$. Because of the assumptions made the conditional p.d.f. of $\underline{\tilde{Y}}(k)$ is Gaussian. The log-likelihood for N-observations $\tilde{Y}^{(N)} = (\tilde{Y}'(1),\ldots,\tilde{Y}'(N))'$ is by Bayes' rule given by

$$\log p(\tilde{Y}^{(N)}|u^{(N)},\theta) = \sum_{j=1}^{N}\log p(\tilde{Y}(j)|\tilde{Y}^{(j-1)},u^{(j)},\theta) =$$

$$= \sum_{j=1}^{N}\log p(\tilde{Y}(j)|\tilde{Y}^{(j-1)},u^{(j)},\theta) =$$

$$= -\tfrac{1}{2}(mN\log 2\pi + N\log\det\Sigma(\theta) + N\operatorname{tr}(\Sigma^{-1}(\theta)D_N(\theta))$$

where $D_N(\theta) = N^{-1}\sum_{j=1}^{N}w(j,\theta)w'(j,\theta)$ is the sample prediction-error covariance of the realized innovations $w(j,\theta) = \tilde{Y}(j) - \hat{\tilde{Y}}(j,\theta)$ where $\hat{\tilde{Y}}(j,\theta)$ is the prediction generated by the steady-state Kalman filter. Using the relation $\underline{\tilde{Y}}(k) = g(\tilde{Y}^{(k-1)},u^{(k)},\theta) + \underline{\varepsilon}(k,\theta)$ and the rule for transformation of random variables we can relate the conditional distribution of $\underline{\tilde{Y}}(k)$ to that of $\underline{\varepsilon}(k,\theta)$ as follows

$$p(\tilde{Y}(k)|\tilde{Y}^{(k-1)},u^{(k)},\theta) = p_{\varepsilon(k)}(w(k,\theta)|\theta)|\det(\partial\varepsilon(k)/\partial\tilde{Y}(k))|$$

where $|\det(\partial\varepsilon(k)/\partial\tilde{Y}(k))| = 1$.

Let the scalar measure of the prediction errors

$$l(k,\theta,\varepsilon(k,\theta)) = -\log p_{\varepsilon(k)}(w(k,\theta)|\theta) = -\log p(\tilde{Y}(k)|\tilde{Y}^{(k-1)},u^{(k)},\theta)$$

then the criterion

$$V_N(\theta) = N^{-1}\log p(\tilde{Y}^{(N)} \mid u^{(N)},\theta) = \tfrac{1}{2}(m\log 2\pi + \log\det\Sigma(\theta) +$$

$$+ \operatorname{tr}(\Sigma^{-1}(\theta)D_N(\theta)).$$

The estimate $\hat{\theta}(N)$ which minimizes $V_N(\theta)$ is now the ML-estimate. Before we can apply theorem 5.3 assumption C2 has to be checked, namely if

$$\lim_{N\to\infty} E_{\tilde{Y}^{(N)}|\theta}\{\underline{V}_N(\theta)\} = \tfrac{1}{2}m\log 2\pi + \log\det\Sigma(\theta) +$$

$$+ \operatorname{tr}\Sigma^{-1}(\theta)\lim_{N\to\infty} E_{\tilde{Y}^{(N)}|\theta}\{\underline{D}_N(\theta)\}$$

exists. We have seen that the model in PEM-form is

$$\underline{\tilde{Y}}(k) = L_1(z,\theta)\underline{\tilde{Y}}(k-1) + L_2(z,\theta)u(k) + \underline{\varepsilon}(k,\theta)$$

$$= \underline{\hat{\tilde{Y}}}(k,\theta) + \underline{\varepsilon}(k,\theta)$$

where the predictor $\underline{\hat{\tilde{Y}}}(k,\theta)$ is generated by the steady-state Kalman filter and where $L_1(z,\theta)$ and $L_2(z,\theta)$ are stable for <u>all</u> considered $\theta \in B(\theta_0,\varepsilon) \subset \Theta$.

The parameter search is over all stable processes, i.e. $\|E\{\underline{\tilde{Y}}(k)\}\| < \infty$, for all k and all $\theta \in B(\theta_0,\varepsilon) \subset \Theta$ and hence $\|E\{\underline{\hat{\tilde{Y}}}(k,\theta)\}\| < \infty$, for all k, that is, the expected value of the Kalman predictors are bounded. Suppose the 'true' model is

$$\underline{\tilde{Y}}(k) = \hat{\tilde{Y}}(k,\theta_0) + \underline{\varepsilon}(k,\theta_0)$$

such that $\Sigma(\theta_0)$ is minimum. The prediction-error

$$\underline{w}(j,\theta) = \underline{\tilde{Y}}(k) - \underline{\hat{\tilde{Y}}}(k,\theta) = \Delta\underline{f}_k(\theta,\theta_0) + \underline{\varepsilon}(k,\theta_0)$$

where $\Delta\underline{f}_k(\theta,\theta_0) \triangleq \underline{\hat{\tilde{Y}}}(k,\theta_0) - \underline{\hat{\tilde{Y}}}(k,\theta)$ is the difference between the Kalman predictors of the true model and the model with parameter value $\theta$. Because the expected values of the Kalman predictors are bounded, the variance of $\underline{w}(j,\theta) - E\{\Delta\underline{f}_k(\theta,\theta_0)\}$, given by $\Sigma(\theta_0)$ is bounded and hence $E\{\underline{w}(j,\theta)\underline{w}'(j,\theta)\}$ is bounded for all j and all $\theta \in B(\theta_0,\varepsilon)$.

From this it follows that

$$\lim_{N\to\infty} E_{\tilde{\underline{Y}}(N)|\theta}\{\underline{D}_N(\theta)\} = \lim E_{\tilde{\underline{Y}}(N)|\theta}\{N^{-1}\sum_k(\Delta\underline{f}_k(\theta,\theta_0)+\underline{\varepsilon}(k,\theta_0))(\text{—})'\}$$

$$= \lim_{N\to\infty} E_{\tilde{\underline{Y}}(N)|\theta}\{(N^{-1}\sum_k \Delta\underline{f}_k(\theta,\theta_0)\Delta\underline{f}_k'(\theta,\theta_0)+\Sigma(\theta_0)\}$$

$$= Q(\theta,\theta_0) + \Sigma(\theta_0),$$

because $E\{\Delta\underline{f}_k(\theta,\theta_0)\underline{\varepsilon}'(k,\theta_0)\} = 0$.

The parameter identifiability condition implies that w.p. one $Q(\theta,\theta_0) \neq 0$ unless $\theta = \theta_0$. (In fact the conditional mean of $\tilde{\underline{Y}}(k)$ is given by $\hat{\tilde{Y}}(k,\theta)$.)

The limit of $V_N(\theta)$ is given by

$$\overline{V}(\theta) = \tfrac{1}{2}m\log 2\pi + \log\det\Sigma(\theta) + \mathrm{tr}(\Sigma^{-1}(\theta)[Q(\theta,\theta_0)+\Sigma(\theta_0)]$$

which is bounded with minimum value $\overline{V}(\theta_0)$.

Applying theorem (5.3) we have that the ML-estimate obtained by minimizing $V_N(\theta)$ is strongly consistent and asymptotically efficient see section (5.3).

Example (5.3):

Consider the LSF-model

$$A_0\underline{x}(k+1) = A_1\underline{x}(k) + \overline{B}u(k) + \overline{\underline{w}}(k),\ k = k_0,k_0+1,\ldots$$

$$\underline{y}(k) = C\underline{x}(k) + \underline{v}(k)$$

with initial condition $x(0) = 0$; $x(k) \in \mathbb{R}^2$; $u(k) \in \mathbb{R}^2$; $y(k) \in \mathbb{R}^2$ with *known* covariances $\mathrm{cov}\{\overline{\underline{w}}(k)\overline{\underline{w}}'(k)\} = \Sigma_{\overline{w}} = \overline{Q}$ and $\mathrm{cov}\{\underline{v}(k)\underline{v}'(k)\} = \Sigma_v = R$.

$$A_0 = \begin{bmatrix} 1 & a_{12}^0 \\ a_{21}^0 & 1 \end{bmatrix};\ A_1 = \begin{bmatrix} a_{11}^1 & a_{12}^1 \\ a_{21}^1 & a_{22}^1 \end{bmatrix};\ \overline{B} = \begin{bmatrix} \overline{b}_{11} & 0 \\ 0 & \overline{b}_{22} \end{bmatrix};\ C = \begin{bmatrix} c_{11} & 0 \\ 0 & c_{22} \end{bmatrix}.$$

The reduced form matrices are

$$A = A_0^{-1}A_1 = \begin{bmatrix} a_{11} & a_{12} \\ a_{21} & a_{22} \end{bmatrix};\ B = A_0^{-1}\overline{B} = \begin{bmatrix} b_{11} & b_{12} \\ b_{21} & b_{22} \end{bmatrix}.$$

We assume A to be stable; (A,B,C) to be minimal and $\{u(k)\}$ to be 'persistently exciting' of order 3. Let $\alpha' = (a_{11},a_{12},a_{21},a_{22},b_{11},b_{12},b_{21},b_{22},c_{11},c_{22})$ be the vector of parameters of the LRF-model and $T \in GL(2)$ with $T = [t_{ij}]$ and $T^{-1} = [t^{ij}]$. Consider the function

$$F(T,\alpha) = (TA(\alpha)T^{-1},TB(\alpha),C(\alpha)T^{-1})$$

and more in particular $\tilde{C}(\alpha) = C(\alpha)T^{-1}$. It is easily seen that $\tilde{C}(\alpha)$ contradicts the specification C unless $t^{12} = t^{21} = 0$. $\tilde{C}(\alpha)$ does not contradict C except for some scaling factor. Rescale C be putting $c_{11} = c_{22} = 1$ then $T = I$ is the only allowable 'transformation' thus $F(T,\alpha) \neq F(I,\alpha)$ for $T \neq I$ and hence $\alpha$ is identifiable. The transfer-model

$$\underline{y}(k) = G(z,\alpha)u(k) + \underline{\eta}(k)$$

with $G(z,\alpha)u(k) = (zI-A)^{-1}Bu(k) = \sum_{i=1}^{\infty} A^{i-1}(\alpha)B(\alpha)u(k-i) = \sum_{i=1}^{\infty} G_i u(k-i)$ thus A and B are identifiable from $\{G_i\}$. Now the relation between the process equations of the LSF-model and the LRF-model will be considered. Let $\theta' = (a^0_{12},a^0_{21},a^1_{11},a^1_{12},a^1_{21},a^1_{22},\bar{b}_{11},\bar{b}_{22})$ and consider the function

$$\bar{F}(T,\theta) = (TA_0(\theta),TA_1(\theta),T\bar{B}(\theta))$$

and more in particular $\tilde{B}(\theta) = T\bar{B}(\theta)$. Again it is easily seen that $\tilde{B}(\theta)$ contradicts $\bar{B}(\theta)$ unless $t_{12} = t_{21} = 0$. Now consider the submatrix $\tilde{A}_0(\theta) = T_D A_0(\theta)$ with $T_D = \text{diag}(t_{11},t_{22})$ then $\tilde{A}_0(\theta)$ contradicts the specification $A_0(\theta)$ unless $t_{11} = t_{22} = 1$ and hence $\bar{F}(T,\theta) \neq \bar{F}(I,\theta)$ for $T \neq I$. From this it follows that $\theta$ is identifiable.

## 5.6. Prediction Error Estimation and Jöreskog's LISREL Procedure.

Consider the static stationary LSF-model from section (5.5) with $A_0 = 0$, $\bar{B} = 0$ and $D = 0$, i.e.,

$$-A_{1,(\theta)}\underline{x}(k) = \underline{\bar{w}}(k)$$

$$\underline{Y}(k) = C_{(\theta)}\underline{x}(k) + \underline{v}(k), \qquad k = 0,1,2,\ldots$$

with initial condition $\underline{x}(0) \sim N(0,\Sigma_{x,(\theta)})$, where $\Sigma_{x,(\theta)} = A^{-1}_{1,(\theta)}\Sigma_{\bar{w},(\theta)}A'^{-1}_{1,(\theta)}$. The best unconditional and conditional prediction of $Y(k)$ is zero for $k = 0,1,2,\ldots$ and the 'prediction error' $\varepsilon(k) = Y(k)$ is the observation $Y(k)$ itself. From section (5.5) we have that a ML estimate $\hat{\theta}(N-1)$ for $N$ observations $Y(0),\ldots,Y(N-1)$ can be obtained by minimizing the prediction error criterion

$$V_N(\theta,Y^{(N-1)}) = (m/2)\log 2\pi + (\tfrac{1}{2})\log\det\Sigma_{\varepsilon,(\theta)} + \\ + \tfrac{1}{2}\mathrm{tr}(\Sigma^{-1}_{\varepsilon,(\theta)}D_N(\theta)),$$

where the sample 'prediction error' covariance

$$D_N(\theta) = N^{-1}\sum_{j=0}^{N-1}Y(j)Y'(j) = S$$

and

$$\Sigma_{\varepsilon,(\theta)} = E\{\underline{\varepsilon}(j)\underline{\varepsilon}'(j)\} = E\{\underline{Y}(j)\underline{Y}'(j)\} = \Sigma_{Y,(\theta)}$$

for all j.

The covariance matrix $\Sigma_{Y,(\theta)} = C_{(\theta)}A^{-1}_{1,(\theta)}\Sigma_{\bar{w}}A^{-1}_{1,(\theta)}C'_{(\theta)} + \Sigma_{v,(\theta)}$. The above prediction error criterion can be rewritten as

$$V_N(\theta,Y^{(N-1)}) = (m/2)\log 2\pi + (\tfrac{1}{2})\log\det\Sigma_{Y,(\theta)} + \\ +(\tfrac{1}{2})\mathrm{tr}(\Sigma^{-1}_{Y,(\theta)}S) + \log\det S - m$$

which is the function minimized in the LISREL procedure, see Jöreskog (1978). The prediction error ML estimation procedure applied to a static stationary (LSF) model is equivalent to the LISREL procedure.

## 5.7. Likelihood Ratio and Model Check.

### Likelihood Ratio.

The likelihood ratio can be used for hypothesis testing. Following Goodwin and Payne (1977) we have the following. Suppose s locally independent restrictions of the form $l_i(\theta) = 0$, $i = 1,2,\dots,s$ between the parameters $\theta_j$, $j = 1,2,\dots,n$. Let $\theta' = (\theta_1,\dots,\theta_s : \theta_{s+1},\dots,\theta_n) = (\alpha'\beta')$ where under the null hypothesis the restrictions $l_i(\theta) = 0$, $i = 1,\dots,s$ give rise to particular values for $\theta_1,\dots,\theta_s$, say $\alpha_1,\dots,\alpha_s$ arranged in the vector $\alpha^* = (\alpha_1^*,\dots,\alpha_s^*)'$. Assume N *independent* observations Y(i), $i = 1,\dots,N$ then $\log p(Y^{(N)};\theta) = \sum_{i=1}^{N} \log p(Y(i);\theta)$. Let $\hat{\theta}$ be the unrestriced ML estimate and $\tilde{\theta}$ the ML estimate satisfying the restrictions $l_i(\tilde{\theta}) = 0$. The likelihood ratio is

$$\lambda(Y) = p(Y^{(N)};\hat{\theta})/p(Y^{(N)};\tilde{\theta})$$

Applying a Taylor series around $\hat{\theta}$ we have

$$N^{-1}\log p(Y^{(N)};\theta) \approx N^{-1}\sum_{i=1}^{N}\log p(Y(i);\hat{\theta}) + $$
$$+ N^{-1}\sum_{i=1}^{N}(\theta-\hat{\theta})'\left.\frac{\partial^2 \log p(Y(i);\theta)}{\partial\theta\partial\theta'}\right|_{\theta=\hat{\theta}}(\theta-\hat{\theta}).$$

Let the partioned sample information matrix

$$\bar{R}(\hat{\theta}) = -N^{-1}\sum_{i=1}^{N}\left.\frac{\partial^2 \log(Y(i;\theta)}{\partial\theta\partial\theta'}\right|_{\theta=\hat{\theta}} = \begin{bmatrix} \bar{R}_{\alpha\alpha} & \bar{R}_{\alpha\beta} \\ \bar{R}_{\beta\alpha} & \bar{R}_{\beta\beta} \end{bmatrix}$$

then

$$N^{-1}\log p(Y^{(N)};\theta) \approx N^{-1}\log p(Y^{(N)};\hat{\theta}) - (\tfrac{1}{2})\begin{bmatrix} \alpha-\hat{\alpha} \\ \beta-\hat{\beta} \end{bmatrix}'\begin{bmatrix} \bar{R}_{\alpha\alpha} & \bar{R}_{\alpha\beta} \\ \bar{R}_{\beta\alpha} & \bar{R}_{\beta\beta} \end{bmatrix}\begin{bmatrix} \alpha-\hat{\alpha} \\ \beta-\hat{\beta} \end{bmatrix}$$

The restricted ML estimate $\tilde{\beta}$ for $\beta$ with $\alpha = \alpha^*$ is given by

$$\tilde{\beta} \approx \hat{\beta} - \bar{R}_{\beta\beta}^{-1}\bar{R}'_{\alpha\beta}(\alpha^*-\hat{\alpha})$$

and

$$N^{-1}\log p(Y^{(N)};\tilde{\theta}) \approx N^{-1}\log p(Y^{(N)};\hat{\theta}) -$$

$$- \tfrac{1}{2}(\alpha^{*}-\hat{\alpha})'[\bar{R}_{\alpha\alpha}-\bar{R}_{\alpha\beta}\bar{R}_{\beta\beta}^{-1}\bar{R}'_{\alpha\beta}](\alpha^{*}-\hat{\alpha})$$

and hence

$$2\log\lambda(Y) = 2\log p(Y^{(N)};\hat{\theta}) - 2\log p(Y^{(N)};\tilde{\theta})$$

$$\approx N(\alpha^{*}-\hat{\alpha})'[\bar{R}_{\alpha\alpha}-\bar{R}_{\alpha\beta}\bar{R}_{\beta\beta}^{-1}\bar{R}'_{\alpha\beta}](\alpha^{*}-\hat{\alpha}).$$

If the null hypothesis is true it can be shown that

$$2\log\lambda(Y) \xrightarrow{L} \chi^{2}_{(s)}$$

with a specific alternative hypothesis $H_A$, namely that the true value of $\alpha$ is $\alpha_a \neq \alpha^{*}$ then

$$2\log\lambda(Y) \xrightarrow{L} \chi'_{(s,h)}$$

where $\chi'_{(s,h)}$ is a non-central $\chi^2$-distribution with non-centrality parameter

$$h = N(\alpha_a-\alpha^{*})'(\bar{R}_{\alpha\alpha}-\bar{R}_{\alpha\beta}\bar{R}_{\beta\beta}^{-1}\bar{R}'_{\alpha\beta})(\alpha_a-\alpha^{*}).$$

The power of the test can be increased by increasing the number of data points (N) or maximizing $\det(\bar{R}_{\alpha\alpha}-\bar{R}_{\alpha\beta}\bar{R}_{\beta\beta}^{-1}\bar{R}'_{\alpha\beta})$. Because $\det\bar{R}(\hat{\theta}) = \det\bar{R}_{\beta\beta}\det(\bar{R}_{\alpha\alpha}-\bar{R}_{\alpha\beta}\bar{R}_{\beta\beta}^{-1}\bar{R}'_{\alpha\beta})$ this is equivalent when $\det\bar{R}(\theta)/\det\bar{R}_{\beta\beta}$ is maximized, in particular if $\det\bar{R}(\hat{\theta})$ is maximum. This suggests that ML-estimate between 'competing' estimates with the largest amount of information measured by $\det\bar{R}(\hat{\theta})$.

The Wald Test.

As we have seen in the preceeding sections, under quite general conditions the prediction error estimate $\hat{\theta}(N)$ is strongly consistent and

$$\sqrt{N}(\hat{\theta}(N)-\theta_o) \xrightarrow{L} N(0,P)$$

provided that the true parameter point $\theta_o$ is such that $\bar{V}(\theta_o) = \min_{\theta}\bar{V}(\theta)$. Let $\hat{P}$ be a consistent estimate of P. Assume that under the null hypothesis $\theta_o$ satisfies a set of constraints of the form $h(\theta_o) = 0$ where

$h(\theta_o)$ is a vector of s independent, continuously differentiable functions. It can be shown, see e.g. Palm (1982) or Szroeter (1983) that under the null hypothesis the Wald test statistic

$$\underline{W} \triangleq N h'(\hat{\theta}(N))\hat{\Omega}_h^{-1} h(\hat{\theta}(N)) \xrightarrow{L} \chi^2_{(s)}$$

where

$$\hat{\Omega}_h = \frac{\partial h}{\partial \theta}\bigg|_{\theta=\hat{\theta}(N)} \hat{P} \left[\frac{\partial h}{\partial \theta}\bigg|_{\theta=\hat{\theta}(N)}\right]'$$

provided that $\text{plim}(\hat{\Omega}_h)$ is non-singular and $\partial h/\partial\theta$ is a continuous function of $\theta$ at the true parameter point $\theta_o$. See Szroeter (1983) for a generalized version of the Wald statistic.

From Chapter IV we have seen that if the model is correctly specified the prediction error sequence is white noise. The model can be checked by analyzing the auto-covariance or spectrum of the prediction errors or applying a white noise test, see Mehra and Peschon (1971). A measure of accuracy for the parameter estimates is given by the inverse of the calculated Fisher information matrix and also by det $\overline{R}(\hat{\theta}(N))$. If the components of the input are not 'rich' enough, measured by their variances, compared with the variance of the prediction errors, then it is difficult to identify the parameter vector. A quantitive measure is given by the *signal-to-noise ratio*

$$\frac{d_{ii}(\hat{\theta}(N))}{\sigma_{jj}(u)}, \qquad i = 1,\dots,m,\ j = 1,\dots,p$$

where $d_{ii}(\hat{\theta}(N))$ is the square root of the i-th diagonal element of the prediction error covariance $D_N(\hat{\theta}(N))$ and $\sigma_{jj}(u)$ is the square root of the variance of the deterministic input $\{u(k),\ k = 1,\dots,N\}$.

## 5.8. Structure Selection.

In the sequel we have an informal discussion on structure discrimination, which is currently an area of active research. The basic problem in structure discrimination is to select between a 'simple' model and a more 'complex' model, which may give a better fit to the data; 'simple' in terms of freely adjustable parameters, see e.g. Popper (1977). Intuitively a model with 'many' parameters may give a better fit, but the 'uncertainty' of parameter estimates measured by the (asymptotic) variances will also increase. Two approaches are discussed; one based on the non-central $\chi^2$-distribution and one based on Kullback's information measure.

From the previous section we have seen that

$$2\log\lambda(Y) = 2\log p(Y^{(N)};\hat{\theta}) - 2\log p(Y^{(N)};\tilde{\theta})$$

$$\approx N(\alpha^*-\hat{\theta})'[\bar{R}_{\alpha\alpha}-\bar{R}_{\alpha\beta}\bar{R}_{\beta\beta}^{-1}\bar{R}'_{\alpha\beta}](\alpha^*-\hat{\alpha}).$$

Under a specific alternative hypothesis ($H_A$) with $\alpha_a \neq \alpha^*$ we have that

$$2\log\lambda(Y) \xrightarrow{L} \chi'_{(s,h)}$$

with non-centrality parameter $h = N(\alpha_a-\alpha^*)'[\bar{R}_{\alpha\alpha}-\bar{R}_{\alpha\beta}\bar{R}_{\beta\beta}^{-1}\bar{R}'_{\alpha\beta}](\alpha_a-\alpha^*)$. The power of the test can be increased by increasing the number of data points N or increasing $\bar{R}_{\alpha\alpha} - \bar{R}_{\alpha\beta}\bar{R}_{\beta\beta}^{-1}\bar{R}'_{\alpha\beta}$.

Because $\det\bar{R}(\hat{\theta}) = \det\bar{R}_{\beta\beta}\det(\bar{R}_{\alpha\alpha}-\bar{R}_{\alpha\beta}\bar{R}_{\beta\beta}^{-1}\bar{R}'_{\alpha\beta})$ we have that the power can be increased by maximizing the determinant of the Fisher information matrix. According to Goodwin and Payne (1977) we have that if the structure test can be posed as a test for zero parameters, then a suitable criterion for structure selection is to maximize the ratio of determinants of the Fisher information matrices of two competing models.

Another approach which recently has been followed is based on the information theoretical concepts entropy and information, see e.g. Akaike (1974), Rissanen (1983) and Parzen (1983). This approach seems to be promising. In the sequel we derive an entropy criterion which can be used to discriminate between competing models and discuss Akaike's AIC criterion together with a generalized Akaike's criterion given by Niedźwiecki (1984).

Definition (5.3) : The *entropy* of an m-dimensional random vector $\underline{x}$ having p.d.f. p(x) is defined as

$$H(p) \triangleq -E_x\{\log p(x)\} = -\int_{-\infty}^{\infty}\log p(x)p(x)dx$$

Definition (5.4) : The *information divergence* between the 'true' p.d.f. f(x) and the p.d.f. g(x) used in a model is

$$I(f,g) \triangleq -\int_{-\infty}^{\infty} \log \left(\frac{g(x)}{f(x)}\right) f(x)\,dx$$

The information divergence equals Kullback's mean information $I(\theta_0,\theta)$ as defined in section 5.1 with $f(x) = p(y:\theta_0)$ and $g(x) = p(y:\theta)$. Bowden's entropy function $H(\theta,\theta_0) = -I(\theta_0,\theta)$.

If $\underline{x}$ is Gaussian with mean $\mu$ and covariance $\Sigma$ then

$$H(p) = -E_x\{\log p(x)\} = -E_x\{-\tfrac{1}{2}m \log 2\pi - \tfrac{1}{2}\log\det\Sigma - \tfrac{1}{2}(x-\mu)'\Sigma^{-1}(x-\mu)\}$$

$$= \tfrac{1}{2}m \log 2\pi + \tfrac{1}{2}\log\det\Sigma +$$

$$+ \tfrac{1}{2}\mathrm{tr}(\Sigma^{-1}E_x\{(x-\mu)(x-\mu)'\}$$

$$H(p) = \tfrac{1}{2}m(\log 2\pi + 1) + \tfrac{1}{2}\log\det\Sigma.$$

It can be proved that an m-dimensional random vector $\underline{x}$ with covariance $\Sigma$ has its maximum entropy when its distribution is Gaussian, see Shannon (1948). Moreover in the class of random vectors having covariances with the same trace, the random vectors which are independently, identically Gaussian distributed (innovations!) have maximum entropy, see Goodwin and Payne (1977, p. 14). These results can be used in model selection. Consider the (prediction-error) model

$$\underline{y}(k) = f_k(\theta) + \underline{\varepsilon}(k)$$

with $y(k) \in \mathbb{R}^m$ as output vector. The data $Y^{(N)} = (y'(1),\ldots,y'(N))'$ are approximately modelled as $f_k(\theta)$, $k = 1,\ldots,N$, e.g. as prediction-error model $f_k(\theta) = g(z^{(k)},\theta)$ where $z^{(k)}$ is the vector of previous observations of the output and input. Assume $\{\underline{\varepsilon}(k)\}$ to be an innovation sequence with common covariance $\Sigma$, that is, we postulate a model with maximum entropy. The log-likelihood is given by

$$\log p(Y^{(N)};\theta,\Sigma) = -\tfrac{1}{2}[Nm \log 2\pi + \log\det\Sigma +$$

$$+ \sum_{k=1}^{N}(y(k)-f_k(\theta)'\Sigma^{-1}(y(k)-f_k(\theta))]$$

For any value of $\theta$, say $\tilde{\theta}$, the above expression for $\log p(Y^{(N)};\tilde{\theta},\Sigma)$ can be maximized with respect to $\Sigma$ giving

$$\tilde{\Sigma} = N^{-1}\sum^{N}(y(k)-f_k(\tilde{\theta}))(y(k)-f_k(\tilde{\theta}))' \triangleq D(\tilde{\theta})$$

where $D(\tilde{\theta})$ is the prediction error covariance.
This relation can be used to eliminate $\Sigma$ from the likelihood yielding

$$\log p(Y^{(N)};\theta,\Sigma=D(\theta)) = -\tfrac{1}{2}[Nm(\log 2\pi+1)+N \log\det D(\theta)].$$

The entropy of $p(Y^{(N)};\theta,\Sigma=D(\theta))$ is

$$H(p(Y^{(N)};\theta)) = \tfrac{1}{2}[Nm(\log 2\pi+1)+N \log\det E_{Y^{(N)}|\theta}\{D(\theta)\}.$$

The ML-estimate $\hat{\theta}$ which maximizes the log-likelihood can be seen as the estimate which minimizes the maximum entropy (minmax entropy estimate). An estimate of twice the minimum entropy is given by

$$2\hat{H}(p(Y^{(N)};\hat{\theta},\hat{\Sigma}=D(\hat{\theta})) = Nm(\log 2\pi+1)+N \log\det D(\hat{\theta})$$

where $\hat{\theta}$ is the ML-estimate. It is seen that the entropy is increasing with the number of observations N; the number of output variables m and the log of the generalized variance of the innovations measured by $\det D(\hat{\theta})$. If we have to choose between two or more models then a criterion for choosing between them is to choose the one with minimum entropy, that is the one for which $\log\det D(\hat{\theta})$ is minimum. However it is to be expected that by increasing the number of 'freely adjustable' parameters (and input variables) a better fit can be obtained with a lower generalized error variance but with the cost of an increasing uncertainty of the parameter estimates. The parameter uncertainty can be related to the entropy as follows. Applying a Taylor series around the ML-estimate $\hat{\theta}$ we have

$$\log p(Y^{(N)};\theta,D(\theta)) \approx \log p(Y^{(N)},\hat{\theta},D(\hat{\theta})) + \tfrac{1}{2}(\theta-\hat{\theta})\frac{\partial^2 \log p(Y^{(N)},\hat{\theta},D(\hat{\theta}))}{\partial\theta\partial\theta'}(\theta-\hat{\theta})$$

and hence

$$-2E_{Y^{(N)}|\hat{\theta}}\{\log p(Y^{(N)},\theta,D(\theta)\} \approx -2E_{Y^{(N)}|\hat{\theta}}\{\log p(Y^{(N)},\hat{\theta},D(\hat{\theta})\} +$$

$$+ (\theta-\hat{\theta})'R(\hat{\theta})(\theta-\hat{\theta})$$

where the expected information matrix

$$R(\hat{\theta}) = -E_{Y^{(N)}|\hat{\theta}}\left[\left.\frac{\partial^2 \log p(Y^{(N)},\theta,D(\theta))}{\partial\theta\partial\theta}\right|_{\theta=\hat{\theta}}\right]$$

thus

$$2H(p(Y^{(N)},\theta,D(\theta)) - 2H(p(Y^{(N)},\hat{\theta},D(\hat{\theta})) \approx (\theta-\hat{\theta})'R(\hat{\theta})(\theta-\hat{\theta})$$

and according to definition 5.4 the information divergence

$$2I(p(\hat{\theta}),p(\theta)) \approx (\theta-\hat{\theta})'R(\hat{\theta})(\theta-\hat{\theta})$$

where $p(\hat{\theta}) = p(Y^{(N)},\hat{\theta},D(\hat{\theta}))$ and $p(\theta) = p(Y^{(N)},\theta,D(\theta))$. The information of $p(\hat{\theta})$ compared with $p(\theta)$ is increasing with 'increasing' $R(\hat{\theta})$ and can be used as a measure of fit. The entropy of $p(\hat{\theta})$ *relative* to $p(\theta)$ which can be seen as the information loss of $p(\hat{\theta})$ relative to $p(\theta)$ is

$$2H(p(\hat{\theta}),p(\theta)) = -2I(p(\hat{\theta}),p(\theta)) \approx -(\theta-\hat{\theta})'R(\hat{\theta})(\theta-\hat{\theta})$$

Twice the estimated total entropy $p(\hat{\theta})$, which is the sum of the information loss and the entropy is given by

$$\begin{aligned}2H(p(\hat{\theta})) + 2H(p(\hat{\theta}),p(\theta)) &\approx Nm(\log 2\pi+1) + N\log\det E_{Y^{(N)}|\hat{\theta}}\{D(\hat{\theta})\} - \\ &\quad - (\theta-\hat{\theta})'R(\hat{\theta})(\theta-\hat{\theta}) \\ &\approx c + N\log\det E_{Y^{(N)}|\hat{\theta}}\{D(\hat{\theta})\} - \\ &\quad - N(\theta-\hat{\theta})'\overline{R}(\hat{\theta})(\theta-\hat{\theta})\end{aligned}$$

where $\overline{R}(\hat{\theta}) = N^{-1}R(\hat{\theta})$ is the average expected information matrix. The above expression suggests the following entropy estimate criterion for discriminating between two or more models

$$HC(\hat{\theta}) = \log\det D(\hat{\theta}) - \log\det\overline{R}(\hat{\theta}) = \log(\det D(\hat{\theta})/\det\overline{R}(\hat{\theta})).$$

where $\log\det\overline{R}(\hat{\theta})$ is a scalar measure for $\overline{R}(\hat{\theta})$. Note that if $\det\overline{R}(\hat{\theta})$

approaches zero, that is $\hat{\theta}$ is almost unidentifiable (theorem 5.1b), then $HC(\hat{\theta})$ approaches infinity.

The above criterion resembles some equivalence with the generalized Akaike's criterion

$$L(\hat{\theta}) \triangleq \log \det D(\hat{\theta}) + 2k/N^*$$

proposed by Niedźwiecki (1984), where $N^*$ is the 'effective' number of observations and k the number of freely adjustable parameters. This criterion is based on Akaike's AIC criterion, Akaike (1974), which is discussed in the sequel. From Kullback (1959, chapter V) we have that an estimate of the information $I(\theta_0,\hat{\theta})$ defined before is given by

$$\hat{I}(\theta_0,\hat{\theta}) = -\log\left(\frac{p(Y^{(N)};\hat{\theta})}{p(Y^{(N)};\theta_0)}\right)$$

where the 'true' parameter vector $\theta_0 \in \mathbb{R}^k$ lies on a r-dimensional hyperplane of a k-dimensional space, i.e. (k-r) elements of $\theta_0$ are zero and $\hat{\theta} \in \mathbb{R}^k$ is the ML-estimate with k freely adjustable parameters. Under the null hypothesis that $\theta_0$ is the true parameter

$$2 \log \lambda(Y) = 2 \log \left(\frac{p(Y^{(N)};\hat{\theta})}{p(Y^{(N)};\theta_0)}\right) \xrightarrow{L} \chi^2_{(k-r)}$$

and hence twice the expected information equals asymptotically (-k+r). If we use $2 \log\lambda(Y) = 2 \log p(Y^{(N)};\hat{\theta}) - 2 \log p(Y^{(N)};\theta_0)$ as an estimate for twice the information it is asymptotically biased by an amount of 2(k-r). Correcting for the bias and neglecting $\log p(Y^{(N)};\theta_0)$ and r leads to the following estimated information criterion.

$$AIC(\hat{\theta}) = -2 \log p(Y^{(N)};\hat{\theta}) + 2k$$

For a further discussion we refer to Parzen (1983), Rissanen (1983) and Geweke and Meese (1981).

# VI. Economic Applications

In this chapter only a few economic applications of the feature space model will be considered. It is by no means an exhaustive description but merely gives an indication of the potential use of the feature space model for economic and social applications. See also the economic examples given in the preceeding chapters.

## 6.1. Regression.

In chapter IV we already discussed the Kalman estimator for the regression model in feature space (or state space) form, namely,

$$\beta(k+1) = \beta(k)$$

$$\underline{y}(k) = x'(k)\beta(k) + \underline{\varepsilon}(k), \qquad k = 1,2,\ldots$$

where $\beta(k) \in \mathbb{R}^p$ is the unknown parameter vector; $x(k) \in \mathbb{R}^p$ is a vector of exogenous variables and $\underline{y}(k)$ is a Gaussian output (endogenous) variable. It was shown that the Kalman filtering procedure generates the conditional mean and covariance of $\beta(k)$, given the previous observations $y(k), y(k-1),\ldots, x(k), x(k-1),\ldots$ . An advantage of the filter is that it generates a *time-series* of parameter estimates $\{\hat{\beta}(j)\}$ and a *time-series* of prediction errors $\{r(j)\}$, which can be used to analyse the assumption of time invariance of the parameter vector. See Tempelaar (1983) for an application of the Kalman filter to a structural model of the Dutch economy. It was shown in chapter IV that - if the model is correctly specified - the prediction errors are not autocorrelated, which can be used for a model check, e.g. a white noise test or a test based on Brownian motion, see e.g. Brown et.al. (1975). If the hypothesis of time invariance of the parameter vector is rejected then in a second stage the time-series $\{\hat{\beta}(j)\}$ can be modelled as a time-series model, e.g. as a Markov process and/or regressed on an observable input vector $u_1(k) \in \mathbb{R}^m$, leading to the (LRF) model

$$\underline{\beta}(k+1) = A\underline{\beta}(k) + Bu_1(k) + \underline{w}(k)$$

$$\underline{y}(k) = x'(k)\underline{\beta}(k) + \underline{v}(k), \qquad k = 1,2,\ldots$$

where $\underline{w}(k)$ is process white noise. Under the usual conditions of stochastic reconstructability and controllability the Kalman filter generates a time-series of estimates $\{\hat{\beta}(j)\}$. Again a model check can be performed by using the prediction errors. In this way the feature space model, Kalman filter and prediction error estimation can be used for a 'flexible' regression modelling.

Possible advantages of applying the Kalman filtering procedure are (i) because of its Bayesian character prior knowledge of the parameter vector can be incorporated (ii) the filter produces a time-series of estimated parameter vectors and a time-series of prediction errors, which can be used for a model check and also for a 'flexible' modelling (iii) the Kalman filtering procedure is recursive and can easily be programmed on a computer.

## 6.2. A Case Study.

### *2.1 Outline of This Section*

We have seen in chapter IV that several parameters have to be given numerical values before the Kalman filter can be applied. In economic regression analysis we usually have vague a-priori ideas about these values, so the values have to be chosen more or less intuitively which will have consequences for the resulting estimates and predictions, unless the initial parameter estimates of the filter are estimated by the prediction error method.

In subsection 2.2 we investigate these consequences by applying the filter, with various starting values, to a macro-economic model, describing a relation between investments, profits and capital stock in the USA, between the world wars. Theil's prediction error measure U is used to compare the prediction powers of the various Kalman estimators and the least squares estimator.

In subsection 2.3 we consider a regression model with time-varying stochastic parameters. Again the Kalman filter is applied with various starting values. Further we decompose Theil's measure U to investigate whether a model with time-varying stochastic parameters predicts systematically better than a model with constant parameters.

*2.2 Sensitivity Analysis for a Macro-Economic Model*

The following regression equation is studied

$$\underline{I}(t) = \beta_o + \beta_1 P(t) + \beta_2 P(t-1) + \beta_3 K(t-1) + \underline{v}_2(t), \qquad (2.2.1)$$

$$t = 1,2,\dots,21$$

where $\underline{I}(t)$ represents the net investments in year t+1920 in the USA, P(t) the profits in year t+1920, K(t+1) the capital stock at the end of year t+1919. All quantities are measured in tenths of billions of dollars. The equation can be rewritten as

$$\underline{I}(t) = h(t)\beta + \underline{v}_2(t), \qquad (2.2.2)$$

where $h(t) = (1,P(t),P(t-1),K(t-1))$ and $\beta' = (\beta_o,\beta_1,\beta_2,\beta_3)$. The errors $\underline{v}_2(1),\underline{v}_2(2),\dots$ are assumed to be independent, normally distributed random variables with zero mean and variance $\sigma^2 < \infty$. Tabel 1 gives the set of observations.

Table 1. Time-series data on the variables of the investment equation

| t | 1 | 2 | 3 | 4 | 5 | 6 | 7 | 8 | 9 | 10 | 11 |
|---|---|---|---|---|---|---|---|---|---|---|---|
| I(t) | -2 | 19 | 52 | 30 | 51 | 56 | 42 | 30 | 51 | 10 | -34 |
| P(t) | 124 | 169 | 184 | 194 | 201 | 196 | 198 | 211 | 217 | 156 | 114 |
| K(t-1) | 1828 | 1826 | 1845 | 1897 | 1927 | 1978 | 2034 | 2076 | 2106 | 2157 | 2167 |

| t | 12 | 13 | 14 | 15 | 16 | 17 | 18 | 19 | 20 | 21 |
|---|---|---|---|---|---|---|---|---|---|---|
| I(t) | -62 | -51 | -30 | -13 | 21 | 20 | -19 | 13 | 33 | 49 |
| P(t) | 70 | 112 | 123 | 140 | 176 | 173 | 153 | 190 | 211 | 235 |
| K(t-1) | 2133 | 2071 | 2020 | 1990 | 1977 | 1998 | 2018 | 1999 | 2012 | 2045 |

Source: Theil (1971, p. 456).

As we saw in chapter III equation (2.2.2) can be rewritten as the following

(LRF) model

$$\beta(t+1) = \beta(t) \tag{2.2.3}$$

$$\underline{I}(t) = h(t)\beta(t) + \underline{v}_2(t). \tag{2.2.4}$$

Before we can apply the Kalman filter we must have a starting value for $\hat{\beta}(0)$, the initial estimate of $\beta$, for its 'error covariance' matrix $\Sigma_{\tilde{\beta}}(0)$ and for $\sigma^2$. Throughout the analysis we have taken $\hat{\beta}(0) = 0$, for $\Sigma_{\tilde{\beta}}(0)$ a diagonal matrix $\delta I_4$ with all diagonal elements equal to $\delta$, where the following values of $\delta$ are considered: 100,50,40,30,20,10,5,1 and for $\sigma^2 = \tilde{\sigma}^2$ the values 1000,100,10,1.

We use Theil's prediction error measure

$$U = \{n^{-1}\sum_{i=1}^{n}(P_i-A_i)^2\}^{\frac{1}{2}}/\{(n^{-1}\sum_{i=1}^{n}P_i^2)^{\frac{1}{2}}+(n^{-1}\sum_{i=1}^{n})A_i^2)^{\frac{1}{2}}\}$$

to compare the accuracy of the one-period ahead predictions of the Kalman and least squares estimates. $P_i$ $(i=1,\ldots,n)$ are the predictions and $A_i$ $(i=1,\ldots,n)$ are the realizations of the variable under consideration. The better the predictions are, the smaller U, with limiting value 0 in the case of perfect predictions: $P_i = A_i$, $i = 1,\ldots,n$. The above measure can be decomposed into three components, namely what is called the bias $U_m$, the variance $U_s$, and the covariance proportion $U_c$. Roughly speaking one can say that the lower the values of $U_m$ and $U_s$ the smaller the systematic errors in the predictions. See for details Theil (1965). In our case U is calculated using the formula

$$U = [17^{-1}\sum_{t=5}^{21}\{\hat{I}(t)-I(t)\}^2]^{\frac{1}{2}}/[\{17^{-1}\sum_{t=5}^{21}(\hat{I}(t))^2\}^{\frac{1}{2}}+\{17^{-1}\sum_{t=5}(I(t))^2\}^{\frac{1}{2}}]$$

Here $\hat{I}(t)$ denotes the one-period ahead prediction of the investments for period and is determined by

$$\hat{I}(t) = h(t)\bar{\beta}(t-1).$$

where $\bar{\beta}(t-1)$ is a Kalman or the least squares estimate, obtained by using the realizations of the variables until period (t-1). I(t) is the actual value of the investments in period t. The results for the Kalman estimates for the various starting values are presented in table 2.

Table 2. Computed values of U using Kalman estimates with starting values

| | $\tilde{\sigma}^2$ | | | |
|---|---|---|---|---|
| $\delta$ | 1000 | 100 | 10 | 1 |
| 100 | 0.16 | 0.15 | 0.14 | 0.13 |
| 50 | 0.17 | 0.15 | 0.14 | 0.13 |
| 10 | 0.24 | 0.16 | 0.15 | 0.14 |
| 5 | 0.30 | 0.17 | 0.15 | 0.14 |
| 1 | 0.40 | 0.24 | 0.16 | 0.15 |

The least squares estimate yields U = 0.17. From table 2 it can be seen that the prediction powers of the various Kalman estimates are rather insentive to the starting values as long as the diagonal elements $\Sigma_{\tilde{\beta}}(0)$ are larger than $\sigma^2$. In table 3 several Kalman estimates are presented together with the least squares estimates. From table 3 one can see that if $\delta = 1$ and $\tilde{\sigma}^2 = 1000$, the starting value $\hat{\beta}(0) = 0$ dominates all estimates.

## *2.3 A Linear Regression Model with Time-Varying Stochastic Parameters*

It might be argued that in this non-stationary world the time constancy of the parameter vector $\beta$ is an unrealistic assumption. We relax this assumption and consider the parameter vector to be a stochastic process, obtained by adding to the right-hand side of (2.2.3) a stochastic variable. We then have the (LRF) model

$$\underline{B}(t+1) = \underline{B}(t) + \underline{v}_1(t) \tag{2.3.1}$$

$$\underline{I}(t) = h(t)\underline{B}(t) + \underline{v}_2(t). \tag{2.3.2}$$

where $\underline{B}'(t) = (\underline{B}_o(t), \underline{B}_1(t), \underline{B}_2(t), \underline{B}_3(t))$ and $(\underline{v}_1'(t), \underline{v}_2(t))'$, $t = 1,2,\ldots,21$ is a sequence of independent normally distributed column vectors of dimension 4+1 with zero mean and covariance matrix

$$\begin{bmatrix} \Sigma_{11} & 0 \\ 0 & \sigma^2 \end{bmatrix},$$

where it is assumed that $\Sigma_{11}$ is a diagonal matrix with diagonal elements $\sigma_{ii}^2$; $i = 1,2,3,4$.

Table 3. Estimated parameter vector $\overline{\beta}(t) \times 100$.

| | least squares | | | | Kalman filter with starting values $\delta = 100,\ \tilde{\sigma}^2 = 1$ | | | | Kalman filter with starting values $\delta = 1,\ \tilde{\sigma}^2 = 1000$ | | | |
|---|---|---|---|---|---|---|---|---|---|---|---|---|
| | $\dot{\beta}_o(t)$ | $\dot{\beta}_1(t)$ | $\dot{\beta}_2(t)$ | $\dot{\beta}_3(t)$ | $\hat{\beta}_o(t)$ | $\hat{\beta}_1(t)$ | $\hat{\beta}_2(t)$ | $\hat{\beta}_3(t)$ | $\hat{\beta}_o(t)$ | $\hat{\beta}_1(t)$ | $\hat{\beta}_2(t)$ | $\hat{\beta}_3(t)$ |
| t= 5 | 5015 | 49 | 62 | -35 | 243 | 52 | 25 | -7 | 0 | 2 | 2 | 1 |
| 6 | 56 | 44 | 36 | -6 | 6 | 44 | 35 | -6 | 0 | 2 | 3 | 1 |
| 7 | 388 | 43 | 39 | -8 | 118 | 44 | 35 | -6 | 0 | 2 | 3 | 1 |
| 8 | 1464 | 35 | 56 | -14 | 708 | 36 | 45 | -9 | 0 | 2 | 3 | 1 |
| 9 | 1058 | 36 | 52 | -12 | 593 | 37 | 44 | -9 | 0 | 2 | 3 | 1 |
| 10 | 1168 | 47 | 46 | -13 | 676 | 51 | 35 | -10 | 0 | 4 | 2 | 1 |
| 11 | 1101 | 46 | 44 | -12 | 727 | 52 | 36 | -10 | 1 | 8 | 5 | 0 |
| 12 | 1026 | 45 | 41 | -12 | 689 | 51 | 34 | -10 | 1 | 14 | 9 | -1 |
| 13 | 909 | 48 | 36 | -11 | 676 | 51 | 34 | -10 | 1 | 16 | 13 | -2 |
| 14 | 915 | 48 | 37 | -11 | 680 | 51 | 34 | -10 | 1 | 17 | 14 | -2 |
| 15 | 915 | 48 | 37 | -11 | 680 | 51 | 34 | -10 | 1 | 17 | 14 | -2 |
| 16 | 858 | 51 | 34 | -11 | 641 | 53 | 32 | -10 | 1 | 17 | 14 | -2 |
| 17 | 853 | 51 | 34 | -11 | 637 | 53 | 32 | -10 | 1 | 17 | 14 | -2 |
| 18 | 700 | 57 | 28 | -10 | 524 | 59 | 27 | -9 | 1 | 17 | 14 | -2 |
| 19 | 812 | 53 | 31 | -10 | 614 | 55 | 30 | -9 | 1 | 17 | 14 | -2 |
| 20 | 904 | 50 | 32 | -11 | 687 | 53 | 31 | -10 | 1 | 18 | 14 | -2 |
| 21 | 1013 | 48 | 33 | -11 | 783 | 50 | 32 | -10 | 1 | 19 | 14 | -2 |

We must have a starting value for $\hat{B}(0)$, the initial estimate of the mean of $\underline{B}(0)$, for its 'error covariance' matrix $\Sigma_{\tilde{B}}(0)$ and $\sigma^2$. We have taken $\hat{B}(0) = 0$, $\Sigma_{\tilde{B}}(0)$, a diagonal matrix with all diagonal elements equal to 100 and $\tilde{\sigma}^2 = 1$. The Kalman filter with these starting values gave the best predictions for the model in subsection (2.2), see table 2. The covariance matrix $\Sigma_{11}$ must be specified too. There was no a-priori knowledge on $\Sigma_{11}$, so we considered several values for the variances $\sigma^2_{ii}$; $i = 1,2,3,4$. Some results are summarized in table 4, where also the decomposition of U is presented in order to see whether the predictions have been improved systematically.
From the table it can be seen that the predictions can be slightly improved by specifying the constant $\beta_o$ in (2.2.1) to be a stochastic process. The prediction power decreases however if we allow the other parameters to vary stochastically in time.

Table 4. Computed values of U and a decomposition into $U_m$, $U_s$ and $U_c$ for some values of $\sigma^2_{ii}$; $i = 1,2,3,4$.

| $\sigma^2_{11}$ | $\sigma^2_{22}$ | $\sigma^2_{33}$ | $\sigma^2_{44}$ | U | $U_m$ | $U_s$ | $U_c$ |
|---|---|---|---|---|---|---|---|
| 0 | 0 | 0 | 0 | 0.133 | 0.61 | 0.02 | 0.36 |
| 0.5 | 0 | 0 | 0 | 0.127 | 0.50 | 0.01 | 0.49 |
| 0 | 0.5 | 0 | 0 | 0.157 | 0.64 | 0.01 | 0.34 |
| 0 | 0 | 0.5 | 0 | 0.144 | 0.66 | 0.02 | 0.31 |
| 0 | 0 | 0 | 0.5 | 0.237 | 0.74 | 0.00 | 0.26 |
| 0.5 | 0.5 | 0 | 0 | 0.156 | 0.64 | 0.01 | 0.34 |
| 0.1 | 0 | 0 | 0 | 0.125 | 0.54 | 0.01 | 0.45 |
| 1 | 0 | 0 | 0 | 0.131 | 0.56 | 0.01 | 0.43 |
| 1.5 | 0 | 0 | 0 | 0.133 | 0.60 | 0.01 | 0.39 |

## 6.3. Univariate Time-Series Modelling.

Time-series models are commonly classified into two categories; time-series models with 'fitting functions' and time-series models as difference equations, the so-called ARMA (AutoRegressive Moving Average) models. They will be shortly discussed. A - for econometrics - rather new type of model, the so-called state space model for stationary multivariate time-series will also be discussed. For illustrative purposes a well known prediction method, called the single exponential smoothing (SES) method will be related to Kalman filtering, before discussing the time-series models.

Single Exponential Smoothing and Kalman Filtering.

Consider an univariate stationary time-series $\{\underline{y}(i)\}$ , $i = 1,\ldots,n$ modelled as

$$\underline{y}(k) = \theta + \underline{v}(k), \qquad k = 1,2,\ldots,n$$

where $\theta$ is an unknown constant and $\underline{v}(k)$ is white noise with variance $\sigma_v^2$. The model can be rewritten as the feature space model

$$\theta(k+1) = \theta(k)$$

$$\underline{y}(k) = \theta(k) + \underline{v}(k).$$

The Kalman prediction equation for this model is (with preliminary estimate $\hat{y}(1|0) = y(0)$)

$$\hat{y}(k+1|k) = \hat{y}(k|k-1) + K(k)\underline{r}(k), \qquad k = 0,1,\ldots,n$$

where $\hat{y}(k+1|k)$ is the prediction for period $(k+1)$ in period $k$; the Kalman gain $K(k) = 1/k$, see Otter (1978) and $r(k) = y(k) - \hat{y}(k|k-1)$ is the prediction error. As well known the (SES) algorithm is

$$\hat{\underline{y}}(k+1|k) = \hat{\underline{y}}(k|k-1) + \alpha\underline{r}(k)$$

where $\alpha$ is the smoothing constant. It is seen that the (SES) algorithm is equivalent to the Kalman predictor except for the time invariant smoothing constant $\alpha$. If the model is correctly specified the time-varying gain $K(k) = 1/k$ provides an optimal (MSE) prediction estimate $\hat{y}(k+1|k)$, (Because the Kalman estimate is a minimum error variance estimate.) but if the model is not correctly specified, divergence of the filter may occur (see chapter IV) which is prevented in the SES method by the time invariant smoothing constant $\alpha$. By adding process noise $\underline{w}(k)$ to the unknown constant $\theta$, we can deal with the misspecification, see also the section on divergence of the Kalman filter in chapter IV. We then have the following feature model

$$\underline{\theta}(k+1) = \underline{\theta}(k) + \underline{w}(k)$$

$$\underline{y}(k) = \underline{\theta}(k) + \underline{v}(k),$$

where $\underline{w}(k)$ denotes process white noise with variance $\sigma_w^2$. It can be shown, see Otter (1978) that the steady state Kalman prediction equation is

$$\hat{\underline{y}}(k+1|k) = \hat{y}(k|k-1) + K\underline{r}(k),$$

which equals the (SES) algorithm. The steady state gain $k = \alpha = A/(A+2)$ with $A \triangleq k + \sqrt{(k^2+4k)}$ where $k = \sigma_w^2/\sigma_v^2$ the ratio process noise/measurement noise. It may be concluded that the (SES) algorithm is a special Kalman predictor for a feature space model with process noise.

Univariate Time-Series Models with Fitting Functions.

A 'basic' univariate time-series model is

$$\underline{y}(k) = \underline{s}(k) + \underline{v}(k), \qquad k = 1,2,\ldots$$

where $\underline{s}(k)$ is some 'signal' to be filtered from the observation y(k), which is corrupted with measurement noise. This 'signal' s(k) can be modelled in many ways, depending on the structure of the time-series $\{\underline{y}(i)\}$ , i = 1,...,n. For example Theil developed an adaptive prediction procedure for the following model

$$\underline{y}(k) = \underline{s}(k) + \underline{v}(k)$$

$$\underline{s}(k+1) = \underline{s}(k) + \underline{\eta}(k)$$

$$\underline{\eta}(k+1) = \underline{\eta}(k) + \underline{\xi}(k)$$

where $\underline{y}(k)$ is the observed time-series; $\underline{s}(k)$ is the trend component and $\underline{\eta}(k)$ is a change of trend. $\underline{v}(k)$ and $\underline{\xi}(k)$ are respectively measurement white noise and process white noise. The model is a special feature space model, namely

process equation:

$$\begin{bmatrix} \underline{s}(k+1) \\ \underline{\eta}(k+1) \end{bmatrix} = \begin{bmatrix} 1 & 1 \\ 0 & 1 \end{bmatrix} \begin{bmatrix} \underline{s}(k) \\ \underline{\eta}(k) \end{bmatrix} + \begin{bmatrix} 0 \\ 1 \end{bmatrix} \underline{\xi}(k)$$

output equation:

$$\underline{y}(k) = (1 \quad 0) \begin{bmatrix} \underline{s}(k) \\ \underline{\eta}(k) \end{bmatrix} + \underline{v}(k),$$

with as feature vector $(\underline{s}(k)\underline{\eta}(k))$. As shown by Vishwakarma (1970) Theil's adaptive prediction procedure is a special Kalman filter. If the signal s(k) is a vector of time 'fitting' functions, it is often written as a first-order difference equation, i.e.

$$s(k+1) = As(k)$$

where $s(k) \in \mathbb{R}^p$, see Van Winkel (1970). It is seen that again the model

process equation:

$$s(k+1) = As(k)$$

output equation:

$$\underline{y}(k) = Cs(k) + \underline{v}(k)$$

is a feature space model with as feature vector a vector of deterministic time functions. C is a row vector of regression parameters.

<u>Example (6.1)</u>:

Harvey (1982) considers the following seasonal model

$$\underline{y}(k) = T(k) + s(k) + \underline{v}(k)$$

$$T(k) = T(k-1) + b(k) + \underline{w}_1(k)$$

$$b(k) = b(k-1) + \underline{w}_2(k)$$

$$s(k) = \sum_{j=1}^{s-1} s(k-j) + \underline{w}_3(k)$$

where $\underline{y}(k)$ is the observed univariate time-series; T(k) is the trending component and s(k) the seasonal component. It is assumed that $\{\underline{v}(k)\}$ and $\{\underline{w}_i(k)\}$ are uncorrelated white noise sequences. The model can easily be rewritten as the following (LSF) model

process equation:

$$\begin{bmatrix} 1 & -1 & 0 \dots 0 \\ 0 & 1 & \\ \vdots & & 1 & \vdots \\ & & & \\ 0 & \dots & & 1 \end{bmatrix} \begin{bmatrix} T(k) \\ b(k) \\ s(k) \\ \vdots \\ s(k-s+2) \end{bmatrix} = \begin{bmatrix} 1 & 0 & & \dots\dots & 0 \\ 0 & 1 & 0 & & 0 \\ 0 & 0 & 1 & \dots & 1 \\ 0 & 0 & 1 & 0 \dots & 0 \\ \vdots & & & & \vdots \\ 0 & \dots & 0 & 1 & 0 \end{bmatrix} \begin{bmatrix} T(k-1) \\ b(k-1) \\ s(k-1) \\ \\ \vdots \\ s(k-s+1) \end{bmatrix} + \begin{bmatrix} \underline{w}_1(k) \\ \underline{w}_2(k) \\ \underline{w}_3(k) \\ 0 \\ \vdots \\ 0 \end{bmatrix}$$

or

$$A_o\underline{x}(k) = A_1\underline{x}(k-1) + \underline{w}(k)$$

output equation:

$$\underline{y}(k) = (1 \quad 0 \quad 1 \quad 0 \dots 0)\underline{x}(k) + \underline{v}(k)$$

or

$$\underline{y}(k) = C\underline{x}(k) + \underline{v}(k).$$

Univariate ARMA Modelling.

A systematic treatment is given in the next section, but to give an impression the following analysis is presented. Consider the following univariate difference equation (ARMA(p,q) model)

$$\underline{y}(k) = a_1\underline{y}(k-1) + \dots + a_p\underline{y}(k-p) + \underline{\varepsilon}(k) + b_1\underline{\varepsilon}(k-1) + \dots$$
$$\dots + b_q\underline{\varepsilon}(k-q)$$

or

$$a(z)\underline{y}(k) = b(z)\underline{\varepsilon}(k),$$

where $\underline{y}(k)$ is an observed variable; $\underline{\varepsilon}(k)$ a white noise variable with variance $\sigma^2$ and $a(z) = 1 - a_1z^{-1} - a_2z^{-2} - \dots - a_pz^{-p}$ and $b(z) = 1 + b_1z^{-1} + b_2z^{-2} + \dots + b_qz^{-q}$ are polynomials in the lag operator $z^{-1}$. From the ARMA model we have the (MA) model

$$\underline{y}(k) = a^{-1}(z)b(z)\underline{\varepsilon}(k) = \sum_{i=0}^{\infty}\alpha_i\underline{\varepsilon}(k-i)$$

if the roots of $a^{-1}(z)$ are outside the unit circle and the (AR) model

$$b^{-1}(z)a(z)\underline{y}(k) = \underline{\varepsilon}(k)$$

or

$$\underline{y}(k) = \sum_{j=1}^{\infty} \pi_j \underline{y}(k-j) + \underline{\varepsilon}(k)$$

if the roots of $b^{-1}(z)$ are outside the unit circle.

AR Modelling and Kalman Filteren.

Suppose that in the AR model

$$\underline{y}(k) = \sum_{j=1}^{\infty} \pi_j \underline{y}(k-j) + \underline{\varepsilon}(k) = \sum_{j=1}^{p} \pi_j \underline{y}(k-j) + \sum_{j=p+1}^{\infty} \pi_j \underline{y}(k-j) + \underline{\varepsilon}(k)$$

the series

$$\sum_{j=p+1}^{\infty} \pi_j \underline{y}(k-j) \approx c$$

Define $\pi \triangleq (\pi_1,\ldots,\pi_p,c)'$ and $c(k) \triangleq (y(k-1),\ldots,y(k-p),1)$ then we have the following feature space model

$$\begin{aligned} \pi(k+1) &= \pi(k) \\ \underline{y}(k) &= \underline{c}(k)\pi(k) + \underline{\varepsilon}(k), \qquad k = 1,2,\ldots \end{aligned}$$

with as feature vector $\pi(k)$. Assume $y(0),y(-1),\ldots,y(-p)$ to be known then the Kalman filter generates a time-series of estimates $\{\hat{\pi}(j)\}$ and a time-series of prediction errors $\{r(j)\}$, which can be used for a model check. Note that prior information on $\pi(k)$, provided by the stationarity and invertibility conditions can be incorporated in the filter. See for details Otter and Tempelaar (1980).

## 6.4. Multivariate Time-Series Modelling.

ARMA Modelling

Following Anderson and Moore (1979) we have that an ARMA (n,m) process is defined by a p-dimensional vector difference equation with constant coefficients of the form

$$\underline{y}(k) + A_1\underline{y}(k-1) + \dots + A_n\underline{y}(k-n) = B_o\underline{v}(k) + \dots + B_m\underline{v}(k-m)$$

The process $\{\underline{v}(k)\}$ is, without loss of generality, assumed to be standard white noise and $\{\underline{y}(k)\}$ is the output process. If the difference equation is defined for $k \geqq 0$ some form of initialization is needed, e.g. $y(-1) = y(-2) = \dots = y(-n) = 0$. According to Anderson and Moore the difference equation can be rewritten for $m \leqq n$ as the following (LRF) model

$$\underline{x}(k+1) = A\underline{x}(k) + \underline{w}(k), \qquad \text{initial condition } x(0) = 0$$

$$\underline{y}(k) = C\underline{x}(k) + \underline{\varepsilon}(k)$$

where

$$A = \begin{bmatrix} -A_1 & I & \dots & 0 \\ -A_2 & & & \vdots \\ \vdots & & & \\ & & & I \\ -A_n & 0 & \dots & 0 \end{bmatrix}; \; C = (I \;\; 0 \; \dots \; 0]; \; \underline{w}(k) = \begin{bmatrix} B_1 - A_1 B_o \\ B_2 - A_2 B_o \\ \vdots \quad \vdots \\ B_m - A_m B_o \\ -A_n B_o \end{bmatrix} \underline{v}(k)$$

or $\underline{w}(k) = D\underline{v}(k)$ and $\underline{\varepsilon}(k) = B_o\underline{v}(k)$. Note that the process noise and measurement noise are correlated. By substituting the prediction error sequence $\{\overline{v}(k)\}$ of the Kalman filter for the white noise sequence $\{\underline{v}(k)\}$ we have the so-called innovation representation of the process.

(AR) Modelling and Kalman Filtering.

Consider the multivariate AR-(p) model

$$\underline{y}(k) = A_1\underline{y}(k-1) + \dots + A_p\underline{y}(k-p) + \underline{\varepsilon}(k), \qquad k = 1,\dots,n$$

where $\underline{y}(k) \in \mathbb{R}^m$ and $\underline{\varepsilon}(k)$ is white noise with covariance

$$\Sigma_\varepsilon = \sigma_\varepsilon^2 I.$$

The model can be rewritten as

$$\underline{y}_j(k) = a_{1,j}\underline{y}(k-1) + a_{2,j}\underline{y}(k-2) + \dots + a_{p,j}\underline{y}(k-p) + \underline{\varepsilon}_j(k),$$

$$j = 1,\dots,m$$

or

$$\underline{y}_j(k) = \underline{c}(k)\pi_j$$

where $\underline{c}(k) \triangleq (\underline{y}'(k-1),\ldots,\underline{y}'(k-p)$ and $\pi_j' = (a_{1,j},\ldots,a_{p,j})$ where $a_{i,j}$ denotes the j-th row of $A_i$. The AR model can be rewritten as m feature space models of the form

$$\pi_j(k+1) = \pi_j(k)$$
$$\underline{y}_j(k) = \underline{c}(k)\pi_j(k) + \underline{\varepsilon}(k), \qquad j = 1,\ldots,m.$$

The vector $\pi_j(k)$ can be estimated by the Kalman filtering procedure.

<u>State Space Modelling of Multivariate Time-Series.</u>

A rather new area - at least in econometrics - is the so-called state space modelling of stationary processes. The basic idea behind state space modelling is how to describe parsimoniously the relation between *past* (inputs or outputs) and *future* (outputs). As shown in chapter III, by the canonical correlation technique a stationary multivariate Gaussian time-series $\underline{y}(k) \in \mathbb{R}^p$ with zero mean can be modelled as the following stationary state space model

$$\underline{x}(k+1) = A\underline{x}(k) + \underline{w}(k)$$
$$\underline{y}(k) = C\underline{x}(k) + \underline{v}(k)$$

where the state vector $\underline{x}(k) \in \mathbb{R}^n$ is Gaussian with $\mathrm{cov}\{x(k)x'(k)\} = I$; $\underline{w}(k)$ is white noise with covariance $\Sigma_w = I - AA'$, and uncorrelated with $\underline{x}(k)$ and $\underline{v}(k)$ is white noise with covariance $\Sigma_v = R_o - CC'$ with $R_o = E\{\underline{y}(i)\underline{y}'(i)\}$. The state vector x(k) consists of the first n canonical variables of the past outputs. The matrices A and C can be calculated from a factorization of a finite generalized Hankel matrix by means of the canonical variables technique. In chapter III also the estimation of the state space model is discussed. A (MSE) predictor is given by $\underline{y}^p(k+1) = CA\underline{x}(k)$.

It would be interesting to compare state space modelling and prediction with the more 'classical' prediction methods in econometrics. See for a 'pre'-state space modelling of multivariate time-series Otter and Schuur (1982). For an extensive study of multivariate time-series analysis and system theory we refer to Aoki (1983).

## 6.5. Structural Modelling.

### ARX Modelling and Reduced Form.

Consider the structural ARX model

$$A_o\underline{y}(k) = A_1 y(k-1) + \ldots + A_p y(k-p) + B_o u(k) + \ldots$$

$$\ldots + B_q u(k-q) + \underline{\varepsilon}(k),$$

where $\underline{y}(k) \in \mathbb{R}^m$ is the output vector; $u(k) \in \mathbb{R}^s$ is a deterministic input vector and $\underline{\varepsilon}(k)$ is white noise with covariance $\Sigma_\varepsilon = \sigma^2 I$. The reduced form model is

$$\underline{y}(k) = \Pi_1 y(k-1) + \ldots + \Pi_p y(k-p) + \Pi_{p+1} u(k) + \ldots$$

$$\ldots + \Pi_{p+q+1} u(k-q) + \underline{w}(k),$$

where $\Pi_j = A_o^{-1} A_j$, $j = 1,\ldots,p$ and $\Pi_{p+i+1} = A_o^{-1} B_i$, $i = 0,\ldots,q$ and $\underline{w}(k) = A_o^{-1}\underline{\varepsilon}(k)$. It is assumed that $A_o^{-1}$ exists. The j-th structural equation can be rewritten as

$$\underline{y}_j(k) = (\underline{y}^j(k) U_j(k)) \begin{bmatrix} \gamma_j \\ \beta_j \end{bmatrix} + \underline{\varepsilon}_j(k), \qquad j = 1,\ldots,m$$

$$= \underline{Z}_j(k)\delta_j + \underline{\varepsilon}_j(k)$$

where $\underline{y}^j(k)$ is a $(1 \times m_j)$ vector of components of $\underline{y}(k)$ appearing in the j-th structural equation and $U_j(k)$ is a $(1 \times s_j)$ vector of components of $\{y(k-i),\ i=1,\ldots,p\}$ and $\{u(k-i),\ i=0,\ldots,q\}$.

The j-th reduced form equation can be rewritten as

$$\underline{y}_j(k) = U_j^*(k)\Pi_j + \underline{w}_j(k), \qquad j = 1,\ldots,m$$

where $U_j^*(k)$ is a $(1 \times s_j^*)$ vector of components of $\{y(k-i),\ i=1,\ldots,p\}$ and $\{u(k-i),\ i=0,\ldots,q\}$.

The j-th structural equation is in (LRF) form

$$\delta_j(k+1) = \delta_j(k)$$

$$\underline{y}_j(k) = \underline{Z}_j(k)\delta_j(k) + \underline{\varepsilon}_j(k).$$

This model contradicts the assumptions we have made for the LRF-model because $\mathrm{cov}\{\underline{Z}_j(k)\underline{\varepsilon}_j(k)\} \neq 0$, thus it is not allowed to apply the Kalman filter directly to this model. Following Tempelaar (1983) we can substitute $\hat{y}^j(k)$ for $\underline{y}^j(k)$ in $\underline{Z}_j(k)$ where $\hat{y}^j(k)$ is obtained by using the Kalman filter for the LRF-models

$$\pi_j(k+1) = \pi_j(k), \qquad j = 1,\dots,m$$

$$\underline{y}_j(k) = U_j^*(k)\pi_j(k) + \underline{w}(k)$$

thus $\hat{y}_j(k) = U_j^*(k)\hat{\pi}_j(k)$, where $\hat{\pi}_j(k)$ is generated by the filter. It is easily seen that the 'systematic' part $\hat{y}^j(k)$ is uncorrelated with $\underline{\varepsilon}_j(k)$, thus by substituting $\hat{y}^j(k)$ for $\underline{y}^j(k)$ in $\underline{Z}_j(k)$ in a second stage Kalman estimates $\{\hat{\delta}_j(k)\}$ can be computed for the structural model. An advantage of the above procedure is that also time-varying parameters in the structural model can be estimated.

State Space Modelling of Input-Output Processes.

Consider the stationary $\Sigma I/O$:

$$y(k) = \sum_{i=0}^{\infty} G_i u(k-i)$$

with output vector $y(k) \in \mathbb{R}^p$ and input vector $u(k) \in \mathbb{R}^q$ with $q \geqq p$. In econometrics this equation is called the final form equation. From section (3.6) we have that if the relation between past inputs and future outputs is finite dimensional then a state space realization exists with state vector $x \in \mathbb{R}^n$ where n is the rank of the Hankel matrix. However the observations are often noisy which makes it difficult to determine the rank of the Hankel matrix. The following procedure can be applied to obtain an *approximate* state space realization from a sample, see section (3.6): (i) Estimate by least-squares the impulse-response functions $\{G_i\}$, (ii) Form a finite Hankel matrix, (iii) Apply a SVD, (iv) obtain by the PHC-procedure an approximate balanced realization $\Sigma_{B,s}(A,B,C,D)$ where the first s singular values have been used, (v) Add stochastic components to the state equation and output equation in order to get a stationary LRF-model, (vi) Transform the LRF-model into the following PE-form as described in section (5.5):

$$\hat{\underline{x}}(k+1) = A\hat{\underline{x}}(k) + Bu(k) + K\underline{\varepsilon}(k)$$

$$y(k) = C\hat{\underline{x}}(k) + Du(k) + \underline{\varepsilon}(k)$$

where $\{\varepsilon(k)\}$ is an innovation sequence with covariance $\Sigma_\varepsilon$, (vii) 'Refine' the matrices A,B,C,D and estimate the gain K and $\Sigma_\varepsilon$ by using the PE-estimation method.
State space modelling is a new area in econometrics and it seems to be promising because of the parsimony in the description of relations.

## 6.6. Models with 'Unobservables'.

### Dynamic Factor Modelling.

In the chapters III and V it is shown that the linear structural model of Jöreskog is a static stationary LSF-model which can easily be extended to a dynamic version. The non-linear ML-estimation procedure of Jöreskog, called LISREL is a special case of the prediction error estimation method as discussed in chapter V, by considering the independent Gaussian outputs $\{y(j)\}$ as 'prediction errors'. Also procedures were given in chapter III in order to estimate the dimension of the factor space. By Kalman filtering the factor input and output vectors can be estimated and the prediction error estimation method gives under general conditions consistent ML-estimates.
In the author's opinion dynamic factor modelling might be important for econometrics because a more parsimonious description of input-output relations may be obtained and also for applications in other social sciences, e.g. in psychology because of its *dynamic* aspects (either in space or time). See Jöreskog (1977) for applications in psychology.

### Robinson's Model with Unobservables.

Robinson (1977) considers the following static model with unobservables

process equation:

$$\underline{x}(k) = Bu(k) + \underline{w}(k)$$

output equation:

$$\underline{y}(k) = C\underline{x}(k) + Du(k) + \underline{v}(k)$$

where $\underline{x}(k) \in \mathbb{R}^H$ is a vector of unobservables; $u(k) = (u_1'(k)u_2'(k)u_3'(k))' \in \mathbb{R}^{L+\overline{P}+Q}$ is a vector of deterministic inputs; $B = (B_1:B_2:0)$; $D = (D_1:0:D_3)$, $\{\underline{w}(k)\}$ and $\{\underline{v}(k)\}$ are white noise sequences. It is easily seen that the model is a static stationary (LSF) model with as feature vector the vector of unobservables.

Models with 'Errors-in-Variables'.

As we have seen in chapter III the output equation of the (LSF) model and (LRF) model is

$$\begin{bmatrix} \underline{y}(k) \\ \underline{u}(k) \end{bmatrix} = \begin{bmatrix} C_y(k) & 0 \\ 0 & C_u(k) \end{bmatrix} \begin{bmatrix} \underline{x}_y(k) \\ \underline{x}_u(k) \end{bmatrix} + \begin{bmatrix} D_1(k) \\ D_2(k) \end{bmatrix} u_2(k) + \begin{bmatrix} \underline{v}_1(k) \\ \underline{v}_2(k) \end{bmatrix}$$

where $\underline{y}(k) \in \mathbb{R}^p$ is the observed output and $\underline{u}(k) \in \mathbb{R}^q$ is the observed input; $\underline{x}_y(k)$ and $\underline{x}_u(k)$ are respectively the (unobservable) feature output vector and $\underline{x}_u(k)$ the (unobservable) feature input vector. $u_2(k)$ is a deterministic input vector and $\underline{v}_1(k)$ and $\underline{v}_2(k)$ are *measurement* white noise vectors. Let $C_y(k) \equiv I$ and $C_u(k) \equiv I$; $D_1(k) \equiv 0$ and $D_2(k) \equiv 0$; $\underline{x}_y(k) = \overline{\underline{y}}(k)$, the 'true' (unobservable) output vector without measurement noise and $\underline{x}_u(k) = \overline{\underline{u}}(k)$ the 'true' unobservable input vector without measurement noise. The process equation of the 'true' input-output vector is

$$\begin{bmatrix} A_{o,1} & A_{o,2} \\ 0 & I \end{bmatrix} \begin{bmatrix} \overline{\underline{y}}(k+1) \\ \overline{\underline{u}}(k+1) \end{bmatrix} = \begin{bmatrix} A_{1,1} & A_{1,2} \\ 0 & A_{1,3} \end{bmatrix} \begin{bmatrix} \overline{\underline{y}}(k) \\ \overline{\underline{u}}(k) \end{bmatrix} + \begin{bmatrix} B_1 \\ B_2 \end{bmatrix} u_1(k) + \begin{bmatrix} \underline{w}_1(k) \\ \underline{w}_2(k) \end{bmatrix}$$

where $u_1(k) \in \mathbb{R}^m$ is an observable input vector and $\underline{w}_1(k)$ and $\underline{w}_2(k)$ are process noise vectors. The complete model is again a (LSF) model with as feature vector the vector of true input and output variables which can be estimated by the Kalman filter, when $A_{o,1} = I$ and $A_{o,2} = 0$.

Example (6.2):

Mehra (1976) considers the following 'errors-in-variables' model

$$\underline{y}(k) = \alpha + \beta\underline{x}(k) + \underline{\delta}(k), \qquad k = 1,2,...$$

where $\underline{y}(k)$ is a Gaussian observable random variable; $\underline{x}(k)$ is an unobservable Gaussian random variable from a population with mean $\mu$ and covariance $\sigma_x^2$; $\underline{\delta}(k)$ is white noise with covariance $\sigma_\delta^2$ and uncorrelated with $\underline{x}(k)$. The variable $\underline{x}(k)$ is measured with error, i.e.

$$\underline{z}(k) = \underline{x}(k) + \underline{\varepsilon}(k),$$

where $\underline{\varepsilon}(k)$ is white noise with covariance $\sigma_\varepsilon^2$. The two equations can be written as the output equation of a (LRF) model i.e.

$$\begin{bmatrix} \underline{y}(k) \\ \underline{z}(k) \end{bmatrix} = \begin{bmatrix} \beta \\ 1 \end{bmatrix} \underline{x}(k) + \begin{bmatrix} \alpha \\ 0 \end{bmatrix} + \begin{bmatrix} \underline{\delta}(k) \\ \underline{\varepsilon}(k) \end{bmatrix}$$

or

$$\underline{Y}(k) = C\underline{x}(k) + D + \underline{v}(k)$$

Now $E\{\underline{Y}(k)\} = \mu_Y = C\mu + D$ and $\mathrm{cov}\{\underline{Y}(k)\underline{Y}'(k)\} = \Sigma = \sigma_x^2 CC' + \Sigma_v$ where it is assumed that $\underline{\delta}(k)$ and $\underline{\varepsilon}(k)$ are uncorrelated. Following Rothenberg (1971) we have that the six unknowns $\alpha,\beta,\mu,\sigma_\varepsilon^2,\sigma_\delta^2$ and $\sigma_x^2$ are not identifiable from $\mu_Y$ and $\Sigma$. More specific we have the following five equations with six unknowns; $\mu_z = \mu$, $\mu_y = \alpha + \beta\mu$, $\sigma_z^2 = \sigma_x^2 + \sigma_\varepsilon^2$, $\sigma_y^2 = \beta^2\sigma_x^2 + \sigma_\delta^2$ and $\sigma_{zy} = \beta\sigma_x^2$.
Assume now that $\underline{x}(k)$ is generated by a first order Markov process, thus the process equation is

$$\underline{x}(k+1) = \phi\underline{x}(k) + \underline{w}(k)$$

with initial state $x(0) \sim N(\mu,\sigma_x^2)$ and where $|\phi| < 1$.
The stationary covariance is $\sigma_x^2 = \phi^2\sigma_x^2 + \sigma_w^2$. The sequence $\{\underline{x}(k),\underline{z}(k)\}$ is stationary. Define $c(i) \triangleq E\{\underline{z}(k)\underline{z}(k+i)\}$, $i = 0,1,2,...$ with consistent estimates $\hat{c}(i) = (1/N)\sum_{k=1}^{N-i} z(k)z(k+i)$. Now $c(0) = \sigma_z^2 = \sigma_x^2 + \sigma_\varepsilon^2$; $c(1) = \phi\sigma_x^2,...,c(k) = \phi^k\sigma_x^2$ thus $\phi = c(2)/c(1)$; $\sigma_x^2 = c^2(1)/c(2)$; $\sigma_\varepsilon^2 = c(0) - c^2(1)/c(2)$ and $\sigma_w^2 = (1/c(2))(c^2(1)-c^2(2))$; $\sigma_x^2,\phi,\sigma_\varepsilon^2$ and $\sigma_w^2$

can be obtained from the autocovariance function of z(k). Once $\sigma_x^2$ and $\sigma_\varepsilon^2$ can be identified, $\alpha,\beta,\mu,\sigma_\delta^2$ are also identifiable. By imposing a *dynamic* structure the parameters are identifiable. The (LRF) model is

$$\underline{x}(k+1) = \phi\underline{x}(k) + \underline{w}(k)$$

$$\underline{Y}(k) = C\underline{x}(k) + D + \underline{v}(k)$$

with initial condition $\underline{x}(0) \sim N(\mu,\sigma_x^2)$.

Rational Expectations.

In Wallis (1980) an econometric model is described, in which the output vector $\underline{y}(k) \in \mathbb{R}^m$ is linearly related to an observable input $u(k) \in \mathbb{R}^p$ and an (unobservable) prediction of y(k), denoted by y*(k), of the economic agents, using the information $\Omega(k-1) = \{y(k-1),y(k-2),u(k-1),...\}$ with $y^*(k) = E\{\underline{y}(k)|\Omega(k-1)\}$. The reduced form model is

$$\underline{y}(k) = Cy^*(k) + Du(k) + \underline{\varepsilon}(k).$$

The prediction y*(k) is subject to adaptation and modelled as

$$y^*(k+1) - y^*(k) = (I-A)[y(k)-y^*(k)]$$

or

$$y^*(k+1) = Ay^*(k) + By(k)$$

with B = (I-A). It is easily seen that the expectation model is a stationary (LRF) model with as feature vector the prediction y*(k), namely

process equation:

$$y^*(k+1) = Ay^*(k) + By(k)$$

output equation:

$$\underline{y}(k) = Cy^*(k) + Du(k) + \underline{\varepsilon}(k),$$

where y(k) is *deterministic* in the process equation. y*(k) can be estimated by the Kalman filtering procedure.

Geweke's Permanent Income Model.

Geweke (1981) considers the model

$$c_i(k) = c_i(z^{-1})Z(k) + \underline{\varepsilon}_i(k)$$

$$\underline{y}(k) = Z(k) + \underline{\delta}(k)$$

where $c_i(k)$ is the aggregate expenditures on good i, i = 1,...,N in constant prices; Z(k) is the unobserved permanent income at time k, whereas y(k) is the observed income; $\underline{\varepsilon}_i(k)$ and $\delta(k)$ are white noise components to be interpreted as transitory expenditure and transitory income respectively $c_i(z^{-1})$, i = 1,...,N are polynomials in the lag operator $z^{-1}$ with maximum degree p.

The above model can be rewritten as the following output equation of a (LRF) model with as feature vector the vector of (lagged) unobservable permanent incomes, i.e. $x'(k) = (Z(k),\ldots,Z(k-p))$

$$\begin{bmatrix} c_1(k) \\ c_2(k) \\ \vdots \\ c_N(k) \\ \underline{y}(k) \end{bmatrix} = \begin{bmatrix} c_{11} & \cdots\cdots & c_{1p} \\ c_{21} & \cdots\cdots & c_{2p} \\ \vdots & & \vdots \\ c_{N1} & \cdots\cdots & c_{Np} \\ 1 & 0 \ldots & 0 \end{bmatrix} \begin{bmatrix} Z(k) \\ Z(k-1) \\ \vdots \\ Z(k-p) \\ \phantom{0} \end{bmatrix} + \begin{bmatrix} \underline{\varepsilon}_1(k) \\ \vdots \\ \vdots \\ \underline{\varepsilon}_N(k) \\ \underline{\delta}(k) \end{bmatrix}$$

or

$$\underline{Y}(k) = Cx(k) + \underline{v}(k).$$

A dynamical evolution of the permanent income could be

$$\begin{bmatrix} Z(k+1) \\ Z(k) \\ \vdots \\ Z(k-p+1) \end{bmatrix} = \begin{bmatrix} a_{11} & \cdots\cdots & a_{1p} \\ 1 & \cdots\cdots & 0 \\ \vdots & & \vdots \\ 0 & \ldots\ 1 & 0 \end{bmatrix} \begin{bmatrix} Z(k) \\ Z(k-1) \\ \vdots \\ Z(k-p) \end{bmatrix} + \begin{bmatrix} b_1 \\ 0 \\ \vdots \\ 0 \end{bmatrix} y(k)$$

or

$$x(k+1) = Ax(k) + By(k), \qquad \text{initial condition } x(0) = y(0)$$

where y(k) is the observed income.

Avery's Monetary Policy Model.

Avery (1979) considers a policy model in which a policy variable is considered to be an unobservable. The model is actually a simple static (LSF) model, namely,

$$\underline{y}^*(k) = \gamma u(k) + \underline{\varepsilon}(k), \qquad k = 1,\ldots,N$$

$$\underline{z}(k) = \beta \underline{y}^*(k) + \underline{v}(k)$$

where $\underline{y}^*(k)$ is the unobservable policy variable; $u(k)$ is a $(K \times 1)$ vector of deterministic inputs called causal variables; $\underline{z}(k)$ is a $(m \times 1)$ vector of outputs called indicator variables and $\underline{\varepsilon}(k)$ and $\underline{v}(k)$ are white noise components. In chapter VII it is seen that for the general (LRF) model optimal control algorithms exist.

# VII. Self-Tuning Control

## 7.1. Introduction.

In control literature there is a growing interest in adaptive control procedures. Adaptive control deals with the question of how to control (regulate) an 'uncertain' system, uncertain in the sense that its structure is unknown or changing over time and/or its model parameters are unknown. According to Kreiselmeier (1983) there are two approaches; the indirect one and the direct one, also called model reference approach. In the indirect approach the unknown model parameters are identified (estimated) and the current parameter estimates are used to update the control parameters. The term 'indirect' means that the control parameters are not adapted directly but indirectly through the model parameter estimates. The indirect approach is referred to as self-tuning or self-optimizing adaptive control and is subject of this study. In the model reference approach, the parameters of a suitably chosen controller structure are adapted directly in such a way that the output follows the output of a prespecified reference model. See for references e.g. Åström (1973), Goodwin (1981), Kendrick (1981), Saridis (1977), Landau (1974), Monopoli (1974) and Åström (1983).
For the single-input single-output case there is some progress in deriving stable control identification procedures, see. e.g. Goodwin (1981), but according to Isermann (1982) there is 'a big field to be developed for the multivariable case'. Aim of all control, adaptive or not, is to bring the output of a system 'close' to a prespecified output, indicated by the stability of the so-called closed loop system. Unfortunately an analytic study of the stability of closed loop systems in case of adaptive controllers is rather difficult because the control identification procedures result in non-linear closed loop systems, see e.g. Åström (1973).

In this chapter the following approach is discussed; if for a model with *known* parameters the application of a (optimal) controller results in a stable closed loop (CL) system and if the adaptive estimated controller, in which the parameters are replaced by parameter estimates, converges to the controller, then the (CL)-system is asymptotically stable. The study involves therefore the following steps: (i) a study of optimal controllers, which, for a model with known parameters, results in a stable (CL) system and (ii) studying the convergence of the estimated controller. This convergence is known as the self-tuning property of the adaptive controller. From optimal control theory it is known that for the state space model or in our terms the (LRF) model the so-called linear quadratic Gaussian (LQG) control is optimal and results in a stable (CL) system, provided that the model parameters are known, see e.g. Bertsekas (1976) or Kwakernaak (1972). A brief summary of the main LQG algorithms is given in section 7.2 together with minimum variance (MV) control algorithms in section 7.3. In section 7.5 the question of estimation in closed loop is discussed, because identifiability and estimation problems may occur, when applying linear closed loop controllers. In section 7.6 the self-tuning property of the adaptive versions of the LQG controller and MV controller is discussed and the two adaptive controllers are applied to a small macro-economic model of the US economy in section 7.7.

## 7.2. Linear Quadratic Gaussian (LQG) Control.

Consider the stationary (LRF) model

$$\underline{x}(k+1) = A\underline{x}(k) + Bu(k) + \underline{w}(k)$$
$$\underline{y}(k) = C\underline{x}(k) + \underline{v}(k), \qquad k = 0,1,\ldots,N-1$$

with initial state $\underline{x}(0) \sim N(\mu_x(0),\Sigma_x(0))$. The feature vector (target vector) $x(k) \in \mathbb{R}^n$ has to be controlled towards zero by means of the unconstrained control vector $u(k) \in \mathbb{R}^m$. The observable output vector is $y(k) \in \mathbb{R}^p$ and $\{\underline{w}(k)\}$ and $\{\underline{v}(k)\}$ are white noise processes uncorrelated with the initial state with covariances respectively $\Sigma_w$ and $\Sigma_v$, where it is assumed that $\Sigma_v^{-1}$ exists. It is further assumed that the pair (A,B) is controllable; the pair (A,C) is uniformly completely stochastically reconstructable and the pair $(A,\sqrt{\Sigma_w})$ is uniformly completely stochastically controllable.

Aim is to minimize the following cost functional

$$J_1 = E\{\underline{x}'(N)Q\underline{x}'(N) + \sum_{k=0}^{N-1}(\underline{x}'(k)Q\underline{x}(k) + u'(k)Ru(k))\}$$

where $Q = Q'$ is a positive semidefinite weighting matrix; $R = R' > \varepsilon I$ is a weighting matrix with $\varepsilon$ positive. From Bertsekas (1976) we have the following result. Under the assumption that the pair (A,F) is controllable where $Q = F'F$ the optimal control equation or controller, which stabilizes the (LRF) model is given by

$$u^*(k) = -L(k)\hat{x}(k)$$

where the gain

$$L(k) = (R+B'K(k+1)B)^{-1}B'K(k+1)A$$

K(k+1) is the solution of the Riccati equation

$$K(k) = A'[K(k+1)-K(k+1)B(R+B'K(k+1)B)^{-1}B'K(k+1)]A + Q$$

with terminal condition $K(N) = Q$; $\hat{x}(k)$ is the conditional mean of $\underline{x}(k)$ generated by the Kalman filter.

Remark: When x(k) is observable, that is $y(k) \equiv x(k)$ then $\hat{x}(k)$ is replaced by x(k).

Steady State Solution.

It is shown by Bertsekas that under the conditions given before, the controller tends to the following one, with a time invariant gain, called the steady state solution, which minimizes the criterion

$$J_2 = \lim_{N\to\infty} N^{-1} E\{\sum_{k=0}^{N-1}(x'(k)Qx(k)+u'(k)Ru(k))\}$$

namely

$$u_s^*(k) = -L\hat{x}(k)$$

where the gain

$$L = (R+B'KB)^{-1}B'KA$$

and K is the solution of the algebraic Riccati equation (ARE)

$$K = A'(K-KB(R+B'KB)^{-1}B'K)A + Q$$

The conditional mean $\hat{x}(k)$ is generated by the steady state Kalman filtering equations

$$\hat{x}(k+1) = (A+BL)\hat{x}(k) + \bar{\Sigma}C'\Sigma_v^{-1}(y(k+1)-C(A+BL)\hat{x}(k))$$

where

$$\bar{\Sigma} = \Sigma - \Sigma C'(C\Sigma C'+\Sigma_v)^{-1}C\Sigma.$$

$\Sigma$ is the solution of the algebraic Riccati equation

$$\Sigma = A(\Sigma-\Sigma C'(C\Sigma C'+\Sigma_v)^{-1}C\Sigma)A' + \Sigma_w$$

Stability of the Closed Loop System.

Aim of the control algorithms is to stabilize the system, which can be studied by considering the so-called closed loop (CL) system. The (CL) system can be obtained by substituting the controller into the process model. Consider the (LRF) model with an observable feature vector $x(k) \in \mathbb{R}^n$

$$\underline{x}(k+1) = A\underline{x}(k) + Bu(k) + \underline{w}(k).$$

From the foregoing we have that the steady state (LQG) controller is given by

$$\underline{u}(k) = -L\underline{x}(k)$$

where the gain

$$L \triangleq (R+B'KB)^{-1}B'KA$$

and K is the solution of the algebraic Riccati equation given before. Substitution of the controller into the right-hand side of the (LRF) model yields the (CL) system

$$\underline{x}(k+1) = (A-BL)\underline{x}(k) + \underline{w}(k),$$

The stability of the (CL) system depends on the stability of the matrix (A-BL). It can be proved, see Bertsekas (1976), that the matrix (A-BL) is a stable matrix, i.e., $\lim_{k \to \infty} (A-BL)^k = 0$.

A (LRF) Model with Uncontrollable Input and Non-Zero Reference Trajectory.

The (LRF) model given above is not the most suitable model for economic applications and needs some respecification by partitioning the input vector into a controllable and uncontrollable part. Consider the following (LRF) model with observable target vector $x(k) \in \mathbb{R}^n$

$$\underline{x}(k+1) = A\underline{x}(k) + Bu(k) + C\underline{\bar{u}}(k+1) + \underline{\tilde{w}}(k)$$

with initial state x(0). The unconstrained control vector is $u(k) \in \mathbb{R}^m$ and $\underline{\bar{u}}(k) \in \mathbb{R}^s$ is an uncontrollable Gaussian input vector called *exogenous noise* uncorrelated with $\underline{\tilde{w}}(k)$. Assume the following Markov process for $\underline{\bar{u}}(k)$

$$\underline{\bar{u}}(k+1) = T\underline{\bar{u}}(k) + \underline{\varepsilon}(k),$$

with initial state $\bar{u}(0)$ and where $\underline{\varepsilon}(k)$ is white noise with covariance $\Sigma_\varepsilon$. Let the reference trajectory be given by

$$x^*(k+1) = Gx^*(k)$$

with initial state x*(0). The three equations can be written, following Engwerda (1982), as the following (LRF) model

$$\begin{bmatrix} I & 0 & -0 \\ 0 & I & 0 \\ 0 & 0 & I \end{bmatrix} \begin{bmatrix} \underline{x}(k+1) \\ x^*(k+1) \\ \underline{\bar{u}}(k+1) \end{bmatrix} = \begin{bmatrix} A & 0 & 0 \\ 0 & G & 0 \\ 0 & 0 & T \end{bmatrix} \begin{bmatrix} \underline{x}(k) \\ x^*(k) \\ \underline{\bar{u}}(k) \end{bmatrix} + \begin{bmatrix} B \\ 0 \\ 0 \end{bmatrix} u(k) + \begin{bmatrix} \underline{\tilde{w}}(k) \\ 0 \\ \underline{\varepsilon}(k) \end{bmatrix}$$

or

$$\underline{z}(k+1) = \tilde{A}\underline{z}(k) + \tilde{B}u(k) + \underline{w}(k)$$

where

$$\tilde{A} = \begin{bmatrix} A & 0 & CT \\ 0 & G & 0 \\ 0 & 0 & T \end{bmatrix} : \tilde{B} = \begin{bmatrix} B \\ 0 \\ 0 \end{bmatrix}$$

with initial state $z'(0) = (x'(0)x'^*(0)\bar{u}'(0))$.

Consider the steady state cost functional

$$J_3 = \min_{U(\infty)} \lim_{N\to\infty} N^{-1} E\{\sum_{k=0}^{N-1} (\underline{z}'(k) \begin{bmatrix} I \\ -I \\ 0 \end{bmatrix} Q(I-I0)\underline{z}(k) + \underline{u}'(k)R\underline{u}(k))\}$$

with $Q = Q'$ positive semidefinite and $R = R' > \varepsilon I$ where $U(\infty) \triangleq$ $\triangleq (\underline{u}'(0),\underline{u}'(1),\ldots,\underline{u}'(\infty))$. From the preceeding section we have that under the conditions given the steady state control law is given by

$$\underline{u}_s^*(k) = -L\underline{z}(k)$$

where

$$L = (R+\tilde{B}'K\tilde{B})^{-1}\tilde{B}'K\tilde{A}$$

K is the positive definite solution of the Riccati equation (ARE)

$$K = \tilde{A}'[K-K\tilde{B}(R+\tilde{B}'K\tilde{B})^{-1}\tilde{B}'K]\tilde{A} + \tilde{Q}$$

where $\tilde{Q} \triangleq \begin{bmatrix} I \\ -I \\ 0 \end{bmatrix} Q(I-I0)$. It is assumed that the pair $(\tilde{A},F)$ is controllable where $\tilde{Q} = F'F$. By suitable matrix partitioning we have

$$\underline{u}_s^*(k) = L_1\underline{x}(k) + L_2x^*(k) + L_3\underline{\bar{u}}(k)$$

where

$$L_1 = -(B'K_{11}B+R)^{-1}B'K_{11}A$$

$$L_2 = -(B'K_{11}B+R)^{-1}B'K_{12}G$$

$$L_3 = -(B'K_{11}B+R)^{-1}B'[K_{11}CT+K_{13}T]$$

$K_{11}$ is the solution of the matrix Riccati equation

$$K_{11} = A'[K_{11}-K_{11}B(R+B'K_{11}B)^{-1}B'K_{11}]A + Q$$

and $K_{12}$ and $K_{13}$ are solutions of a matrix equation of the form $AXB + C = X$ with known A, B and C, i.e.

$$K_{12} = A'[K_{12}-K_{11}B(R+B'K_{11}B)^{-1}B'K_{12}]G - Q$$

$$K_{13} = A'[K_{11}-K_{11}B(R+B'K_{11}B)^{-1}B'K_{11}]CT + A'[K_{13}-K_{11}B(R+ +B'K_{11}B)^{-1}B'K_{13}]T$$

It is easily seen that the pair $(\tilde{A},\tilde{B})$ is not controllable. Following Kwakernaak (1972, theorem 6.11) we have that (i) if the pair (A,B) is controllable and (ii) the moduli of G and T are strictly less than one then the (CL) system is stable. In general the above conditions seem to be too severe for economic applications which is further illustrated in section 7.7.

Remark: The ARMAX model

$$\underline{x}(k+1) = Ax(k) + A_1x(k-1),\ldots,A_px(k-p) + B\underline{u}(k) + B_1u(k-1) + \ldots$$
$$\ldots + B_qu(k-q) + C_o\bar{u}(k+1),\ldots,C_{r+1}\bar{u}(k-r) + \underline{\varepsilon}(k)$$

in which x(k+1) is the target vector; u(k) the control vector and $\bar{u}(k+1)$ an uncontrollable input vector can be written as the following (LRF) model with uncontrollable input, i.e.

$$\underline{x}(k+1) = Ax(k) + B\underline{u}(k) + C\tilde{u}(k+1) + \underline{\varepsilon}(k)$$

where $C \triangleq (A_1,\ldots,A_p,B_1,\ldots,B_q,C_o,\ldots,C_{r+1})$ and $\tilde{u}'(k+1) \triangleq (x'(k-1),\ldots$ $\ldots,x'(k-p),u'(k-1),\ldots,u'(k-q),\bar{u}'(k+1),\ldots,\bar{u}'(k-r))$.

## 7.3. Minimum Variance (MV) Control.

Consider the (LRF) model with observable target feature vector $x(k) \in \mathbb{R}^n$

$$\underline{x}(k+1) = Ax(k) + B\underline{u}(k) + C\bar{u}(k+1) + \underline{w}(k), \qquad k = 0,1,2,\ldots$$

with initial state x(0). The control vector $u(k) \in \mathbb{R}^m$ with $m \leqq n$ and $\bar{u}(k+1) \in \mathbb{R}^p$ is deterministic exogenous noise assumed to be known in period k. The white noise vector $\underline{w}(k)$ is assumed to be uncorrelated with $\underline{x}(k)$. It is further assumed that the rank of B equals m.
Consider the one-period ahead cost functional

$$J^*(k+1|k) = \min_{u(k)} E\{(\underline{x}(k+1)-x^*(k+1))'Q(\underline{x}(k+1)-x^*(k+1)) + u'(k)Ru(k)\}, \qquad k = 0,1,2,\ldots$$

given $x(k),\ldots,u(k-1),\ldots,\bar{u}(k+1),\bar{u}(k),\ldots$ .
It is assumed that either $Q = Q' \geqq 0$ and $R = R' > 0$ or $Q = Q' > 0$ and

$R = R' \geqq 0$.

Using Åström's Lemma 3.1, Åstrom (1970), we have that the cost functional is minimized by the following controller, referred to as (MV) controller

$$u_{mv}(k) = -(B'QB+R)^{-1}B'Q[Ax(k)+C\bar{u}(k+1)-x^*(k+1)].$$

Note that the Hessian $B'QB + R$ is positive definite. If $Q = I$ and $R = 0$ the (MV) controller reduces to

$$\tilde{u}_{mv}(k) = -B^+[Ax(k)+C\bar{u}(k+1)-x^*(k+1)]$$

where $B^+ \triangleq (B'B)^{-1}B'$ is a generalized inverse of B. This controller will be used in a simulation study to be discussed in section 7.7. Note that $B^+ = B^{-1}$ if the dimension of $u(k)$ equals the dimension of the feature vector $x(k)$, i.e., $m = n$. See for a generalization of this case Grimble (1981).

Stability of the (MV) controller with $Q = I$ and $R = 0$.

In order to study the stability of the (CL) system the process equation is transformed into the so-called *echelon canonical form*. From Wonham (1974, theorem 5.4) we have that if the pair (A,B) is controllable, with $r(B) = m$ then there exists a non-singular transformation matrix S, such that $\tilde{A} = SAS^{-1}$ and $\tilde{B} = SB$ with

$$\tilde{A} \triangleq \begin{bmatrix} \begin{matrix} k_1 \end{matrix} & \begin{bmatrix} 0 & 1 & 0 & & & \cdots & & & & 0 \\ & & \ddots & & & & & & & \\ 0 & \cdot & \cdot & 1 & 0 & \cdots & & & & 0 \\ * & * & * & * & & \cdots & & * & * & * \end{bmatrix} \\ k_2 & \begin{bmatrix} 0 & \cdot & \cdot & \cdot & 0 & 1 & 0 & \cdots & & 0 \\ & & & & & & \ddots & & & \\ 0 & \cdot & \cdot & \cdot & & 0 & 1 & 0 & \cdots & 0 \\ * & * & * & * & \cdots & * & * & & * & * & * \end{bmatrix} \\ & \vdots \\ k_m & \begin{bmatrix} 0 & & \cdots & & & 0 & 1 & 0 \\ & & & & & & & \ddots \\ 0 & & & \cdots & & & 0 & 1 \\ * & * & * & * & \cdots & * & * & \cdots & * & * & * \end{bmatrix} \end{bmatrix} \qquad \tilde{B} \triangleq \begin{bmatrix} 0 & 0 & \cdots & 0 \\ \vdots & & & \\ 0 & & & \\ 1 & 0 & & \\ 0 & & & \\ \vdots & & & \vdots \\ & 0 & & \\ 0 & 1 & 0 & \\ & & & \\ \vdots & & & \\ & & & \\ 0 & 0 & \cdots & 1 \end{bmatrix}$$

where $k_1 \geq k_2 \geq k \geq \dots \geq k_m \geq 1$ with $k_1 + k_2 + \dots + k_m = n$ are the Kronecker indices of A and B and * denotes a 'free' parameter. The transformation of the (LRF) model with $\tilde{x}(k+1) = Sx(k)$ leads to

$$\underline{\tilde{x}}(k+1) = \tilde{A}\underline{\tilde{x}}(k) + \tilde{B}\underline{u}(k) + SC\bar{u}(k) + S\underline{w}(k).$$

Substitution of the (MV) controller for the *transformed* model (the MV controller with $Q = S'S$ for the *original* model) into the above equation yields

$$\underline{\tilde{x}}(k+1) = F\underline{\tilde{x}}(k) + \tilde{M}SC\bar{u}(k+1) + \tilde{B}\tilde{B}^{+}Sx^{*}(k+1) + S\underline{w}(k),$$

where $F \triangleq (I-\tilde{B}\tilde{B}^{+})\tilde{A}$ and $\tilde{M} \triangleq (I-\tilde{B}\tilde{B}^{+})$.
By simple calculation it can be shown that

$$F = \mathrm{diag}(D_1,\dots,D_m)$$

is nilpotent of order n, i.e. $F^n = 0$, where

$$\underset{(k_i \times k_i)}{D_i} \triangleq \begin{bmatrix} 0 & 1 & 0 & \dots & 0 \\ \vdots & & \ddots & & \vdots \\ \vdots & & & \ddots & 0 \\ & & & & 1 \\ 0 & & \dots\dots & & 0 \end{bmatrix}$$

and $\tilde{M} = \bar{I}$, where $\bar{I}$ is the 'identity' matrix with $k_i$-th diagonal element equal to zero. Transforming the above (CL) system back yields

$$\underline{x}(k+1) = S^{-1}FS\underline{x}(k) + S^{-1}\bar{I}SC\bar{u}(k+1) + x^{*}(k+1) -$$

$$- S^{-1}\bar{I}Sx^{*}(k+1) + \underline{w}(k).$$

From the (CL) system we can draw the following conclusions:

(i) The (CL) system is BIBO stable, if the exogenous noise sequence $\{\bar{u}(k+1)\}$ and the reference trajectory $\{x^{*}(k+1)\}$ are bounded.

(ii) Without exogenous noise and reference trajectory, any initial state can be controlled towards zero within n steps.

(iii) If the dimension of the control vector equals n, i.e. $m = n$ then $\bar{I}$ is zero and the expected output equals after n stages the reference value. If however $m < n$ the expected value is after n steps a linear combination of the exogenous noise $\{\bar{u}(k+1)\}$ and reference trajectory $\{x^*(k+1)\}$. The weighting matrix $S^{-1}\bar{I}S$ is 'increasing' with m decreasing, i.e. the less the number of controls the more the output is influenced by the exogenous noise.

## 7.4. Duality of Estimation (Filtering) and Control.

From chapter IV we have seen that the steady state Kalman prediction equation for the stationary (LRF) model

$$\underline{x}(k+1) = A\underline{x}(k) + \underline{w}(k)$$
$$\underline{y}(k) = C\underline{x}(k) + \underline{v}(k)$$

is given by the equation

$$\hat{x}(k+1|k) = A\hat{x}(k|k-1) + A\Sigma C'(C\Sigma C'+\Sigma_v)^{-1}[y(k)-C\hat{x}(k|k-1)]$$

where the steady state covariance matrix $\Sigma$ is the solution of the matrix Riccati equation

$$\Sigma = A[\Sigma-\Sigma C'(C\Sigma C'+\Sigma_v)^{-1}C\Sigma]A' + \Sigma_w$$

provided that the pair (A,C) is stochastically reconstructable.
From the previous sections it is seen that for the stationary (LRF) model with observable feature vector x(k),

$$\underline{x}(k+1) = A\underline{x}(k) + Bu(k) + \underline{w}(k)$$

the steady state optimal control is given by

$$u(k) = -(B'KB+R)^{-1}B'KAx(k),$$

where K is the solution of the matrix Riccati equation

$$K = A'[K-KB(B'KB+R)^{-1}B'K]A + Q$$

The filtering and control problem are related in the following way:

| Filtering | Control |
|---|---|
| $\Sigma$ | K |
| A | A' |
| C' | B |
| $\Sigma_v$ | R |
| $\Sigma_w$ | Q |
| reconstructability | controllability |
| (time-varying) gain | control vector |
| error equation | (CL) system |

The duality of filtering and control can be used in designing numerical procedures for control and filtering (estimation). The 'duals' of the MV control algorithm are the generalized least squares (GLS) if $Q > 0$ and $R = 0$ and the Ridge estimator if $Q = I$ and $R > 0$, see Vinod (1978). It is worthwhile to study the duality of (i) stable control procedures and parameter consistency; (ii) of robust control and robust estimation; (iii) of stable Ridge estimators and stable controllers. A more systematic approach of duality can be found in Kwakernaak (1972), Kalman and Bucy (1961) or Åström (1970).

## 7.5. Estimation in Closed Loop.

From the previous sections we have seen that for the (LRF) model

$$\underline{x}(k+1) = A\underline{x}(k) + B\underline{u}(k) + C\bar{u}(k+1) + \underline{w}(k)$$

the (MV) controller and the steady state (LQG) controller are linear functions of the observed outputs, inputs and reference values. The controllers are of the closed loop type, that is, they are functions of the observed outputs. For instance the (MV) controller with $Q = I$ and $R = 0$ is given by the equation

$$\underline{u}_{mv}(k) = F_1\underline{x}(k) + F_2\bar{u}(k+1) + F_3x^*(k+1)$$

where $F_1 = -B^+A$, $F_2 = -B^+C$ and $F_3 = B^+$.
Substitution of the controller into the model yields the (CL) system

$$\underline{x}(k+1) = (A+BF_1)x(k) + (C+BF_2)\bar{u}(k+1) + BF_3x^*(k+1) + \underline{w}(k)$$

$$= G_1x(k) + G_2\bar{u}(k+1) + G_3x^*(k+1) + \underline{w}(k).$$

The conditional probability density function of $\underline{x}(k+1)$ given $x(k)$, $\bar{u}(k+1)$ and $x^*(k+1)$ is Gaussian with conditional mean

$$E\{\underline{x}(k+1) \mid x(k),\bar{u}(k+1),x^*(k+1)\} = G_1x(k) + G_2\bar{u}(k+1) + G_3x^*(k+1).$$

According to the identifiability definition given in chapter V, the parameter identifiability problem is to derive the process parameters $\{A,B,C\}$ uniquely from the reduced form parameters $\{G_1,G_2,G_3\}$ which can be obtained from the external inputs $x(k)$, $\bar{u}(k+1)$ or $x^*(k+1)$.
By considering the model and controller as one structural model, called the structural closed loop (SCL) model, in which the output target vector $x(k+1)$ and control vector are considered to be output vectors (endogenous) vectors the identifiability problem can be studied in the usual econometric way, see for details Otter (1981b). In system theory this is known as the *joint input/output* method, see e.g. Phadke and Wu (1974).
For the above case we have as (SCL) model

$$\begin{bmatrix} I & -B \\ 0 & I \end{bmatrix} \begin{bmatrix} \underline{x}(k+1) \\ \underline{u}_{mv}(k) \end{bmatrix} = \begin{bmatrix} A \\ F_1 \end{bmatrix} \underline{x}(k) + \begin{bmatrix} C \\ F_2 \end{bmatrix} \bar{u}(k+1) + \begin{bmatrix} 0 \\ F_3 \end{bmatrix} x^*(k+1) \begin{bmatrix} \underline{w}(k) \\ 0 \end{bmatrix}$$

or

$$\tilde{A}_o\underline{\tilde{x}}(k+1) = \tilde{A}_1\underline{x}(k) + \tilde{C}\bar{u}(k+1) + \tilde{D}x^*(k+1) + \underline{\tilde{w}}(k)$$

with conditional mean

$$E\{\underline{\tilde{x}}(k+1) \mid x(k),\bar{u}(k+1),x^*(k+1)\} = \tilde{G}_1x(k) + \tilde{G}_2\bar{u}(k+1) + \tilde{G}_3x^*(k+1)$$

where

$$\tilde{G}_1 = \begin{bmatrix} G_{1,1} \\ G_{1,2} \end{bmatrix} = \tilde{A}_o^{-1}\tilde{A}_1 = \begin{bmatrix} A+BF_1 \\ F_1 \end{bmatrix}$$

$$\tilde{G}_2 = \begin{bmatrix} G_{2,1} \\ G_{2,2} \end{bmatrix} = \tilde{A}_o^{-1}\tilde{C} = \begin{bmatrix} C+BF_2 \\ F_2 \end{bmatrix}$$

and

$$G_3 = \begin{bmatrix} G_{3,1} \\ G_{3,2} \end{bmatrix} = \tilde{A}_o^{-1}\tilde{D} = \begin{bmatrix} BF_3 \\ F_3 \end{bmatrix}$$

The identifiability problem is to derive $\{\tilde{A}_o,\tilde{A}_1,\tilde{C},\tilde{D},\Sigma_w\}$ uniquely from the reduced form parameters $\{\tilde{G}_1,\tilde{G}_2,\tilde{G}_3,\Sigma_{\tilde{w}}\}$. $F_1,F_2$ and $F_3$ can be uniquely derived from $G_{1,2},G_{2,2}$ and $G_{3,2}$ respectively. If $r(F_3) = r(F_3:g_i) = m$ for $i = 1,\dots,n$ where $g_i$ is the i-th row of $G_{3,1}$ then B can be derived from $G_{3,1}$; C from $G_{2,1}$ and A from $G_{1,1}$. If the reference trajectory is zero for all k, then identifiability problems may arise. External inputs must 'excite' the closed loop system in order to make the parameters identifiable. This is illustrated by the following examples.

Example (7.1). A market model as (CL) system.

Consider the following dynamic variant of a market model, described in Goldberger (1964, p. 316)

$$\text{demand: } \underline{q}(k) = az(k-1) + bp(k-1) + \underline{\varepsilon}_1(k)$$

$$\text{supply: } \underline{p}(k) = c\underline{q}(k) \qquad\qquad + \underline{\varepsilon}_2(k)$$

where q(k) = quantity of a good, p(k) = price and z(k) = personal income. For the entrepeneur the target (output) variable could be q(k) and his control variable p(k). The process model for the entrepeneur is the demand equation (siso system). The supply equation can be seen as a closed loop linear control law and the reduced form is given by

$$\begin{bmatrix} \underline{q}(k) \\ \underline{p}(k) \end{bmatrix} = \begin{bmatrix} a & b \\ ca & cb \end{bmatrix} \begin{bmatrix} z(k-1) \\ p(k-1) \end{bmatrix} + \begin{bmatrix} \underline{w}_1(k) \\ \underline{w}_2(k) \end{bmatrix} = \begin{bmatrix} a \\ ca \end{bmatrix} z(k-1) + \begin{bmatrix} b \\ cb \end{bmatrix} p(k-1) + \begin{bmatrix} \underline{w}_1(k) \\ \underline{w}_2(k) \end{bmatrix}$$

The reduced form in turn can be seen as a process model for, let us say the government with one control z(k) and two outputs (targets) namely q(k) and p(k). By suitable manipulation of z(k) (income policy) the government can control both q(k) and p(k).

In the following examples it is shown how the process parameters can be made identifiable.

Example (7.2). Closed loop controllers with (time)varying gains.

Consider the following (LRF) model with observable feature vector $x \in \mathbb{R}^n$

$$\underline{x}(k+1) = Ax(k) + Bu_i(k) + \underline{w}(k), \qquad k = 0,\dots,N$$

and closed loop controller $u_i(k) \in \mathbb{R}^m$ with (time)varying gains

$$u_i(k) = F_i x(k), \qquad i = 1,\dots,\bar{s}.$$

The observation model is given by

$$\begin{bmatrix} x'(1) \\ \vdots \\ \underline{x}'(N) \end{bmatrix} = \begin{bmatrix} x'(0) & x'(0)F_1' \\ \vdots & \vdots \\ x'(N-1) & x'(N-1)F_s' \end{bmatrix} \begin{bmatrix} A' \\ B' \end{bmatrix} + \begin{bmatrix} \underline{w}'(0) \\ \vdots \\ \underline{w}'(N) \end{bmatrix}$$

or

$$\underline{Y} = X\beta + \underline{W}$$

where the dimensions of $Y, X, \beta$ and $\underline{W}$ are respectively $(N\times n)$, $(N\times(n+m))$, $((n+m)\times n)$ and $(N\times n)$. Now A and B can be estimated if rank(X) = n + m where it is assumed that $N \geqq n + m$. By matrix partitioning we have that

$$X = \begin{bmatrix} x'(0) & 0 & \dots & 0 \\ 0 & x'(1) & & \vdots \\ \vdots & & & \vdots \\ 0 & \dots\dots & & x'(N-1) \end{bmatrix} \begin{bmatrix} I & F_1' \\ I & \vdots \\ \vdots & \vdots \\ I & F_s' \end{bmatrix} = \tilde{X}Z$$

which means that A and B can be estimated if the rank of the $Nn \times (n+m)$ matrix Z equals (n+m), which is consistent with Goodwin and Payne (1977, theorem 5.6.3).

Example (7.3). A closed loop controller of 'sufficiently' high order.

Consider the following single-input, single-output model

$$\underline{y}(k+1) = a_1 y(k) + \dots + a_p y(k-p) + b_o u(k) + b_1 u(k-1) + \dots$$
$$\dots + b_p u(k-p) + \underline{\varepsilon}(k)$$

and the controller

$$\underline{u}(k) = f_o y(k) + \ldots + f_q y(k-q) + e_q u(k-1) + \ldots + e_q u(k-q)$$

where it is assumed that $q > p$.

The (SCL) system is

$$\begin{bmatrix} 1 & -b_o \\ 0 & 1 \end{bmatrix} \begin{bmatrix} \underline{y}(k+1) \\ u(k) \end{bmatrix} = \begin{bmatrix} a_o, \ldots, a_p, 0, \ldots, 0, b_1, \ldots, b_p, 0, \ldots, 0 \\ f_o, \quad \ldots \quad , f_q, e_1, \quad \ldots \quad , e_q \end{bmatrix} \begin{bmatrix} y(k) \\ \vdots \\ y(k-p) \\ \vdots \\ y(k-q) \\ u(k-1) \\ \vdots \\ u(k-p) \\ \vdots \\ u(k-q) \end{bmatrix} + \begin{bmatrix} \underline{\varepsilon}(k) \\ 0 \end{bmatrix}$$

The reduced form matrix is

$$\begin{bmatrix} 1 & -b_o \\ 0 & 1 \end{bmatrix}^{-1} \begin{bmatrix} a_o, \ldots, a_p, 0, \ldots, 0, b_1, \ldots, b_p, 0, \ldots, 0 \\ f_o, \quad \ldots \quad , f_q, e_1, \quad \ldots \quad , e_q \end{bmatrix} =$$

$$= \begin{bmatrix} a_o + b_o f_o, a_1 + b_o f_1, \ldots, a_p + b_o f_p, b_o f_{p+1}, \ldots, b_o f_q, b_1 + b_o e_1, \ldots \\ f_o, \quad \ldots \quad , f_p, f_{p+1}, \ldots, f_q, \quad e_1, \ldots \end{bmatrix}$$

$$\begin{matrix} \ldots, b_p + b_o e_p, b_o e_{p+1}, \ldots, b_o e_q \\ \ldots, \quad e_p, e_{p+1}, \ldots \quad , e_q \end{matrix} \Bigg]$$

$$= \begin{bmatrix} g_{1,o}, \ldots, g_{1,p}, g_{1,p+1}, \ldots, g_{1,q}, g_{1,q+1}, \ldots, g_{1,2q} \\ g_{2,o}, \ldots, g_{2,p}, g_{2,p+1}, \ldots, g_{2,q}, g_{2,q+1}, \ldots, g_{2,2q} \end{bmatrix}$$

It is easily seen that the parameters $\{a_i\}$ and $\{b_j\}$, $i = 1,\ldots,p$ and $j = 0,\ldots,p$ can be identified from the reduced form parameters $g_{i,j}$ $i = 1,2$, $j = 0,\ldots,2q$ if the order of the controller (q) is greater than the order of the model (p). If $q \leqq p$ the parameters are unidentifiable

Example (7.4). A closed loop controller with noise.

Consider the following single-input single-output model

$$\underline{x}(k+1) = a\underline{x}(k) + b\underline{u}(k) + \underline{\varepsilon}_1(k)$$

with closed loop controller

$$\underline{u}(k) = f\underline{x}(k) + \underline{\varepsilon}_2(k)$$

It is assumed that $\{\underline{\varepsilon}_1(k)\}$ and $\{\underline{\varepsilon}_2(k)\}$ are uncorrelated white noise processes with variances respectively $\sigma_1^2$ and $\sigma_2^2$ and uncorrelated with $\underline{x}(k)$. The (SCL) system is

$$\begin{bmatrix} 1 & -b \\ 0 & 1 \end{bmatrix} \begin{bmatrix} \underline{x}(k+1) \\ \underline{u}(k) \end{bmatrix} = \begin{bmatrix} a \\ f \end{bmatrix} \underline{x}(k) + \begin{bmatrix} \underline{\varepsilon}_1(k) \\ \underline{\varepsilon}_2(k) \end{bmatrix}$$

with reduced form

$$\begin{bmatrix} \underline{x}(k+1) \\ \underline{u}(k) \end{bmatrix} = \begin{bmatrix} a + bf \\ f \end{bmatrix} \underline{x}(k) + \begin{bmatrix} \underline{\varepsilon}_1(k) + b\underline{\varepsilon}_2(k) \\ \underline{\varepsilon}_2(k) \end{bmatrix}$$

The conditional distribution of $(\underline{x}(k+1)\ \underline{u}(k))'$ given $x(k)$ is Gaussian with conditional mean

$$E\left[\begin{bmatrix} \underline{x}(k+1) \\ \underline{u}(k) \end{bmatrix} \middle|\, x(k)\right] = \begin{bmatrix} a + bf \\ f \end{bmatrix} x(k) = \begin{bmatrix} g_1 \\ g_2 \end{bmatrix} x(k)$$

and conditional covariance

$$E\left[\begin{bmatrix} \underline{\varepsilon}_1(k) + b\underline{\varepsilon}_2(k) \\ \underline{\varepsilon}_2(k) \end{bmatrix} [\underline{\varepsilon}_1(k) + b\underline{\varepsilon}_2(k), \underline{\varepsilon}_2(k)]\right] = \begin{bmatrix} \sigma_1^2 + b^2\sigma_2^2, & b\sigma_2^2 \\ b\sigma_2^2, & \sigma_2^2 \end{bmatrix} = \begin{bmatrix} \sigma_{11} & \sigma_{12} \\ \sigma_{21} & \sigma_{22} \end{bmatrix}$$

Now $\sigma_2^2$ and b can be identified from the reduced form covariances $\sigma_{22}$ and $\sigma_{12}$ respectively and a from the reduced form parameter $g_1$. Note that if the closed loop controller is *without* noise, the parameters a and b can not be identified from $g_1$. From the foregoing it is seen that, in order to identify the process parameters in a closed loop system, one must 'probe' the system with external inputs (reference values, exogenous noise) or to use controllers with (time)varying gains, which is the case if we use controllers, in which the gains are based on *time-varying* parameter estimates, to be discussed in the next section.

## 7.6. Self-Tuning Control.

From the previous section it is known that for the (LRF) model

$$\underline{x}(k+1) = A\underline{x}(k) + B\underline{u}(k) + C\bar{u}(k+1) + \underline{w}(k)$$

the optimal (MV) controller is given by

$$\underline{\tilde{u}}_{mv}(k) = F(\theta_o)\underline{z}(k)$$

where $F(\theta_o) \triangleq -(B^+A:B^+C:B^+)$; $\underline{z}(k) \triangleq (\underline{x}'(k)\bar{u}'(k+1)x'^*(k))'$ and where the parameters of A,B and C are collected in the p-dimensional parameter vector $\theta_o$. With the additional assumptions on the exogenous noise and reference trajectory the optimal steady state (LQG) controller is given by

$$\underline{u}^*(k) = L(\theta_o)\underline{z}(k)$$

where the gain $L(\theta_o) \triangleq (R+\tilde{B}'K\tilde{B})^{-1}\tilde{B}'K\tilde{A}$ and K is the positive definite solution of the Riccati equation provided that the (CL) system is stable. For the (LQG) controller the exogenous noise value $\bar{u}(k+1)$ is to be interpreted as the (MSE) prediction of $\underline{\bar{u}}(k+1)$, namely $\bar{u}(k+1) = T\bar{u}(k)$ given the value $\bar{u}(k)$.

Let $\hat{\theta}(k)$ be a recursive estimate of $\theta_o$ based on the observations $\{z(k),\ldots,z(0),u(k-1),\ldots,u(0)\}$ for k = 1,2,... with initial estimate $\hat{\theta}(0)$. Let the estimated adaptive (MV) controller, based on the *certainty equivalence* principle, denoted by (CEMV) controller, be

$$\hat{\underline{\tilde{u}}}_{mv}(k) = F(\underline{\hat{\theta}}(k))\underline{z}(k)$$

and the estimated adaptive steady state (LQG) controller, denoted by (CESL) controller, be

$$\hat{\underline{u}}(k) = L(\underline{\hat{\theta}}(k))\underline{z}(k)$$

Definition (7.1) : The (CEMV) controller, respectively the (CESL) controller are said to be self-tuning if $\text{plim}(\underline{\tilde{u}}_{mv}(k)-\underline{\hat{\tilde{u}}}_{mv}(k)) = 0$ respectively $\text{plim}(\underline{u}(k)-\underline{\hat{u}}(k)) = 0$.

Assume the following: (i) the (CL) system is stable and the exogenous noise is finite, i.e. $\|z(k)\| < \infty$ and $\|u(k)\| < \infty$ for every k; (ii) $F(\hat{\theta}(k))$ and $L(\hat{\theta}(k))$ are continuous for every outcome $\hat{\theta}(k)$, k = 1,2,...

Proposition (7.1): A sufficient condition for the (CEMV) controller, respectively the (CESL) controller to be self-tuning is that the parameter estimator is consistent, i.e. $\text{plim}(\underline{\hat{\theta}}(k)) = \theta_o$.

Proof : By assumption we have for the (CEMV) controller that $F(\hat{\theta}(k))$ is bounded and continuous for every outcome $\hat{\theta}(k)$. If $\text{plim}(\underline{\hat{\theta}}(k)) = \theta_o$, then $\text{plim}(F(\underline{\hat{\theta}}(k))) = F(\text{plim}(\hat{\theta}(k))) = F(\theta_o)$ and hence $\text{plim}(\underline{\tilde{u}}_{mv}(k)-\hat{\tilde{u}}_{mv}(k)) = \text{plim}([F(\theta_o)-F(\underline{\hat{\theta}}(k)]\underline{z}(k)) = $ $= \text{plim}[F(\theta_o)-F(\underline{\hat{\theta}}(k)]\,\text{plim}(\underline{z}(k)) = 0$ because $\|z(k)\| < \infty$ for every k. The same applies *mutatis mutandis* for the (CESL) controller.

From proposition (7.1) we have that the estimated controllers are self-tuning if consistent recursive parameter estimators are used, provided that the (CL) system is stable. From mathematical statistics it is known that the recursive least squares estimator is consistent, provided that the input variables are statistically independent from the white noise $\{\underline{w}(k)\}$, which, in our recursive procedure of parameter identification and control, is not the case. The estimated controller $\underline{\hat{\tilde{u}}}_{mv}(k)$ or $\underline{\hat{u}}(k)$ is a (non-linear) function of previous inputs, exogenous noise and previous outputs and hence of previous white noise $\{\underline{w}(k-1),\underline{w}(k-2),...\}$. The recursive least squares estimates are no longer consistent. The prediction error method, as discussed in chapter V, will give consistent estimates, provided that the (CL) system is stable and the exogenous noise is bounded for all k, see also Ljung (1976).
In the next section a *simple* recursive estimation procedure will be considered in a simulation study.

## 7.7. Self-Tuning Control of a Macro-Economic System.

### Introduction.

From the previous sections we have seen that for the (LRF) model, the steady state (LQG) control and MV control stabilizes the system, provided that the pair (A,B) is controllable, whereas for the extended (LRF) model with exogenous noise, the (CL) system is stable, provided that the exogenous noise and reference trajectory are (Lyapunov) stable. It was shown that the estimated adaptive versions of the controllers, based on the certainty equivalence principle, are self-tuning if the control inputs are finite and the parameter estimates are consistent.

The conditions imposed on the model in order to derive stable controllers may differ from 'real life' (economic) conditions. It is for instance to be expected the control to have low impact on the output in macro-economic situations (the controllability condition). Further the controls may be bounded, whereas the reference trajectory may be exponentially growing and above all, the (CL) system is already assumed to be stable and not as a *result* of a controller.

Aim of the simulation study is to study the (induced) effects on a economic system, when applying the estimation control schemes of the previous sections. The economic system is a quaterly estimated model of the US economy with two outputs and one control (input). The model is extended by adding an additional control variable in order to study the differences between applying one and two controls.

In particular the following topics will be studied: (i) the stability of the (CL) system, (ii) the self-tuning property and convergence rate of the controllers and (iii) the consistency of the parameter estimates.

### Simulation Models and the Estimation Control Procedure.

Consider the following reduced form model

$$\begin{bmatrix} \underline{C}(k) \\ \underline{I}(k) \end{bmatrix} = \begin{bmatrix} a_{11} & a_{12} \\ a_{21} & a_{22} \end{bmatrix} \begin{bmatrix} \underline{C}(k-1) \\ \underline{I}(k-1) \end{bmatrix} + \begin{bmatrix} b_{11} & b_{12} \\ b_{21} & b_{22} \end{bmatrix} \begin{bmatrix} \underline{u}_1(k-1) \\ \underline{u}_2(k-1) \end{bmatrix} +$$

$$+ \begin{bmatrix} c_1 \\ c_2 \end{bmatrix} x(k) + \begin{bmatrix} \underline{v}_1(k-1) \\ \underline{v}_2(k-1) \end{bmatrix}, \ k = 1,2,\ldots$$

where

$\underline{C}(k)$ = Gross Consumption in the US in quarter k, in billions of dollars.

$\underline{I}(k)$ = Bruto Private Investments, in billions of dollars.

$\underline{u}_1(k)$ = Governmental obligations in quarter k, which equals the governmental expenditures in quarter (k+1).

$\underline{u}_2(k)$ = Governmental taxes in quarter k.

$x(k)$ = Exogenous noise variable.

$\underline{v}(k) \triangleq (\underline{v}_1(k)\underline{v}_2(k))'$ is a white noise vector with $\mathrm{cov}\{\underline{v}(k)\underline{v}'(s)\} = \Sigma\delta_{ks}$.

An Estimated Macro-Economic Model for the US with One Control.

Assume $b_{12} = b_{22} = 0$ and $u_2(k) = 0$ and $x(k) \equiv 1$ for $k = 0,1,2,\ldots$ then the above model coincides with the reduced form model of Samuelson's accelerator model. Kendrick (1981) estimated the model with the following least squares estimates

$$A = \begin{bmatrix} 1.041 & 0.002 \\ 0.093 & 0.752 \end{bmatrix}, \ B = \begin{bmatrix} -0.004 \\ -0.100 \end{bmatrix}, \ C = \begin{bmatrix} -1.312 \\ 0.448 \end{bmatrix} \text{ and } \Sigma = \begin{bmatrix} 9 & 0 \\ 0 & 10 \end{bmatrix}$$

This estimated model is used as 'true' system in our simulation study with one control variable and with starting value $C(0) = 460.1$; $I(0) = 113.1$ and $\bar{u}_1(0) = 153.64$. The reference trajectory is $C^*(k) = 1.0075C^*(k-1)$ and $I^*(k) = 1.0075I^*(k-1)$ with starting value $C^*(0) = C(0)$ and $I^*(0) = I(0)$, Note that the reference trajectories violate the restriction on G in order to stabilize the (CL) system. Simulation experiments are also performed with time-varying exogenous noise.

A Simulation Model with Two Controls.

An additional control variable $u_2(k)$ is added to the original estimated model representing the taxes in quarter k (in billions of dollars) with arbitrarily chosen coefficients $b_{12} = -0.05$ and $b_{22} = -0.05$.

Recursive Estimation, Simulation and Control Procedures.

In the simulation study the following two simple recursive estimation schemes are applied.
Consider the system

$$\underline{y}(k+1) = Ay(k) + Bu(k) + Cx(k+1) + \underline{v}(k), \qquad k = 0,1,2,...$$
$$= Pz(k) + \underline{v}(k)$$

where the $n \times (n+m+1)$ matrix $P \triangleq (A\ B\ C)$ and $z'(k) \triangleq (\underline{y}'(k)\underline{u}'(k)x'(k+1))$ with initial value $z(0)$. When $\underline{x}(k+1)$ is considered to be a Markov process then $x(k+1)$ is the expected value of $\underline{x}(k+1)$, namely $x(k+1) = Tx(k)$, given $\underline{x}(k) = x(k)$. Following Keviczky (1978) and Ljung (1983) we have the (RLS) estimation schemes.

Method Keviczky:

$$\hat{P}(k) = \hat{P}(k-1)+[y(k)-\hat{P}(k-1)z(k-1)]z'(k-1)R(k)$$

$$R(k) = (1/w^2)\{R(k-1)-[R(k-1)z(k-1)][R(k-1)z(k-1)]'\}/$$
$$/[w^2+z'(k-1)R(k-1)z(k-1)]$$

with initial chosen values $w \leqq 1$; $\hat{P}(0)$, $z(0)$ and $R(0)$.

Method Ljung:

$\underline{y}(k+1) = Pz(k) + \underline{v}(k)$ is rewritten as $\underline{y}_i(k+1) = P_i'z(k) + \underline{v}_i(k)$, $i = 1,...,n$ where $P_i'$ is the i-th row of P. According to Ljung we have as estimating scheme

$$\hat{P}_i(k) = \hat{P}_i(k-1)+L_i(k)[y_i(k)-\hat{P}_i'(k-1)z(k-1)]$$

$$L_i(k) = R_i(k-1)z(k-1)/[1/\alpha_i(k)+z'(k-1)R_i(k-1)z(k-1)]$$

$$R_i(k) = R_i(k-1)-R_i(k-1)z(k-1)z'(k-1)R_i(k-1)[1/\alpha_i(k)+$$
$$+z'(k-1)R_i(k-1)z(k-1)]$$

with initial chosen values $\hat{P}_i(0)$, $R_i(0)$ and $\alpha_i(k)$. Ljung gives an indication for 'good' starting values, namely, $R_i(0) = cI$ with $c >> 0$. $\hat{P}_i(0) = 0$ and $1/\alpha_i(k) = 1/\alpha_i = E\{\underline{v}_i^2\}$, for $i = 1,...,n$.

## The Simulation Control Procedure.

From the previous sections it is seen that the (SL) controller and the estimated version need the positive definite solution of the Riccati equation and a solution of the matrix equation A X B + C = X. Both are discussed in the appendix. The simulation control procedure involves the following steps.

Step I : Set $k = 0$; Determine initial values $z(0)$, $y(0)$, $1/\alpha_i$, $\hat{P}(0)$, $\hat{P}_i(0)$, $w^2$, $R(0)$, $R_i(0)$

Step II : $k := k+1$; Generate a 'true' value $y(k)$ by using the simulation model and random generator; update the estimates $\hat{P}(0)$ and $\hat{P}_i(0)$

Step III: Determine the estimated positive definite solution of the Riccati equation and the matrix equation

Step IV: Determine the (CEMV) control $\hat{u}_{mv}(k)$ and the (CESL) control $\hat{u}(k)$ and return to step II until $k = 200$.

## Simulation Results and Conclusions.

The main topics to be studied were the stability of the (CL) system, the self-tuning property and convergence rate of the adaptive controllers and the consistency of the parameter estimates, applying Ljung's simple recursive estimation algorithm.

It appeared that for Kendrick's model of the US economy with one control neither the optimal nor the estimated controllers gave stable (CL) systems, partially due to the small value of the gain parameter $b_{11}$. The controllability matrix is 'almost' singular. The results were even worse if the control values were bounded. A typical output and input sequence for a (CESL) controller is shown in the figures 1 - 3. The weighting matrices are $Q = \text{diag}(10,10)$, $R = 0.01$ and $u_1(k) \in [0,500]$ for all k. (The upper and lower bounds are given by the dotted lines.) Increasing the gain value $b_{11}$ resulted in a better performance of both controllers. See the figures 4 - 6 for a (CESL) controller with $Q = \text{diag}(10,10)$, $R = 0.01$, $u_1(k) \in [0,500]$ and $b_{11} = -0.05$. Note that in the first twenty periods the (CESL) controller is not the optimal one.

As for the model with two controls, all simulation runs resulted in stable (CL) systems, both for the (CESL) and (CEMV) controllers. See the figures 7 - 10 for a typical output and input sequence for a (CEMV)

controller with $u_1(k) \in [0,500]$ and $u_2(k) \in [0,500]$ for all k. If the control values were bounded too much the (CL) system became highly unstable for both controllers. See the figures 11 - 14 for a (CESL) controller with $Q = \text{diag}(10,10)$, $R = 0.01$, $u_1(k) \in [125,175]$ and $u_2(k) \in [125,175]$ for all k. From the figures it can be seen that in most cases the adaptive controllers were self-tuning with a surprisingly fast convergence rate, although the parameter estimates were not consistent. See the figures 15 - 19 for the optimal and estimated feed-back gains of a (CESL) controller with $Q = \text{diag}(10,10)$, $R = 0.01$, $u_1(k) \in [0,500]$, $u_2(k) \in [0,500]$ and $b_{11} = -0.05$, i.e.

$$\hat{u}_1(k) = \hat{l}_{1,11}(k)C(k) + \hat{l}_{1,12}(k)I(k) + \hat{l}_{2,11}C^*(k+1) + \\ + \hat{l}_{2,12}I^*(k+1) + \hat{l}_{3,11}$$

and for the corresponding parameter estimates the figures 20 - 27. The parameter estimates were in most cases not consistent, although the estimates converged rapidly towards the 'true' values. See the figures 28 - 35 for a sequence of parameter estimates when applying a (CESL) controller with one control and gain $b_{11} = -0.004$. The overall conclusion of the simulation experiments is that (adaptive) control of a macro-economic system is rather doubtful and may induce instability, because of the low impact of the control on the output, the bounds on the control values and the exponentially growing reference trajectory. The results sustain Ashby's fundamental statement that 'only (control) variety can destroy variety', see Ashby (1964). For this economic system there seems hardly control 'variety', where the control variety is indicated by (i) the values of the gain matrix B and the controllability matrix (ii) the constraints on the control values and (iii) the number of controls compared with the number of outputs (targets).

Fig. 1

CONSUMPTION

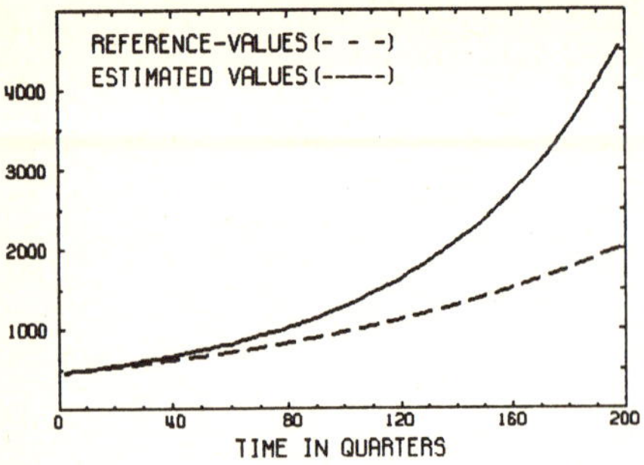


Fig. 4

CONSUMPTION

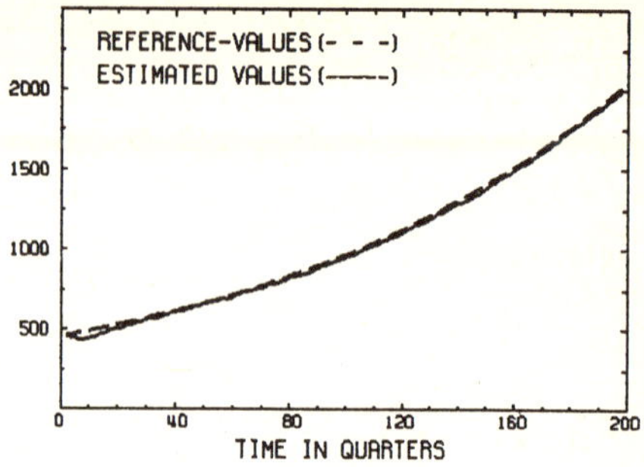


Fig. 2

INVESTMENTS

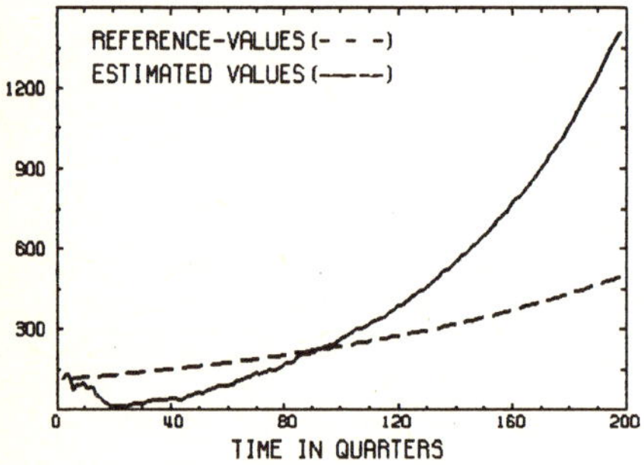


Fig. 5

INVESTMENTS

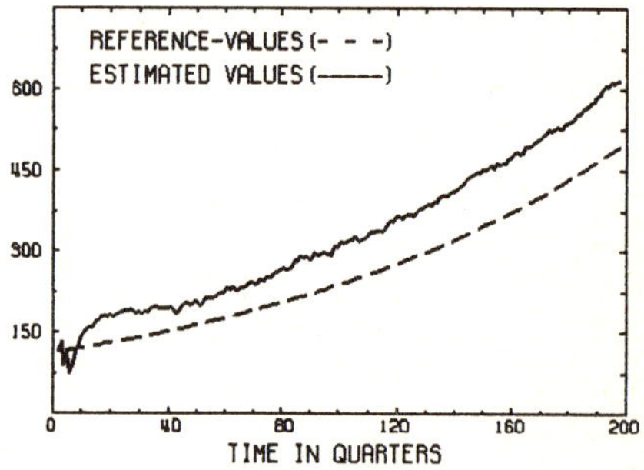


Fig. 3

GOVERNM. EXPENDITURES

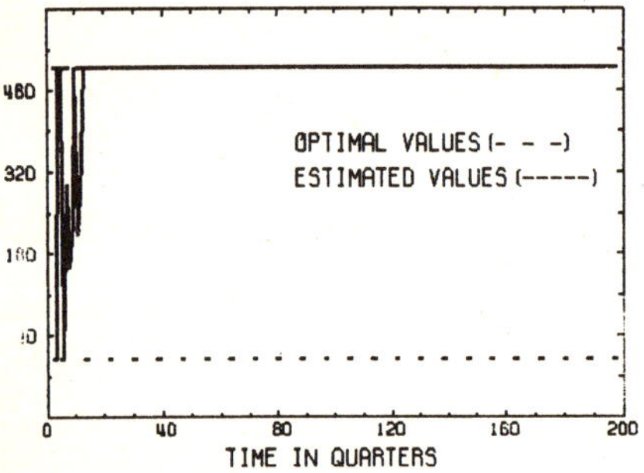


Fig. 6

GOVERNM. EXPENDITURES

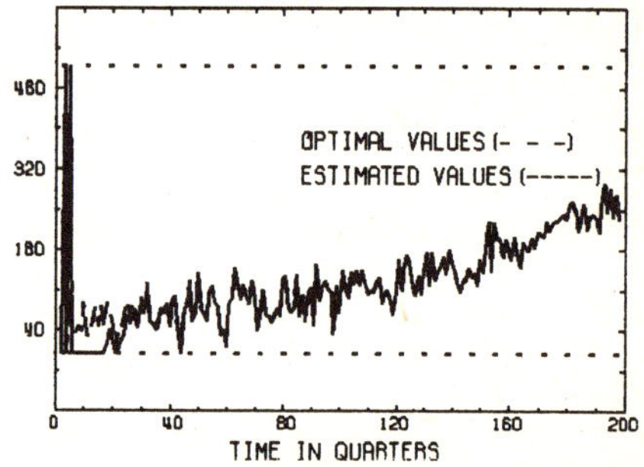


Fig. 7

CONSUMPTION

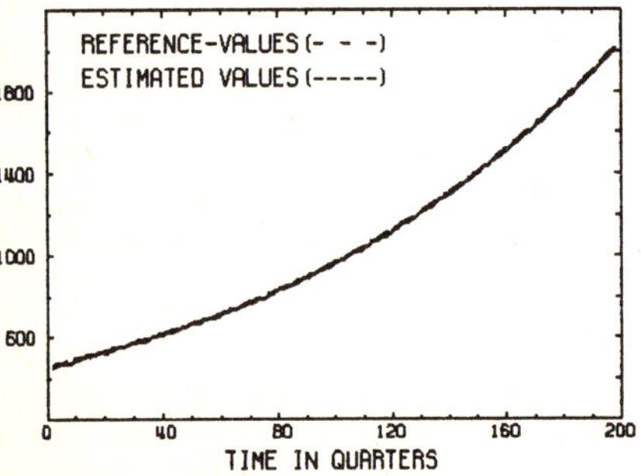


Fig. 8

INVESTMENTS

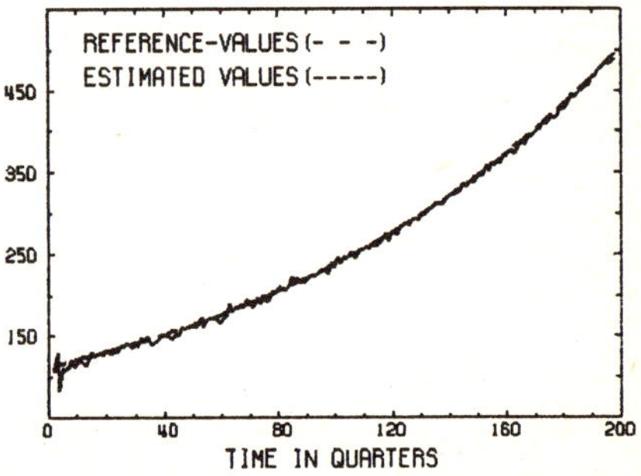

Fig. 9

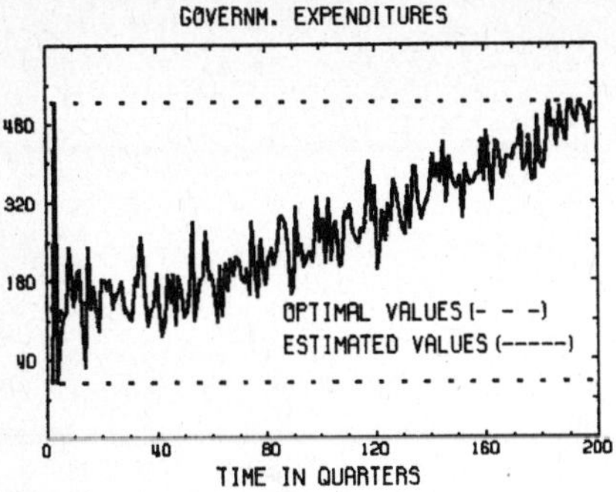


Fig. 10

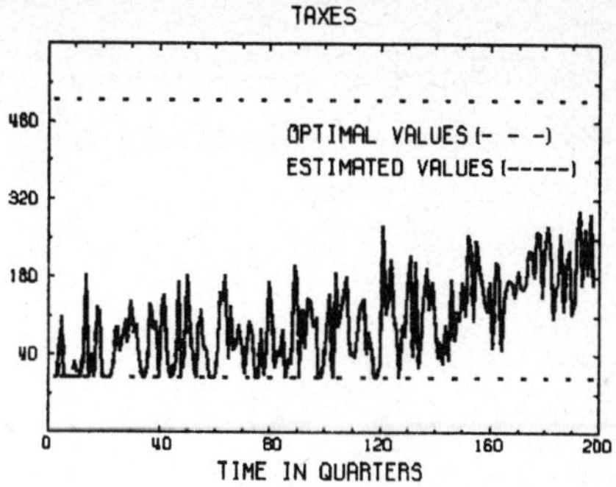


Fig. 11

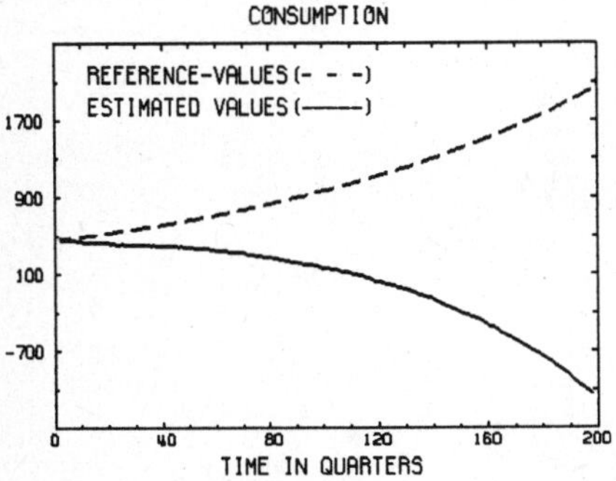


Fig. 12

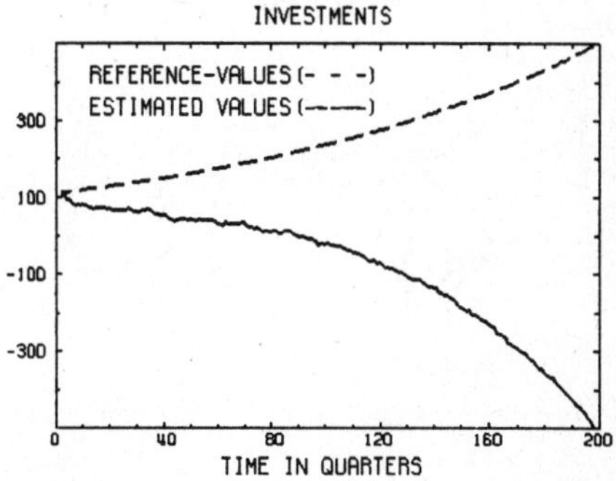


Fig. 13

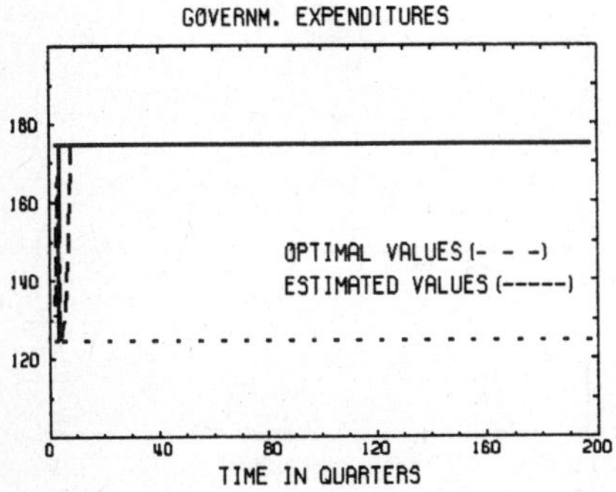


Fig. 14

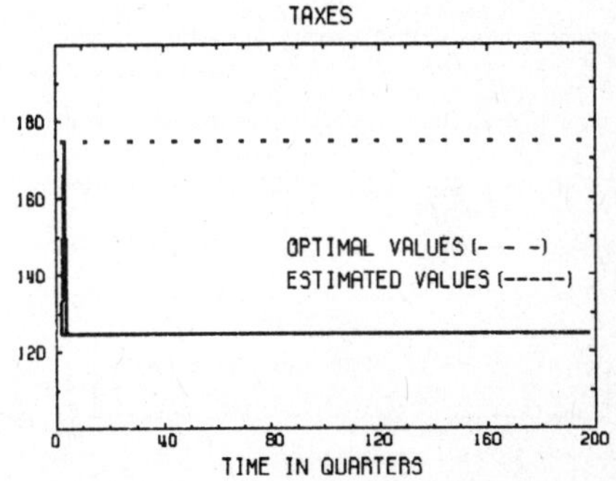


Fig. 15

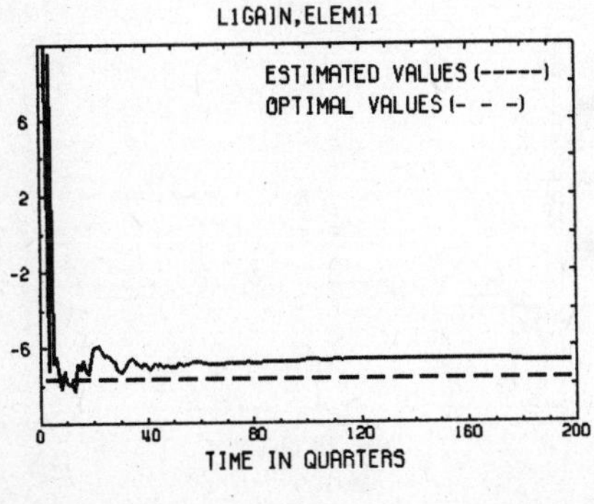


Fig. 16

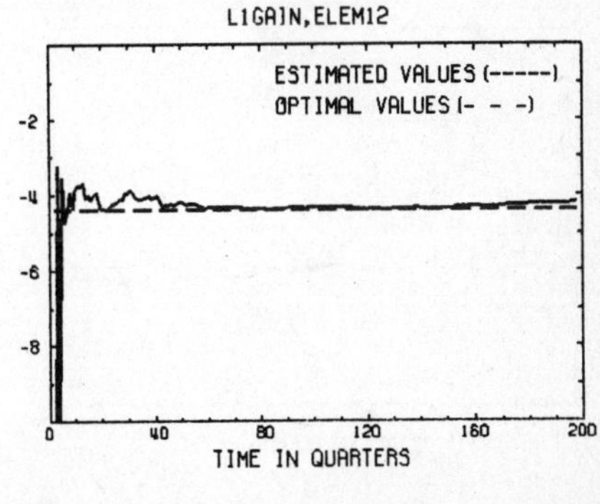

Fig. 17
L2GAIN,ELEM11

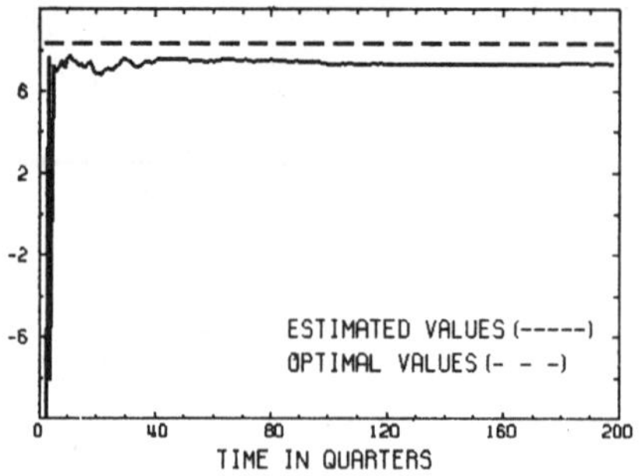


Fig. 18
L2GAIN,ELEM12

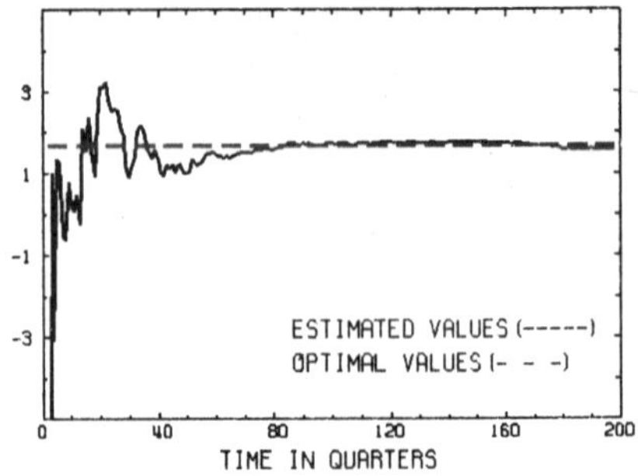


Fig. 19
L3GAIN,ELEM11

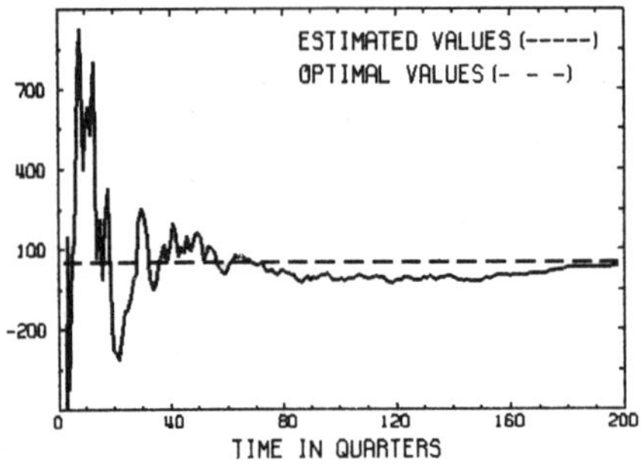


Fig. 20
A11

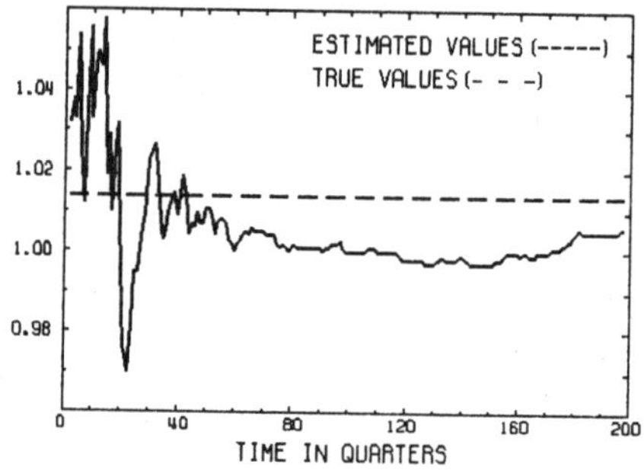


Fig. 21
A12

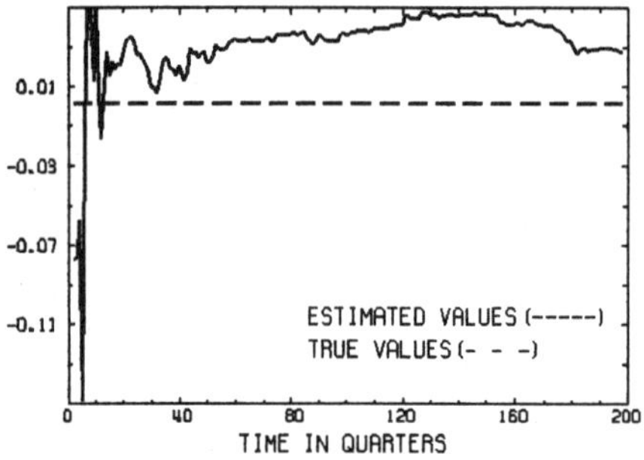


Fig. 22
A21

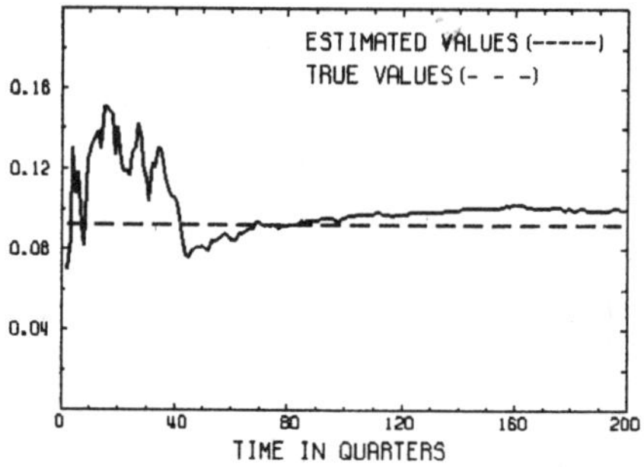


Fig. 23
A22

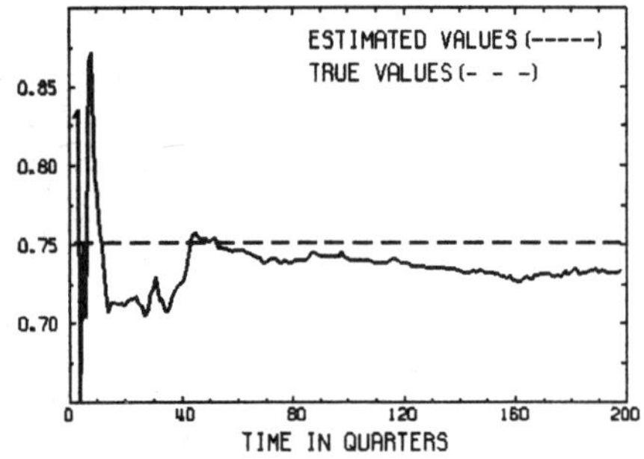


Fig. 24
B11

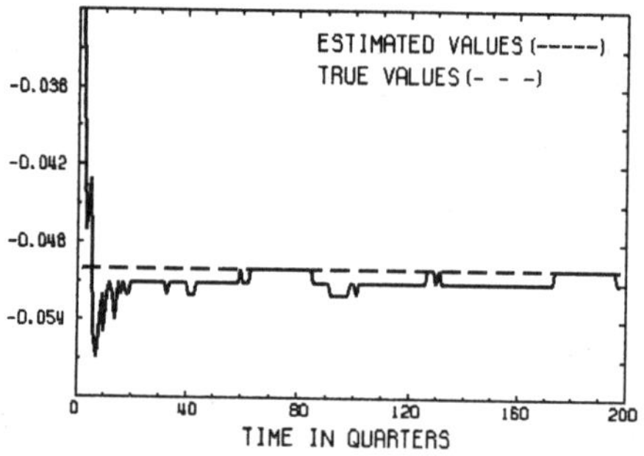

Fig. 25

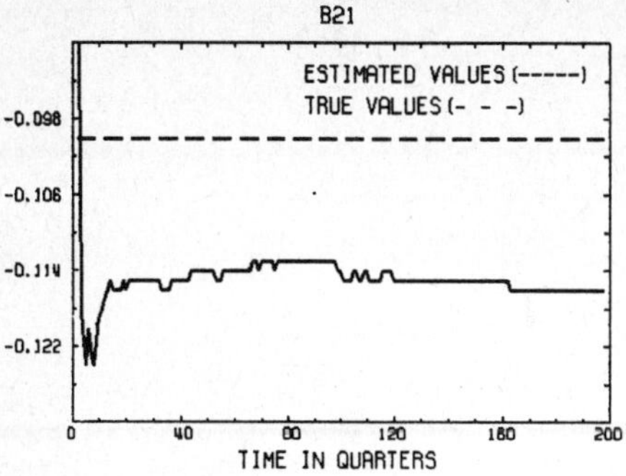


Fig. 26

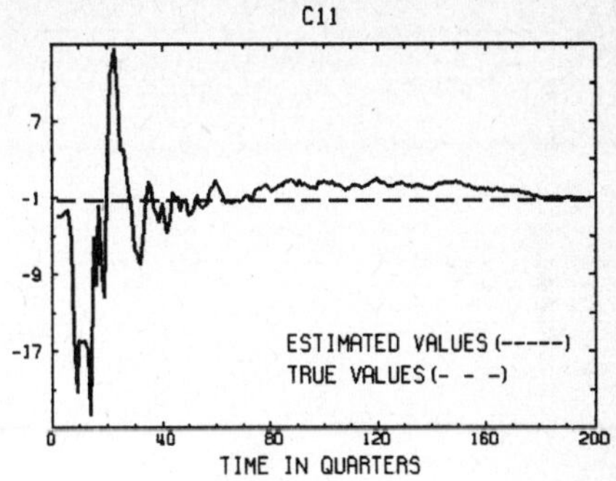


Fig. 27

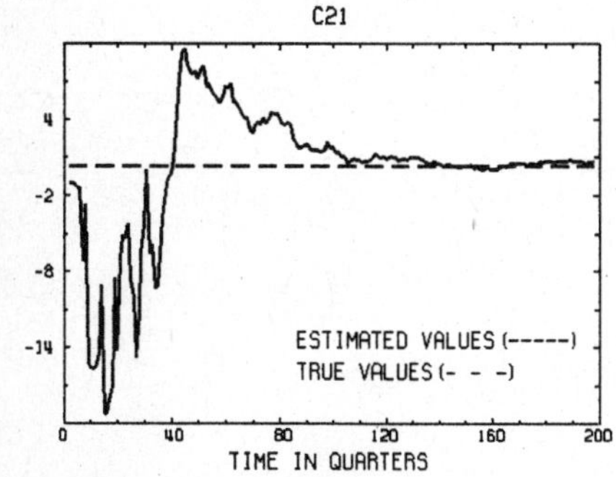


Fig. 28

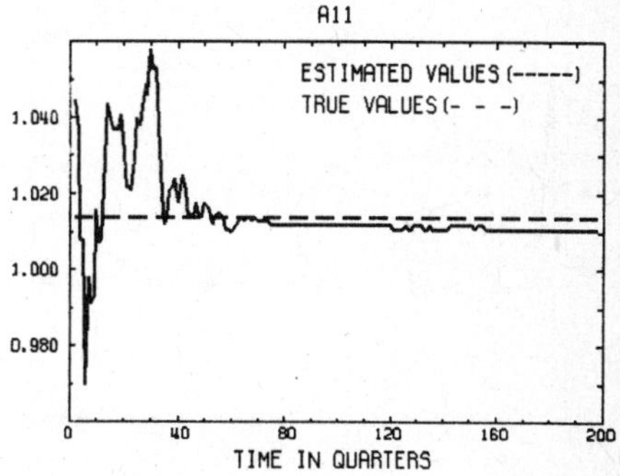


Fig. 29

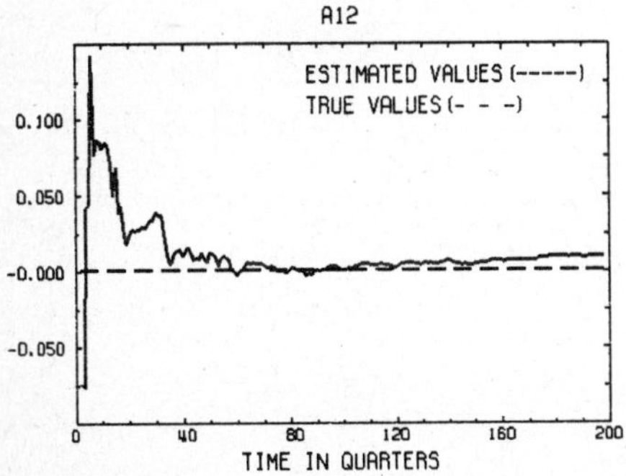


Fig. 30

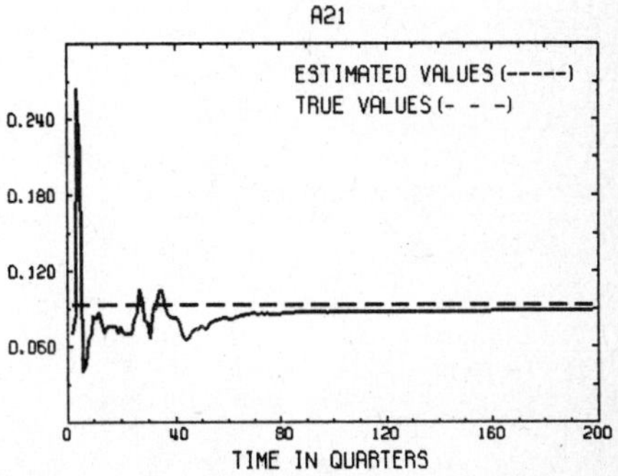


Fig. 31

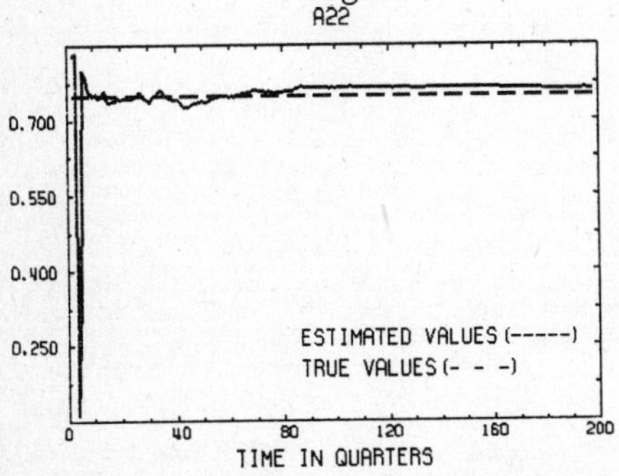


Fig. 32

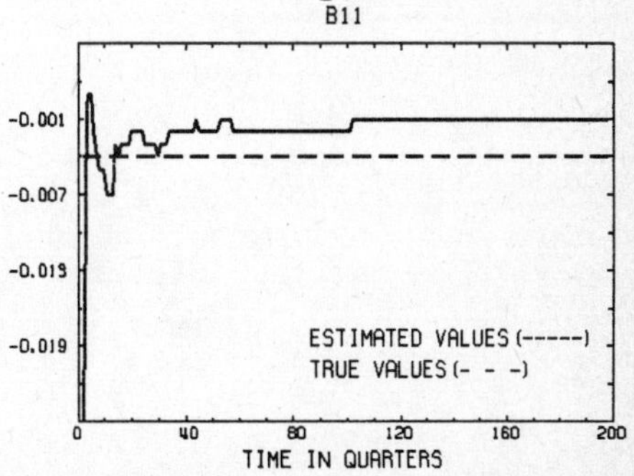

Fig. 33

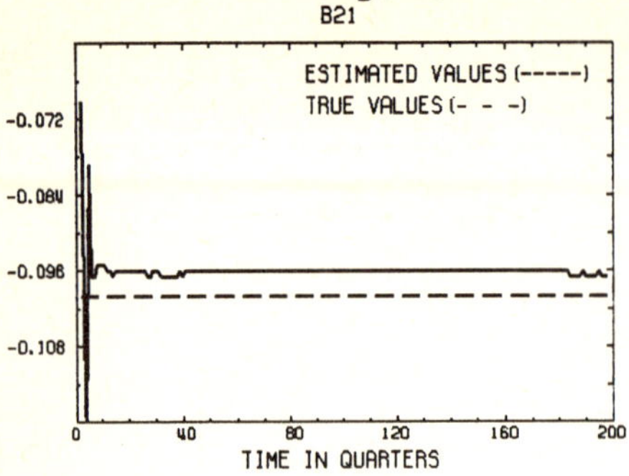


Fig. 34

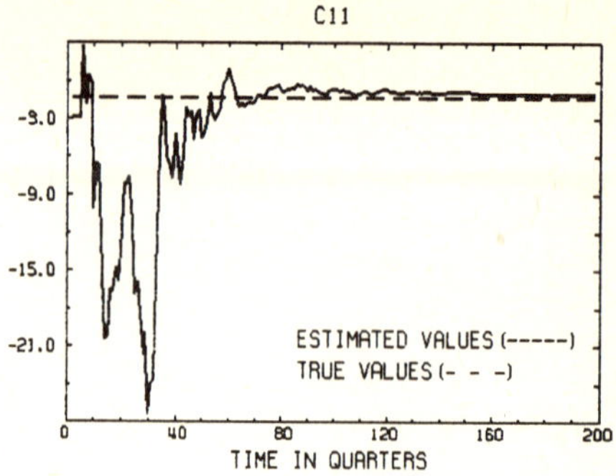


Fig. 35

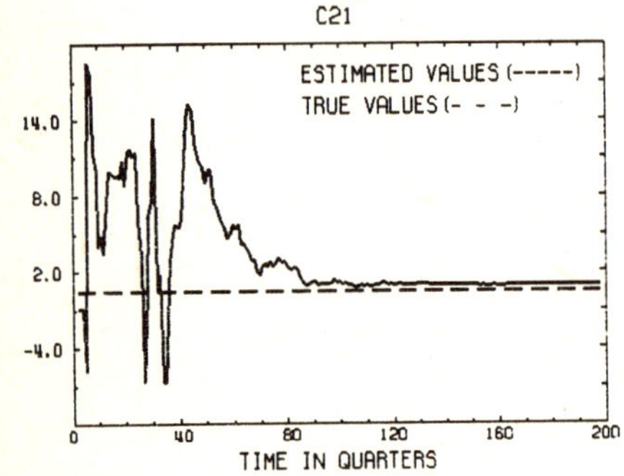

## Appendix

Solution of the Matrix Equation A X B + C = X.

Consider the matrix equation

$$A X B + C = X$$

where the (n×n) matrices A, B and C are known. Let the $n^2$-dimensional vectorized matrix X be $\bar{x}$, i.e.

$$\bar{x} = (x_1', x_2', \ldots, x_n')'$$

where $x_i$ is the i-th column of X. After some calculations it can be shown that

$$(B' \otimes A)\bar{x} + \bar{c} = \bar{x}$$

where $\bar{c}$ is the vectorized matrix C and $\otimes$ denotes the Kronecker product, thus

$$\bar{x} = -(B' \otimes A - I_{n^2})^{-1}\bar{c}$$

where $I_{n^2}$ is the identity matrix of order $n^2$. It is assumed that $(B' \otimes A - I_{n^2})$ exists.

Solution of the ARE.

The algebraic Riccati equation is of the form

$$K = A'[K - KB(R + B'KB)^{-1}B'K]A + Q$$

where A, B (or parameter estimates), Q and R are known with $Q \geqq 0$ and $R > 0$. Aim is to determine the positive definite solution of this equation. This can be done by using recursive methods, namely the so-called direct method or the Newton-Raphson method, to be discussed in the sequel. These methods will converge very fast provided that good initial starting matrices are chosen. Another approach is the Schur eigenvector approach, see Laub (1979).

Direct Method.

Let $P_o$ be an arbitrary chosen positive semi-definite matrix. Determine $P_{k+1}$ from the recursive equation

$$P_{k+1} = A'[P_k-P_kB(R+B'P_kB)^{-1}B'P_k]A + Q, \qquad k = 0,1,2,...$$

and repeat untill $P_k$ converges. From Bertsekas (1976) we have the following theorem.

Theorem : If the pair (A,B) is controllable, Q = C'C and (A,C) observable then $\lim_{k \to \infty} P_k = K$, where K is the positive definite solution of the ARE.

Newton-Raphson Method.

Consider the function

$$f(S) = A'SA-A'SB(R+B'SB)^{-1}B'SA + Q - S$$

Aim is to determine $S_{k+1}$ such that $f(S_{k+1}) = 0$. Applying a Taylor series around $S_k$ yields with neglecting the higher order terms the following equation

$$0 = f(S_{k+1}) = f(S_k) + \frac{\partial f(S_k)}{\partial S} (S_{k+1}-S_k),$$

from which $S_{k+1}$ can be determined as new approximation. Because the derivative of the function f(S) will cause some problems the following approximation is used $(I+X\Delta Y)^{-1} \approx I - X\Delta Y$. The first order approximation is

$$f(S_{k+1}) = 0 = A'(S_k+\Delta)A - A'(S_k+\Delta)B[R+B'(S_k+\Delta)B]^{-1}B'(S_k+\Delta)A + $$
$$+ Q - (S_k+\Delta)$$
$$= (A-BF_k)'S_{k+1}(A-BF_k)-S_{k+1} + Q + F_k'RF_k$$

or

$$S_{k+1} = \Phi_k' S_{k+1} \phi_k + C_k$$

where $\Phi_k \triangleq A - BF_k$ and $C_k = Q + F_k'RF_k$.
This equation is of the Lyapunov type A' X A + Q = X with solution

$X = \sum_{k=1}^{\infty}(A')^k Q A^k$ provided that A is asymptotically stable, that is, for our case if $|\sigma(A-BF_k)| < 1$ for $k = 0,1,2,\ldots$ . If the pair (A,B) is controllable then by a poles assignment algorithm $F_k$ can be determined such that $|\ (A-BF_k)| < 1$, see e.g. Kwakernaak (1972). From Kwakernaak (1972, p. 252) we have the following. If $F_o$ is chosen such that $|\sigma(A-BF_o)| < 1$ then $S_k \geq S_{k+1}$ for $k = 0,1,2,\ldots$ all $\phi_k$ are asymptotically stable and $\lim S_k = K$.

The Newton-Raphson procedure is now as follows:

Step I : Determine $F_o$ such that $|\sigma(A-BF_o)| < 1$

Step II : Determine $\Phi_k = A - BF_k$ and $C_k = Q + F_k'RF_k$ for $k = 0$

Step III: Solve $S_{k+1}$ from the equation $S_{k+1} = \Phi_k S_{k+1}\Phi_k + C_k$;
set $k := k+1$ determine $F_k = (R+B'S_kB)^{-1}B'S_kA$ and return to
step II until $S_{k+1}-S_k \approx 0$.

## References


Aalders, L., Engwerda, J.C. and Otter, P.W.: *'Self-Tuning Control of a Macro-Economic System'*, Proceedings of the 4-th IFAC/IFQRS/IIASA Conference on the Modelling and Control of National Economies, Ed. Basar, T., Pergamon Press, 1984.

Adamjan, V.M., Arov, D.Z. and Krein, M.G., Math. USSR Sfornik, 15, 31, (1978), Am. Math. Soc. Trans., 111-133 (translation of Iz. Akad. Nauk Arrujan. SSR Ser. Mat. 6 (1971, p. 87)).

Akaike, H.: *'A New Look at the Statistical Model Identification'*, IEEE Transactions on Automatic Control, Vol. 19, no. 6, December 1974.

Akaike, H.: *'Markovian Representation of Stochastic Processes by Canonical Variables'*, SIAM Journal of Control, Vol. 13, no. 1, January 1975.

Akaike, H.: *'Canonical Correlation Analysis of Time Series and the Use of an Information Criterion'*, System Identification and Case Studies, Eds. Mehra, R.K. and Lainiotis, D.G., Acad. Press, 1976.

Akaike, H.: *On Entropy Maximization Principle'*, Applications of Statistics, Ed. Krishnaiah, P.R., North-Holland, 1977.

Anderson, B.D. and Moore, J.B.: *'Optimal Filtering'*, Prentice Hall, 1979.

Anderson, T.W.: *'An Introduction to Multivariate Statistical Analysis'*, John Wiley, 1958.

Andrews, H.C.: *'Introduction to Mathematical Techniques in Pattern Recognition'*, Wiley-Interscience, 1972.

Aoki, M.: *'Notes on Economic Time Series Analysis: System Theoretic Perspectives'*, Springer-Verlag in the series 'Lecture Notes in Economics and Mathematical Systems', 1983.

Ashby, W.R.: *'An Introduction to Cybernetics'*, Chapman and Hall, 1964.

Åström, K.J.: *'Introduction to Stochastic Control Theory'*, Acad. Press, 1970.

Åström, K.J. and Wittenmark, B.: *'On Self-Tuning Regulators'*, Automatica, 9, 1973.

Åström, K.J.: *'Maximum Likelihood and Prediction Error Methods'*, Tutorials on System Identification, 5-th IFAC Symposium on Identification, Darmstadt, 1979.

Åström, K.J. and Otter, P.W.: *'Self-Tuning Control of a Simple Macro-Economic Model'*, Internal Paper, Lund Institute of Technology, 1981.

Åström, K.J.: *'Theory and Applications of Adaptive Control: A Survey'*, Automatica, Vol. 19, p.p. 471-486, 1983.

Avery, R.B.: *'Modeling Monetary Policy as an Unobserved Variable'*, Journal of Econometrics, Vol. 10, no. 3, August 1979.

Ayres, F.: *'Theory and Problems of Matrices'*, Schaum Publishing Co, 1962.

Bertsekas, D.P.: *'Dynamic Programming and Stochastic Control'*, Acad. Press, 1976.

Bowden, R.: *'The Theory of Parametric Identification'*, Econometrica, Vol. 41, no. 6, November 1973.

Brown, R.L., Durbin, J. and Evans, J.M.: *'Techniques for Testing the Constancy of Regression Relationships over Time'* (with discussions), Journal of the Royal Statistical Society, B 37, 1975.

Casti, J.L.: *'Dynamical Systems and their Applications; Linear Theory'*, New York, Acad. Press, 1977.

Chow, G.C.: *'Analysis and Control of Dynamic Economic Systems'*, John Wiley, 1974.

Chow, G.C.: *'Selection of Econometric Models by the Information Criterion'*, Research Memorandum 239, March 1979.

Curtain, R.F.: *'Inleiding Systeem Theorie'*, Lecture Notes, Mathematical Institute, Groningen.

Damen, A.A.H., Hof, P.M.J. van den,: *'Approximate Realization based upon an Alternative to the Hankel Matrix: the Page Matrix'*, Systems and Control Letters, 2, 1982.

Dhrymes, P.J.: *'Econometrics'*, New York, 1970.

Eland, T.: *'Idenfication of the Adaptive Feedback of the Human Motor System Using the Response Difference Method'*, Thesis, Delft, 1981.

Engwerda, J.C.: *'Het gedrag van een drietal adaptieve control algoritmen'*, internal paper, Institute of Econometrics, Groningen, 1982.

Eykhoff, P.: *'System Identification'*, John Wiley, 1974.

Geer, J.P. van: *'Inleiding in de Multivariate Analyse'*, Van Loghum Slaterus, 1967.

Geweke, J.R. and Singleton, K.J.: *'Latent Variable Models for Time Series: A Frequency Approach with an Application to the Permanent Income*

*Hypothesis'*, Journal of Econometrics, 17, 1981.

Geweke, J. and Meese, R.: *'Estimating Regression Models of Finite but Unknown Order'*, International Economic Review, Vol. 22, no. 1, February 1981.

Glover, K.: *'Structural Aspects of System Identification'*, Thesis MIT Report ESL-R-516, August 1973.

Glover, K. and Willems, J.C.: *'Parametrizations of Linear Dynamical Systems: Canonical Forms and Identifiability'*, IEEE Transactions on Automatic Control, Vol. AC-19, no. 6, December 1974.

Glover, K.: *'All Optimal Hankel-Norm Approximation of Linear Multivariable Systems and their* $L^{\infty}$*-error Bound'*, Int. J. of Control, Vol. 39, no. 6, pp. 1115-1193.

Goldberger, A.S.: *'Econometric Theory'*, John Wiley, 1964.

Goodwin, G.C. and Payne, R.L.: *'Dynamic System Identification; Experiment Design and Data Analysis'*, Acad. Press, 1977.

Goodwin, G.C., Ramadge, P.J. and Caines, P.E.: *'Discrete Time Stochastic Adaptive Control'*, SIAM-J. Control and Optimization, 1981.

Grimble, M.J. and Fung, P.T.K.: *'Explicit Weighted Minimum Variance Self-Tuning Controllers'*, Proceedings of the 20-th IEEE Conference on Decision and Control, Vol. II, 1981.

Gustavsson, I., Ljung, L. and Söderström, T.: *'Identification of Processes in Closed Loop Identifiability and Accuracy Aspects'*, (Survey Paper), Automatica, Vol. 13, 1977.

Harvey, A.C.: *'An Alternative Framework for Time-Series Model Building and its Implications for Econometrics'*, Discussion Paper, London School of Economics, 1982.

Hesse, M.: *'The Structure of Scientific Inference'*, MacMillan, 1974.

Isermann, R.: *'Parameter Adaptive Control Algorithms - A Tutorial'*, Automatica, Vol. 18, no. 5, 1982.

Jazwinski, A.H.: *'Stochastic Processes and Filtering Theory'*, Acad. Press, 1970.

Jöreskog, K.G.: *'A General Method for Analysis of Covariance Structures'*, Biometrika, 57, 1970.

Jöreskog, K.G.: *'Structural Equation Models in Social Sciences; Specification, Estimation and Testing'*, Applications of Statistics, Ed. Krishnaiah, P.R., North-Holland, 1977.

Jöreskog, K.G. and Sörbom, D.: *'LISREL IV, A General Computer Program for*

*Estimation of Linear Structural Equation Systems by Maximum Likelihood Methods, User's Guide'*, University of Uppsala, Department of Statistics, Sweden, 1978.

Kailath, T.: *'A View of Three Decades of Linear Filtering Theory'*, IEEE Transactions on Information Theory, Vol. IT-20, no. 2, March 1974.

Kalman, R.E. and Bucy, R.S.: *'New Results in Linear Filtering and Prediction Theory'*, J. Basic. Eng. Trans. ASME, Ser. D, 1961.

Kalman, R.E.: *'Identifiability and Problems of Model Selection in Econometrics'*, Invited Lecture at the 4-th World Congress of the Econometric Society, August 1980.

Kalman, R.E.: *'System Identification from Noisy Data'*, Paper presented at the International Symposium on Dynamical Systems, Florida, February 1981.

Kendrick, D.A.: *'Stochastic Control for Economic Models'*, McGraw-Hill, 1981.

Kendrick, D.A.: *'Caution and Probing in a Macro-Economic Model'*, Journal of Econ. Dynamics and Control 4, 1982.

Keviczky, L., Hetthéssy, J., Hilges, M., Kolastari, J.: *'Self-Tuning Adaptive Control of Cement Raw Material Blending'*, Automatica, Vol. 14, 1978.

Kok, J. and Wijk, R. van,: *'Evaluation of Models describing Human Operator Control of Slowly Responding Complex Systems'*, Thesis, Delft University Press, 1978.

Kreiselmeier, G.: *'Adaptive Control'*, invited lecture 1983 Benelux Meeting on Systems and Control, 1983.

Kullback, S.: *'Information Theory and Statistics'*, Wiley and Sons, 1959.

Kung, S.Y. and Lin D.W.: *'Optimal Hankel-Norm Model Reduction: Multivariable Systems'*, IEEE, Vol. AC-26, no. 4.

Kwakernaak, H. and Sivan, D.: *'Linear Optimal Control Systems'*, Wiley-Interscience, 1972.

Landau, I.D.: *'A Survey of Model Reference Adaptive Techniques - Theory and Applications'*, Automatica, Vol. 10, 1974.

Landau, I.D.: *'Near Supermartingales for Convergence Analysis of Recursive Identification and Adaptive Control Schemes'*, Proceedings of the 20-th IEEE Conference on Decision and Control, Vol. 1, December 1981.

Laub, L.: *'A Schur Method for Solving Algebraic Ricatti Equations'*, IEEE

Transactions on Automatic Control, Vol. AC-24, no. 6, 1979.

Levine, M.G.: *'Canonical Analysis and Factor Comparison'*, Sage Publications, 1977.

Ljung, L., Gustavsson, I. and Söderström, T.: *'Identification of Linear Multvariable Systems Operating under Linear Feedback Control'*, IEEE Transactions on Automatic Control, Vol. AC-19, no. 6, December 1974.

Ljung, L.: *'On the Consistency of Prediction Error Identification Methods'*, System Identification; Advances and Case Studies, Eds. Mehra, R.K., Lainiotis, D., Acad. Press, 1976.

Ljung, L. and Söderström, T.: *Theory and Practice of Recursive Identification'*, MIT Press, 1983.

Luenberger, D.G.: *'Canonical Forms for Linear Multivariable Systems'*, IEEE Transactions on Automatic Control, Vol. AC-12, 1967.

Luenberger, D.G.: *'Optimization by Vector Space Methods'*, John Wiley, 1969.

Mehra, R.K. and Peschon, J.: *'An Innovations Approach to Fault Detection and Diagnosis in Dynamic Systems'*, Automatica, Vol. 7, 1971.

Mehra, R.K.: *'Identification in Control and Econometrics: Similarities and Differences'*, Annals of Economic and Social Measurement, 3/1, 1974.

Mehra, R.K.: *'Identification and Estimation of Error-in-Variables Model (EVM) in Structural Form'*, Mathematical Programming Study 5, Ed. Wetz, R., 1976.

Monopoli, R.V.: *'Model Reference Adaptive Control with an augmented Error Signal'*, IEEE Transactions on Automatic Control, Vol. AC-19, 1974.

Mood, A.M., Graybill, F.A. and Boes, D.C.: *'Introduction to the Theory of Statistics'*, McGraw-Hill, 1974.

Moore, B.C.: *'Principal Component Analysis in Linear Systems: Controllability, Observability and Model Reduction'*, IEEE, Vol. AC-26, no. 2, February 1981.

Niedzwiecki, M.: *'On the Localized Estimators and Generalized Akaike's Criterions'*, Proceedings of the 20-th IEEE Conference on Decision and Control, Vol. I, December 1981.

Niedzwiecki, M.: *'On the Localized Estimators and Generalized Akaike's Criteria'*, IEEE, Vol. AC-29, no. 11, November 1984.

Otter, P.W.: *'The Discrete Kalman Filter Applied to Linear Regression Models, Statistical Considerations and an Application'*, Statistica Neerlandica, Vol. 32, no. 1, 1978a.

Otter, P.W.: *'Kalman Filtering in Time-Series Analysis compared with the Box-Jenkins Approach and Exponential Smoothing'*, Paper presented at the European Meeting of the Econometric Society, Geneve, 1978b.

Otter, P.W. and Tempelaar, D.T.: *'Kalman and Box-Jenkins Estimators in a Simulation Study'*, Analysing Time-Series, Ed. Anderson O.D., North-Holland, 1980.

Otter, P.W.: *'Identification and Estimation of Discrete State-Vector Models with Stochastic Inputs'*, Automatica, Vol. 17, no. 2, 1981a.

Otter, P.W.: *'Identification and Estimation of Linear (Economic) Systems, Operating under Linear Closed-Loop Control'*, Dynamic Modelling and Control of National Economies, Eds. Janssen, J.M.L., Pau, L.F. and Strassak, A.J., Pergamon Press, 1981b.

Otter, P.W.: *'On State Space Modelling, Dynamic Factor Analysis and Self-Tuning Control of (Economic) Processes'*, Paper presented at the third International Conference on Mathematical Modelling, Los Angels, 1981c.

Otter, P.W. and Schuur, J.: *'Principal Component Analysis in Multivariate Forecasting of Economic Time-Series'*, Time-Series Analysis: Theory and Practice 1, Ed. Anderson, O.D., North-Holland, 1982.

Palm, F.C. and Kodde, D.A.: *'Computing Wold Criteria for Nested Hypotheses with Econometric Applications'*, Research Memorandum 1982-27, VU, 1982.

Parzen, E.: *'Time-Series Model Identification by Estimating Information'*, Studies in Econometrics, Time-Series and Multivariate Statistics, Eds. Karlin, Amemiya, Goodwin, AC Press, 1983.

Pernabo, L. and Silverman, L.M.: *'Model Reduction via Balanced State Representation'*, IEEE, AC-27, pp. 382-387.

Phadke, M.S. and Wu, S.M.: *'Identification of Multi-input - Multi-output Transferfunction and Noise Model of a Blast Furnace from Closed-Loop Data'*, IEEE Transactions on Automatic Control, Vol. AC-19, no. 6, December 1974.

Picci, G.: *'Some Numerical Aspects of Multivariable Systems Identification'*, Mathematical Programming Study, 18, 1982.

Pindyck, R.S.: *'Optimal Planning for Economic Stabilization'*, North-

Holland, 1973.

Popper, K.: '*The Logic of Scientific Discovery*', Hutchinson, 1977.

Priestley, M.B.: '*Non-Linear Models in Time-Series Analysis*', Paper presented at the Institute of Statisticians 1978 Conference of Time-Series Analysis, Cambridge, 1978.

Rijken van Olst, B.T.: '*Canonical Correlation and Canonical Variables in Econometrics*', Thesis, Knoop, 1981.

Rissanen, J.: '*Information, Prediction and Estimation*', IBM Research K54/282, San José, Cal., 1983.

Robinson, P.M.: '*Identification, Estimation and Large-Sample Theory for Regressions Containing Unobservable Variables*', Latent Variables in Socio-Economic Models, Eds. Aigner, D.J. and Goldberger, A.S., North-Holland, 1977.

Rosen, R.: '*Fundamentals of Measurement and Representation of Natural Systems*', North-Holland, 1978.

Rothenberg , T.J.: '*Identification in Parametric Models*', Econometrica, Vol. 39, no. 3, May 1971.

Sage, A.P. and Melsa, J.L.: '*Estimation Theory with Applications to Communications and Control*', McGraw-Hill, 1971.

Saridis, G.N.: '*Self-Organizing Control of Stochastic Systems*', Marcel Dekker, 1977.

Shannon, C.E.: '*A Mathematical Theory of Communication*', Bell. Syst. Tech. J. 27, 1948.

Standard Mathematical Tables, CRC-Press, 21st edition, 1973.

Szroeter, J.: '*Generalized Wald Methods for testing Nonlinear Implicit and Overidentifying Restrictions*', Econometrica, Vol. 51, no. 2, March 1983.

Tempelaar, D.: '*Analysing Econometric Models with Kalman Filter Methods: An Application to a Short Term Forecasting Model of the Dutch Economy*', Paper presented at the European Meeting of the Econometric Society, Pisa, 1983.

Theil, H.: '*Economic Forecasts and Policy*', North-Holland, 1965.

Theil, H.: '*Principles of Econometrics*', John Wiley, 1971.

Tse, E. and Anton, J.: '*On the Identifiability of Parameters*', IEEE Transactions on Automatic Control, Vol. AC-17, no. 5, 1972.

Tsypkin, Y.Z.: '*Optimality in Identification of Linear Plants*', Int. J. of System Sci., Vol. 14, no. 1, 1983.

Vinod, H.D.: *'A Survey of Ridge Regression and Related Techniques for Improvements Over Ordinary Least Squares'*, Review of Economics and Statistics, Vol. LX, February 1978.

Vishwakarma, K.P.: *'Prediction of Economic Time-Series by means of the Kalman Filter'*, Report 7011, Netherland School of Economics, Rotterdam, 1970.

Vishkwakarma, K.P.: *'Macro-Economic Regulation'*, Thesis, Rotterdam University Press, 1974.

Wall, K.D.: *'Generalized Expectations Modelling in Macro-Econometrics'*, Journ. of Econ. Dynamics and Control, Vol. 2, May 1980.

Wallis, K.F.: *'Econometric Implications of the Rational Expectations Hypothesis'*, Econometrica, Vol. 48, no. 1, January 1980.

Willems, J.C.: *'Systeemleer'*, Eds. H. Buffart, J. Oud, Steinfert Kroese, 1974.

Willems, J.C.: *'Systeem Theorie'*, Lectures Notes (in Dutch), 1981.

Willems, J.L.: *'Stability Theory of Dynamical Systems'*, Nelson, 1970.

Winkel, E.G. and Fraser, B.S.: *'Tijdreeksvoorspellingen en hun bewaking'*, Samson, 1970.

Wonham, W.M.: *'Linear Multivariable Control: A Geometric Approach'*, Springer-Verlag, 1974.

## Subject Index

Vol. 157: Optimization and Operations Research. Proceedings 1977. Edited by R. Henn, B. Korte, and W. Oettli. VI, 270 pages. 1978.

Vol. 158: L. J. Cherene, Set Valued Dynamical Systems and Economic Flow. VIII, 83 pages. 1978.

Vol. 159: Some Aspects of the Foundations of General Equilibrium Theory: The Posthumous Papers of Peter J. Kalman. Edited by J. Green. VI, 167 pages. 1978.

Vol. 160: Integer Programming and Related Areas. A Classified Bibliography. Edited by D. Hausmann. XIV, 314 pages. 1978.

Vol. 161: M. J. Beckmann, Rank in Organizations. VIII, 164 pages. 1978.

Vol. 162: Recent Developments in Variable Structure Systems, Economics and Biology. Proceedings 1977. Edited by R. R. Mohler and A. Ruberti. VI, 326 pages. 1978.

Vol. 163: G. Fandel, Optimale Entscheidungen in Organisationen. VI, 143 Seiten. 1979.

Vol. 164: C. L. Hwang and A. S. M. Masud, Multiple Objective Decision Making – Methods and Applications. A State-of-the-Art Survey. XII, 351 pages. 1979.

Vol. 165: A. Maravall, Identification in Dynamic Shock-Error Models. VIII, 158 pages. 1979.

Vol. 166: R. Cuninghame-Green, Minimax Algebra. XI, 258 pages. 1979.

Vol. 167: M. Faber, Introduction to Modern Austrian Capital Theory. X, 196 pages. 1979.

Vol. 168: Convex Analysis and Mathematical Economics. Proceedings 1978. Edited by J. Kriens. V, 136 pages. 1979.

Vol. 169: A. Rapoport et al., Coalition Formation by Sophisticated Players. VII, 170 pages. 1979.

Vol. 170: A. E. Roth, Axiomatic Models of Bargaining. V, 121 pages. 1979.

Vol. 171: G. F. Newell, Approximate Behavior of Tandem Queues. XI, 410 pages. 1979.

Vol. 172: K. Neumann and U. Steinhardt, GERT Networks and the Time-Oriented Evaluation of Projects. 268 pages. 1979.

Vol. 173: S. Erlander, Optimal Spatial Interaction and the Gravity Model. VII, 107 pages. 1980.

Vol. 174: Extremal Methods and Systems Analysis. Edited by A. V. Fiacco and K. O. Kortanek. XI, 545 pages. 1980.

Vol. 175: S. K. Srinivasan and R. Subramanian, Probabilistic Analysis of Redundant Systems. VII, 356 pages. 1980.

Vol. 176: R. Färe, Laws of Diminishing Returns. VIII, 97 pages. 1980.

Vol. 177: Multiple Criteria Decision Making-Theory and Application. Proceedings, 1979. Edited by G. Fandel and T. Gal. XVI, 570 pages. 1980.

Vol. 178: M. N. Bhattacharyya, Comparison of Box-Jenkins and Bonn Monetary Model Prediction Performance. VII, 146 pages. 1980.

Vol. 179: Recent Results in Stochastic Programming. Proceedings, 1979. Edited by P. Kall and A. Prékopa. IX, 237 pages. 1980.

Vol. 180: J. F. Brotchie, J. W. Dickey and R. Sharpe, TOPAZ – General Planning Technique and its Applications at the Regional, Urban, and Facility Planning Levels. VII, 356 pages. 1980.

Vol. 181: H. D. Sherali and C. M. Shetty, Optimization with Disjunctive Constraints. VIII, 156 pages. 1980.

Vol. 182: J. Wolters, Stochastic Dynamic Properties of Linear Econometric Models. VIII, 154 pages. 1980.

Vol. 183: K. Schittkowski, Nonlinear Programming Codes. VIII, 242 pages. 1980.

Vol. 184: R. E. Burkard and U. Derigs, Assignment and Matching Problems: Solution Methods with FORTRAN-Programs. VIII, 148 pages. 1980.

Vol. 185: C. C. von Weizsäcker, Barriers to Entry. VI, 220 pages. 1980.

Vol. 186: Ch.-L. Hwang and K. Yoon, Multiple Attribute Decision Making – Methods and Applications. A State-of-the-Art-Survey. XI, 259 pages. 1981.

Vol. 187: W. Hock, K. Schittkowski, Test Examples for Nonlinear Programming Codes. V. 178 pages. 1981.

Vol. 188: D. Bös, Economic Theory of Public Enterprise. VII, 142 pages. 1981.

Vol. 189: A. P. Lüthi, Messung wirtschaftlicher Ungleichheit. IX, 287 pages. 1981.

Vol. 190: J. N. Morse, Organizations: Multiple Agents with Multiple Criteria. Proceedings, 1980. VI, 509 pages. 1981.

Vol. 191: H. R. Sneessens, Theory and Estimation of Macroeconomic Rationing Models. VII, 138 pages. 1981.

Vol. 192: H. J. Bierens: Robust Methods and Asymptotic Theory in Nonlinear Econometrics. IX, 198 pages. 1981.

Vol. 193: J. K. Sengupta, Optimal Decisions under Uncertainty. VII, 156 pages. 1981.

Vol. 194: R. W. Shephard, Cost and Production Functions. XI, 104 pages. 1981.

Vol. 195: H. W. Ursprung, Die elementare Katastrophentheorie. Eine Darstellung aus der Sicht der Ökonomie. VII, 332 pages. 1982.

Vol. 196: M. Nermuth, Information Structures in Economics. VIII, 236 pages. 1982.

Vol. 197: Integer Programming and Related Areas. A Classified Bibliography. 1978 – 1981. Edited by R. von Randow. XIV, 338 pages. 1982.

Vol. 198: P. Zweifel, Ein ökonomisches Modell des Arztverhaltens. XIX, 392 Seiten. 1982.

Vol. 199: Evaluating Mathematical Programming Techniques. Proceedings, 1981. Edited by J.M. Mulvey. XI, 379 pages. 1982.

Vol. 200: The Resource Sector in an Open Economy. Edited by H. Siebert. IX, 161 pages. 1984.

Vol. 201: P. M. C. de Boer, Price Effects in Input-Output-Relations: A Theoretical and Empirical Study for the Netherlands 1949–1967. X, 140 pages. 1982.

Vol. 202: U. Witt, J. Perske, SMS – A Program Package for Simulation and Gaming of Stochastic Market Processes and Learning Behavior. VII, 266 pages. 1982.

Vol. 203: Compilation of Input-Output Tables. Proceedings, 1981. Edited by J. V. Skolka. VII, 307 pages. 1982.

Vol. 204: K.C. Mosler, Entscheidungsregeln bei Risiko: Multivariate stochastische Dominanz. VII, 172 Seiten. 1982.

Vol. 205: R. Ramanathan, Introduction to the Theory of Economic Growth. IX, 347 pages. 1982.

Vol. 206: M.H. Karwan, V. Lotfi, J. Telgen, and S. Zionts, Redundancy in Mathematical Programming. VII, 286 pages. 1983.

Vol. 207: Y. Fujimori, Modern Analysis of Value Theory. X, 165 pages. 1982.

Vol. 208: Econometric Decision Models. Proceedings, 1981. Edited by J. Gruber. VI, 364 pages. 1983.

Vol. 209: Essays and Surveys on Multiple Criteria Decision Making. Proceedings, 1982. Edited by P. Hansen. VII, 441 pages. 1983.

Vol. 210: Technology, Organization and Economic Structure. Edited by R. Sato and M.J. Beckmann. VIII, 195 pages. 1983.

Vol. 211: P. van den Heuvel, The Stability of a Macroeconomic System with Quantity Constraints. VII, 169 pages. 1983.

Vol. 212: R. Sato and T. Nôno, Invariance Principles and the Structure of Technology. V, 94 pages. 1983.

Vol. 213: Aspiration Levels in Bargaining and Economic Decision Making. Proceedings, 1982. Edited by R. Tietz. VIII, 406 pages. 1983.

Vol. 214: M. Faber, H. Niemes und G. Stephan, Entropie, Umweltschutz und Rohstoffverbrauch. IX, 181 Seiten. 1983.

Vol. 215: Semi-Infinite Programming and Applications. Proceedings, 1981. Edited by A.V. Fiacco and K.O. Kortanek. XI, 322 pages. 1983.

Vol. 216: H.H. Müller, Fiscal Policies in a General Equilibrium Model with Persistent Unemployment. VI, 92 pages. 1983.

Vol. 217: Ch. Grootaert, The Relation Between Final Demand and Income Distribution. XIV, 105 pages. 1983.

Vol. 218: P. van Loon, A Dynamic Theory of the Firm: Production, Finance and Investment. VII, 191 pages. 1983.

Vol. 219: E. van Damme, Refinements of the Nash Equilibrium Concept. VI, 151 pages. 1983.

Vol. 220: M. Aoki, Notes on Economic Time Series Analysis: System Theoretic Perspectives. IX, 249 pages. 1983.

Vol. 221: S. Nakamura, An Inter-Industry Translog Model of Prices and Technical Change for the West German Economy. XIV, 290 pages. 1984.

Vol. 222: P. Meier, Energy Systems Analysis for Developing Countries. VI, 344 pages. 1984.

Vol. 223: W. Trockel, Market Demand. VIII, 205 pages. 1984.

Vol. 224: M. Kiy, Ein disaggregiertes Prognosesystem für die Bundesrepublik Deutschland. XVIII, 276 Seiten. 1984.

Vol. 225: T.R. von Ungern-Sternberg, Zur Analyse von Märkten mit unvollständiger Nachfragerinformation. IX, 125 Seiten. 1984

Vol. 226: Selected Topics in Operations Research and Mathematical Economics. Proceedings, 1983. Edited by G. Hammer and D. Pallaschke. IX, 478 pages. 1984.

Vol. 227: Risk and Capital. Proceedings, 1983. Edited by G. Bamberg and K. Spremann. VII, 306 pages. 1984.

Vol. 228: Nonlinear Models of Fluctuating Growth. Proceedings, 1983. Edited by R.M. Goodwin, M. Krüger and A. Vercelli. XVII, 277 pages. 1984.

Vol. 229: Interactive Decision Analysis. Proceedings, 1983. Edited by M. Grauer and A.P. Wierzbicki. VIII, 269 pages. 1984.

Vol. 230: Macro-Economic Planning with Conflicting Goals. Proceedings, 1982. Edited by M. Despontin, P. Nijkamp and J. Spronk. VI, 297 pages. 1984.

Vol. 231: G.F. Newell, The M/M/∞ Service System with Ranked Servers in Heavy Traffic. XI, 126 pages. 1984.

Vol. 232: L. Bauwens, Bayesian Full Information Analysis of Simultaneous Equation Models Using Integration by Monte Carlo. VI, 114 pages. 1984.

Vol. 233: G. Wagenhals, The World Copper Market. XI, 190 pages. 1984.

Vol. 234: B.C. Eaves, A Course in Triangulations for Solving Equations with Deformations. III, 302 pages. 1984.

Vol. 235: Stochastic Models in Reliability Theory. Proceedings, 1984. Edited by S. Osaki and Y. Hatoyama. VII, 212 pages. 1984.

Vol. 236: G. Gandolfo, P.C. Padoan, A Disequilibrium Model of Real and Financial Accumulation in an Open Economy. VI, 172 pages. 1984.

Vol. 237: Misspecification Analysis. Proceedings, 1983. Edited by T.K. Dijkstra. V, 129 pages. 1984.

Vol. 238: W. Domschke, A. Drexl, Location and Layout Planning. IV, 134 pages. 1985.

Vol. 239: Microeconomic Models of Housing Markets. Edited by K. Stahl. VII, 197 pages. 1985.

Vol. 240: Contributions to Operations Research. Proceedings, 1984. Edited by K. Neumann and D. Pallaschke. V, 190 pages. 1985.

Vol. 241: U. Wittmann, Das Konzept rationaler Preiserwartungen. XI, 310 Seiten. 1985.

Vol. 242: Decision Making with Multiple Objectives. Proceedings, 1984. Edited by Y.Y. Haimes and V. Chankong. XI, 571 pages. 1985.

Vol. 243: Integer Programming and Related Areas. A Classified Bibliography 1981–1984. Edited by R. von Randow. XX, 386 pages. 1985.

Vol. 244: Advances in Equilibrium Theory. Proceedings, 1984. Edited by C.D. Aliprantis, O. Burkinshaw and N.J. Rothman. II, 235 pages. 1985.

Vol. 245: J.E.M. Wilhelm, Arbitrage Theory. VII, 114 pages. 1985.

Vol. 246: P.W. Otter, Dynamic Feature Space Modelling, Filtering and Self-Tuning Control of Stochastic Systems. XIV, 177 pages. 1985.